Naming Stars

MARINA SKYE

Naming Stars — Backcountry Series Book 3
by Marina Skye

Copyright © 2024 Marina Skye

All rights reserved. No part of this publication may be reproduced, stored in or introduced into a retrieval system, or transmitted, in any form or by any means (electronic, mechanical, photocopying, recording, or otherwise), without the prior written permission of the publisher of this book.

This is a work of fiction. Names, characters, places, and incidents are the product of the author's imagination or are used fictitiously. Any resemblance to actual persons, living or dead, business establishments, events, or locals is entirely coincidental.

Backcountry Series
Barn Notes
Love Drunk
Naming Stars

CHAPTER 1
Try Again

They sat together holding hands on the edge of the bed in complete silence, except for Sawyer's bare heel tapping the wood floor. His knee was bouncing rapidly. He turned to look at the clock again...and again. The moment the third minute had passed, they stood at the same time and rushed into the bathroom. Marina picked up the white stick of truth. There was only one pink line, not two. Marina tucked her face into his chest below his chin and Sawyer let out a long, heavy sigh. His comforting arms wrapped around her and he rested his chin on her head as he stroked her hair.

"It's okay, baby."

"I was hoping it would be positive." She looked up at him, defeat clouding her eyes.

"I know, me too. They say everything happens for a reason. Maybe we were meant to have more time together, just you and I. Just for a bit longer." He tilted his head, looking into her eyes.

"Maybe. Maybe we're trying too hard to make it happen. We had gotten our hopes up, just to be let down. Think I'm too stressed or something?"

"Maybe. I reckon we've both been working hard so maybe we need a break. Not from trying, but from work."

"I don't want a break from trying either." She winked and kissed his soft lips. "It'll happen when it's supposed to."

"Maybe I'm applying too much pressure on you."

"What? No, Sawyer, don't be silly."

"You know what? I think we should take a vacation. Like a nice all-out second honeymoon. Just for a few days. It may be our only chance for a while if we see two pink lines next time."

"That sounds amazing."

"Let's start researching places today. It'll give our minds something else to focus on."

"Sounds good. I love planning things with you."

"Me too, darlin'."

He set up his laptop on the coffee table as she sat on the couch then he brought her a cup of coffee.

"Do you think it's me?" She stared at the ripples in her coffee cup as she blew on it.

"What do you mean?" He sat next to her and took a sip of his steaming coffee.

"Like, my hormone levels or my eggs or something."

"Oh, honey, I doubt it. It could be me for all we know. Maybe it's as simple as being stressed. Lord knows we've both had a lot on our plates. We have a lot going on right now. Or it's just not meant to be at the moment. We'll give it time, try not to stress about it for now. We'll take a vacation and try many, many times while we're off in paradise." He kissed her tenderly, his lips tasting of promises he didn't need to speak aloud for her to hear in her heart.

She set her mug down and grabbed his face in her hands and said, "I love you, Sawyer."

"I love you too, darlin'."

"Are we going with the third place we both had on our dream destination lists?" she asked, sitting back with a notebook on her lap.

"Sure. Unless you wanna go somewhere else."

"Nah, I think it would be perfect." She was quiet for a

moment while he pulled up exotic Bali resorts on the computer, then said, "Doesn't it seem like it should've happened already?"

"What's that?" he asked, typing away.

"Getting pregnant. I mean, think about it. We haven't exactly been careful. It's been over a year that we've been together."

He sat back staring ahead at the computer a moment before turning to her with a raised brow.

"I guess you're right. We haven't been actively trying for long though. Although, you have a point with the whole should've happened already by accident thing." He chuckled, trying to make light of the situation but she didn't crack a smile.

He rested a hand on her knee and asked, "Is there something you're worried about, darlin'?"

"I don't know. I'm hoping we won't have fertility issues. It's upsetting to think that's a possibility at this point."

"We'll just keep trying for now and whenever you want to seek medical advice on this, you know I'll be right there with you holding your hand. We're in this together. Okay?"

"Okay. We shouldn't stress over it yet, I suppose. The less stress, the better."

"Let's just think positively and try to take more time for ourselves instead of staying so busy with work. We can try to get pregnant as much as you want." He pecked her cheek and shot a quick sexy raise of his brows, making her smile. Snuggling was top priority as they continued to plan their vacation.

CHAPTER 2
Cup Runneth Over

"I guess I won't be needing this in there," Sawyer said, taking off his cowboy hat and placing it on the truck's dash. He looked in the rearview mirror and ran his fingers through his hair then exhaled deeply. He got out of the truck and let Marina out of the passenger side. With fingers interlocked and clammy palms squeezed together, they walked into the doctor's office building.

"You nervous?" he asked as they stopped just outside Dr. Chen's door.

"Yeah, a little. Seems like you are too."

He nodded with his head down.

"Thank you for coming with me today."

"Darlin', you don't have to thank me. I wanted to come. There's nowhere I'd rather be than right by your side. This appointment is important for both of us. I'll go to every single one with you. I wouldn't let you do this alone. We're in this together. Remember?"

She took his other hand, holding both and facing him.

"You're a wonderful husband, you know that?"

"You're the perfect wife. No matter what the doctor says today, we're gonna be okay."

"I know." She nodded before he wrapped his arms around her for a quick hug.

They both took a deep breath before the office door opened and the doctor called them in to have a seat. Marina had been to see Dr. Chen once to have blood work labs ordered and a physical. Dr. Chen introduced herself to Sawyer and shook his hand before the three of them took a seat in the squeaky brown leather chairs.

"So, Marina. I'd like to begin by saying that your lab results look great; cell counts and hormone levels are good and your other annual tests came back ideal as well. Sawyer, I'd like to get blood work from you."

"Yes ma'am, whatever you need."

"You don't see any obvious reason for us not having conceived yet?" Marina asked, resting her purse on her lap.

"So far, I see ideal conditions for you, but I'd like to check your egg viability. After Sawyer's lab results come back in about a week or two, we can discuss the next steps. I'd also like to get a semen sample from you, Sawyer."

"Can we go ahead and do that today? Would that move things along quicker?"

"Sure, if you'd like, as long as you've abstained from any sexual activity, including masturbation, for at least two days. Preferably seven. You both still have plenty of time so there isn't any need to rush," Dr. Chen explained.

"I understand that there's still time, it's just that we're both really looking forward to having a baby together. It's our next chapter." Marina squeezed his hand.

"It's been four days by the way. It may also take a while to be able to conceive, or for doing whatever we need to do to have one of our own together, so I'd rather start trying now." Sawyer looked at Marina, wanting to give her the world.

"I can get you a sample cup and materials—" the doctor began as she stood from behind her desk.

Sawyer interrupted, "I don't need materials, I just need her."

He pointed to Marina. Dr. Chen looked at Sawyer, then over at Marina, then back at Sawyer, and cleared her throat.

"Um, normally we don't allow that because of contamination...but if—"

"It's the only way it's happening here. Otherwise, I'll bring a sample from home later." Sawyer shrugged.

Marina bit the inside of her cheek to refrain from smirking. He could be so bold sometimes.

"I see. If the two of you can accomplish a sample without contaminating it, I'll allow it." She straightened her lab coat and slipped her hands into her pockets.

"No problem." Sawyer stood and offered a hand to Marina, who quickly took it and rose to her feet.

"Well then, I'll get you that sample cup." Dr. Chen led the way to the room down the hall, swiping a cup from the nurse's station on her way. She nodded, holding Marina's chart against her chest as Sawyer took the cup and entered the room with his wife. As he locked the door behind him, Marina asked, "So how do you wanna go about—" She was interrupted by Sawyer pinning her against the wall next to the door, his tongue playing a twister game with hers. Her brows rose with surprise as she grabbed the front of his shirt in her fist. He lifted the bottom of hers past her waistline, groping her midriff then fondling her cleavage, which was bulging from her bra.

"These jeans need to come down off your hips," she said quietly as his scruff tickled the side of her face. She unbuttoned his jeans and pulled them down a little while he had his hands full with her breasts. She was causing him to salivate as her slender fingers followed his V-line down the front of his boxer briefs. Oh, God, he was so hard. Closing his eyes for a brief moment, he exhaled a quick, sharp breath in her ear as she wasn't shy in taking hold of him. Her teeth gripped his lower lip, slowly sliding off.

"This feels so naughty being in a doctor's office." She smirked as she kept playing. He braced himself against the wall above her.

"Mmm, you like it though."

"Damn right I do," she said in a sultry voice, staring at the curvature of his carved pecs. That shirt fit snugly and it was turning her on even more. She wanted to rip it off him but didn't want to loosen her grip. "Take that shirt off, cowboy."

"Yes, ma'am." He pulled the material up over his head and dropped it to the floor. He then lifted hers just above her breasts and kissed his way down her chest. His warm breath graced her skin and butterflies rioted in her stomach every time his eyes flicked up to connect with hers.

"I want you against this wall." She pulled on his chin scruff.

"That's not a problem," he growled as he put himself against the wall. Her kisses started at his lips but slowly traveled lower, making him anxious. Although he loved the teasing and her touch, he wasn't one to be put off for long. Her hand had yet to retreat from inside his briefs as she bent lower, kissing along the way. The sensation was getting the best of him as he knotted his fingers in her hair, his nostrils were flared and his breathing ragged and raspy as his head pressed against the wall. She bent over lower, feeling down his ripped torso as she teased him with her eyes and tortured him with her tongue. Once she reached his naval, he looked down at her and nodded, granting her permission. She stood up straight as he grabbed her by the jaw, forcing his lips to hers. She stroked him slowly at first, teasing, before becoming more aggressive. He kept a tight hold of her hair and face with his tongue in her mouth as her nails dug into his ass cheeks.

"Mmm, I love the naughty things you do to me. Quick! Hand me the cup!"

"That didn't take long." She giggled as he screwed the lid onto the sample cup. "Now let's get home and get *me* taken care of."

"Why wait?" He took her by the shoulders, walking her backward, lips locked, until her knees folded at the edge of the chair. She sat and he knelt to his knees, lifting her skirt. Her teeth gripped her bottom lip with anticipation as he slid her panties down, passed her ass then pulled them off. He spread her knees apart and went down on her. She leaned back and her legs wrapped around his shoulders as he enjoyed teasing before getting aggressive. She grabbed a fist full of his hair and covered her mouth to muffle the sounds she was trying hard not to make as she felt so much excitement in the way he pleasured her. Her eyes rolled back before closing and her legs quaked.

"That didn't take long," he joked as he grabbed his shirt from the floor and wiped his beard with the inside of it before putting it on.

"Oh my God, Sawyer." She seemed stunned as she took her panties from him. He laughed, buttoning his jeans. As they exited the room fully clothed and hand in hand, he handed the sample to the nurse at the nurse's station. He sported a grin and nodded on their way out the door.

CHAPTER 3

Feelin' A Buzz

The coffee pot in the barn was brewing as Marina entered the open doorway. The barn note read, "Bee right back." She was curious as to why it was spelled in that fashion but continued with chores after pouring coffee. Athena knocked a knee on the stall door and flung her head up with a whinny.

"Yeah, yeah, I'm coming," Marina acknowledged as she led Foxtrot and Legend out. She came back in for Athena and Dixie, realizing quickly that she should've taken them out one at a time. Athena nipped at Dixie's croup and Dixie kicked at her, jolting forward out of Marina's grip.

"Knock it off! Athena, what's your problem? Why do you have to be so nasty to the others?" She put Athena in the round pen then opened the gate to a pasture for Dixie, who stood at it patiently waiting. She headed back for Tango as Sawyer pulled in. Walking out of the barn next to Tango, whose long, wavy black mane bounced with each high-step trot, Marina asked, "You must not have been gone long. Where'd ya go?"

"It was a quick trip to the hardware store. I told ya I'd *bee* right back." He stood just outside the truck and leaned in to grab a bag.

"I like the view of you bent over like that." She smiled, letting Tango through the gate.

"Ya do, huh?" He shut the truck door and met her just outside the barn.

"Yep. Your butt looks good whether you're bent over or not but it makes me wanna slap it when you bend over."

He laughed before encouraging her, "Slap it anytime, baby."

"Whatcha got in the bag?"

"Bee and hornet spray."

"Oh! I get it now."

"Get what? The note?"

"Yeah." She laughed. "We have a bee problem?"

"Hornets. I couldn't come up with a funny hornet idea for the note though."

"You're so funny. Where are the nests?"

"Oh, I'll get 'em, darlin'. I don't want you getting stung."

"I'm not scared or allergic either. I don't mind helping."

"Still, a sting isn't cozy." He shook a can of spray that he took out of the bag. "They're out here by the faucet." He walked around to the side of the barn by the bathing stall. She followed but he told her over his shoulder to stay back. She kept her distance but watched as he sprayed the nest then ran back a good twenty feet.

"Shit! I think that first spray just pissed them off." He stood near Marina, watching the furious swarm scatter. Marina took the spray from him and hustled back up near the nest, him telling her to stop and wait. She sprayed the nest and kept spraying the air as she backed up out of the chemical cloud. Hornets dropped to the concrete. She handed it back to him and he sprayed the nest again a moment later and knocked it down, stomping on it with his boot.

"That was hot!"

"What was?" she asked, playing coy.

"You takin' on that hornet swarm."

"Nah, I'll still never be as brave as you." She took the hose from the reel and spayed the area down so the horses wouldn't be affected in the bathing stall.

"I beg to differ, darlin'. I'll spray again tomorrow, I'm sure the hornets that survived will come back and start rebuilding."

"They usually do." She reeled the hose up and bent over to shut off the faucet. She had already turned him on by spraying that nest, but her cheeks stuck out from the bottom of her cut-offs just enough to make him brazen.

"Wanna go for a ride this mornin'?" He came up behind her, two hands full of ass cheeks. She squealed with surprise and stood to face him.

Assuming he meant horseback riding, she replied, "Yes, sir."

"What did I tell you happens when you call me that?" He made brief, intense eye contact with her, his jaw clenched and brows furrowed; a sullen look worn on his face that she had never seen used toward her before. Her lips parted, a delicateness about her, and he rushed that last step, closing the gap between them to grab her by the shoulders, slamming her against the outside wall of the barn. He kissed her so fiercely she would've been limp, falling to the grass if she hadn't been grasping his arm. That aggressive, heated passion came out of nowhere and made her weak in the knees. He had never been quite this rough with her but she wasn't complaining. She removed his hat and tossed it to the ground, raking her fingers through his hair. He groaned so she knew he was loving it. He raised her hands above her head, pressing and tightly holding them there against the wall, his fingers locked with hers. His lips had yet to retreat from hers as he took that last small step closer to her, pressing against her. His skin glistened, not just from the sun, but from the heat of the moment. He released one of her hands to have one of his free to unbutton her cut-offs, which he did with ease. Shoving his hand down the front of her panties, he groaned in her ear and said, "Ooh, you're ready for me."

"Your touch unravels me," she whispered.

"Good." That sultry look he gave her sent a hot flash through her body. She grabbed a fist full of his hair and closed her eyes as he suckled her neck. Creating wrinkles down the front of his shirt, her fingertips ran down it, then further, reaching his bulge. Again, he groaned, but his titillating fingers weren't retreating; his focus was entirely on pleasuring her.

"Sawyer, I can't be held accountable for what happens next with you kissing my neck like this." She could feel him grin as his scruff brushed across her neck.

"Your hair smells like peaches. I could eat you up."

She pushed off the wall with her foot and turned him against the wall. He was biting his bottom lip, which drove her even more crazy. He stood with his back up against the wall, feet shoulder-width apart. She unbuttoned his jeans and pulled them down mid-hip then knelt to her knees as he lifted the bottom of his shirt. Grasping the curvature of his hips and her wide eyes looking up at him, she was about to—

But then dust clouded the driveway and they heard gravel shift as tires pulled in and a horn honked.

"Dammit!" He jerked his pants up and she stood quickly to her feet and brushed her knees off. They gathered themselves, disappointed that they didn't get to finish what they started.

"It's Justin," she said, peeking around the corner of the barn and trying to fix her hair.

"Of course, it is. He has the worst timing of anyone I know. It's like he knows when we're trying to get it on. He's buying our coffee all next week." Sawyer sounded pissed but suddenly shifted his mood and said, "I love that I'm the reason your hair is a mess by the way."

She laughed as Sawyer was trying to zip his jeans.

"Hurry, he's out of the truck."

"I'm tryin', darlin'. *He's* not cooperating." He pointed at his crotch as he fumbled to button up.

"Not sure that button is gonna happen right now. Just pull your shirt down over it."

"It doesn't pull down low enough. I'll get the-there, I got it. Walk in front of me for a minute."

They met Justin just outside the front of the barn.

"What's up?" Sawyer asked him, acting casually.

"What were you two doin'?" Justin asked, sliding his hands in his pockets.

"Spraying a hornet nest," Marina answered quickly.

"Ugh, hornets suck. I was on my way out of the office for the day and thought I'd swing in, since you weren't answering your phone, to let you know that either Spunky or Sunny busted a hole in the side of the stall. The wall between them has a hoof-sized breach. One of the ranch hands let me know. Oh, and Cider has a small gash on her leg. That is the chestnut, right?"

"Yeah. Jesus. Brand new barn and they gotta go breakin' shit. Alright, let's go have a look. I'll holler at Doc on the way but I can probably handle it. We'll get her fixed up." Sawyer nodded toward the Jeep.

Sawyer and Marina hopped in the Jeep and followed Justin over to the stables. Resting his hands on his hips, Justin stood next to Sawyer and stared at the hole from inside Spunky's stall. Marina was petting Spunky just outside. Sawyer crossed his arms and said after a moment of silence, "Marina. Go into Sunny's stall."

She did and Sawyer bent down with a squinting eye near the hole. "Stand right here in front of the hole, darlin'." She positioned, standing in front of the hole where instructed. He stood up straight and smirked.

"What?" Justin asked.

"I may just leave the hole."

"Huh?"

"I'm wondering if I even wanna fix it." He couldn't refrain from laughing as he stepped closer to the hole.

"Oh my God, Sawyer!" Marina shook her head and came around the wall to slap his arm playfully. It took Justin a second but then he chuckled.

"It's the perfect height." Sawyer shrugged and patted Spunky's withers then whispered to the paint horse, "Good job. Thanks, buddy."

"You're horrible." She laughed and led the horse back into the stall, forcing the guys to move out of the way amidst their cracking up.

"You two kicking the horses out of their stalls to be in here alone in all your glory?" Justin added to the inappropriate conversation, both of the guys laughing so hard that they were practically leaning on each other.

"Sawyer, what will I ever do with you?" Marina walked out of the barn, the guys following. Sawyer flung his arms out to the sides and replied, "I just gave ya an idea."

Justin laughed before teasing, "I think that was a rhetorical question."

CHAPTER 4
Flippin' A Switch

Marina walked into the bar to find Sawyer standing on a ladder reaching up to take down a hanging light.

"Bob, you shut off this breaker, didn't you?" Gladys hollered as sparks flew and Sawyer dropped the screwdriver. Her hands covered her mouth as did Marina's. Sawyer climbed down the ladder holding his hand with the other.

"Shit! Bob! Goddamn it." He shook his hand around, trying to regain feeling. Marina rushed over to him.

"Sawyer! Oh my God, are you okay?"

"Yeah. I assumed he shut the juice off. I guess next time I better check before using the screwdriver. Shit, that wasn't cozy. It's still tinglin'."

Bob came out of the kitchen. "Did someone holler my name? Why'd the power flicker?"

Gladys smacked him with her dishtowel. "You electrocuted poor Sawyer! Just about fried him crispy."

"What?" Bob looked sincerely confused.

"Hey, Bob, next time I tell ya to kill the switch, make sure it's the right breaker, yeah?"

"Oh, crap! You okay, cowboy?" Bob's eyes were enlarged.

"Yeah, I'm tough. It's just a one-twenty circuit anyway." He picked up the screwdriver that had rolled under a nearby table.

"I'll go flip it." Bob turned to go to the back but Gladys said, "You stay put and let cowboy do it."

"I got it, Bob." Sawyer patted his old friend on the shoulder as he made his way to the back room.

"What's he taking down the lights for?" Marina asked, hands on her hips and looking up at the hanging stained-glass light that had hung there for years.

"He's changing out the lighting. He said it's too dark in this half of the room so he's replacing all the lights so they match throughout. He sure is stubborn. I told him it's just fine the way it is in here."

"I see. I know he talked about wanting to upgrade a while back but he hadn't mentioned it in a while. He just told me to meet him here when I was finished at the office and done picking up the uniforms in town that I had ordered for the program charity ball game. They turned out great, by the way."

Sawyer came out from the back room and greeted Marina with a kiss.

"You want help?" she asked, holding the ladder steady as he climbed back up.

"Nah, darlin'. I got it, but thanks. If you wanna pull that color swatch out of that bag on the table, you and Gladys can decide on wall colors."

"I love deciding on new paint colors."

"I knew you'd be perfect for the job."

Marina dug through the bag excitedly and sat with Gladys at a table.

"You thinking bright or just something light? Don't want dark." Marina asked for Gladys's opinion.

"Well, you two own it now, y'all should be deciding," Gladys said, looking through the swatches.

"Oh, don't be silly! This isn't our place. It's yours still and always will be. I'm excited to help paint though."

"Y'all are too sweet. Let's decide together then."

"I'm loving the deep teal for one wall." Marina slid the swatch across the table.

"It would look great with this bright yellow on the next wall," Gladys suggested.

"Should we do like, an oak or pine wood on the bottom half of the walls all around? Then maybe leave the other walls light gray and hang stuff on them? Maybe some metal western-themed art?" Marina asked.

"I love it." Gladys knew the colors chosen were the couple's wedding colors and thought the joint could use some good luck.

"Thanks for fixing a bunch of stuff around here this afternoon, cowboy. Sorry we had a list for ya. I guess it's been a while since we asked you to fix anything. We know you've been busy," Bob said, looking up from the bottom of the ladder.

"No worries, Bob. It's my job as the owner to take care of stuff around here and it's due for some changes. I've always enjoyed working on stuff around here and helping y'all out anyway. You know that." He secured the new modern light fixture and carefully made his way down the ladder.

"Well, you've never complained. Don't have a choice now that you own it." Bob chuckled.

"You good folks are hard to say no to anyway." Sawyer flashed Gladys a big white smile.

"There are some things that need fixin' already at the new stables too." Marina peered over at Sawyer, who wore a cheeky grin and couldn't contain a chuckle as Marina cleared her throat.

CHAPTER 5
Drownin' Jake

Sawyer came through the front door after finishing evening chores and grabbed his truck keys.

"Gladys just called and asked me to go get Jake. He's up there at the bar totally trashed."

"Really? That's odd for him. It's just now getting dark and it's Wednesday. He okay?" Marina had just gotten cozy on the couch after her shower.

"I don't know. I'll find out when I get there. You wanna come along?"

"Oh, no. It's okay. You should go alone. He'll be more apt to talk to you without me there."

"Okay. I won't be long. Gladys is trying to close up early tonight."

"Take your time, babe. Bring him home to sleep it off if ya need to."

"That's probably gonna happen, unless he'd rather I drop him off at home, but he'll need his truck tomorrow. We'll play it by ear." He gave her a quick peck on the cheek before heading out.

Sawyer graced the bar with his presence, as Gladys says. There was Jake, sitting up at the bar alone, the jukebox playing Restless Road's *Go Get Her*. Bob had called last call...twice. The neon signs seemed brighter up behind the bar, leaving a colored glow across the surface of the newly polished butcher-block-style countertop. Sawyer settled on a stool to the right of Jake and nodded to Bob, who poured him a flaming 'Sawyer' drink. Jake hadn't said a word yet, almost as if he hadn't realized it was Sawyer next to him. Sawyer blew out the flame and took a sip then patted Jake's shoulder.

"You plan on overstaying your welcome tonight?"

"Hey," Jake acknowledged him.

"You feel like talkin' or you just gonna drink till you fall off the stool and make me pick ya up off the floor?"

"I haven't decided yet." Jake shrugged.

"Well, you're drinkin' the strong shit tonight instead of beer so I'm here to listen or hang. Either way, I'll be drivin' ya home."

"I wasn't plannin' on going home."

"Oh?"

"Nah, I'll just sleep in my truck." Jake tipped back his half-empty glass.

Sawyer laughed. "No, ya won't, dude. You can crash at my place."

"'Kay. Thanks."

"Always. I got your back like you always have mine." He watched Jake swirl his glass then asked, "So you and your lady get into it or somethin'? I can stop prying if ya rather."

"Yeah, she's movin' out. Thought I'd let her have space to pack her stuff."

"Since when was she living with you?"

"She wasn't. We weren't that serious. She had a few things she kept there. I just didn't wanna hang around and I didn't have any of the strong stuff at home." Jake knocked back the rest of his drink then stared into the emptiness of the glass.

"If y'all weren't serious, why you up here drownin' your sorrows?"

"I don't know. Just got thinkin'. I'm a year younger than you and haven't met that special person yet. Life flies by, so once I do finally meet her and we get to know each other…man, I'm gonna be past my prime."

Sawyer laughed. "Nah, you're already past your prime. But you got time. Ya can't rush things like that. You'll know when ya meet her. It's usually when ya aren't even lookin'. Just worry about you and she'll come along."

"I guess so. She told me that the reason she refused to come to gatherings was because she was too attracted to you. She didn't think she could control herself and not make a move on ya. So, there's that."

"Yikes. Well, shit. I'm sorry, dude." Sawyer hung his head but turned an eye up at Jake.

"It's not your fault. At least she admitted it and didn't act on it. We aren't splitting on bad terms, just don't feel much for each other. We decided not to waste any more of each other's time."

"Is that really all you're drunk over?"

"Work pissed me off too."

"Ahh. Maybe we should pick guitars in the morning over coffee. Don't have to talk about anything but music."

"Yeah." Jake slapped the countertop. "Yeah, let's do that. Maybe a workout too. Bob, will you close me out?"

"Already did." Bob stacked a glass behind the bar that he had finished polishing.

"But I didn't pay though. Or did I?" Jake stood, tipsy and confused.

"Jake, your money isn't wanted here." Sawyer stood and scooched their stools in.

"Rude. Oh! Because you own the place! I get it. Thanks, Bob." Jake could barely finish the sentence or walk straight.

"Am I gonna need to hold your hand?" Sawyer asked, laughing.

"Shut the hell up. I ain't that drunk and you've been drunker."

"The hell you're not and yeah, I have. Y'all laughed at me too. I won't live that shit down." They waved at Bob and Gladys as they walked out, Eric Church's *Record Year* fading from the jukebox as the heavy door shut behind them. The night was quiet, the gentle chirp of the crickets the only sound drifting in the breeze.

"Need me to get your door for ya too?" Sawyer hit the unlock button.

"Oh, so you think since you bought me drinks, you can take me home?"

"That's how it works." Sawyer laughed, climbing into the truck. They sang along loudly to familiar songs on the way, Jake playing air guitar.

Marina was already asleep when the guys got to the house.

"You can take the spare room or the couch," Sawyer offered quietly as they entered the house.

"I'll take the spare room," Jake said as he reached for the door handle to the master bedroom. Sawyer stumbled removing his boots as he grabbed Jake's arm quickly.

"Shh, other way, dude. You aren't sleeping with my wife."

"Oh, shit, my bad. Okay, maybe I am a little drunk." Jake whispered loudly.

"Yeah, a little bit." Sawyer snickered, shaking his head.

The next morning, Sawyer got up early and was out doing chores when Marina woke. She peeked around the corner before walking from the bedroom, through the living room, and to the kitchen to pour a cup of coffee. She didn't see Jake sleeping on the couch when she walked through and wondered if Sawyer had taken him home already.

"Good morning," he said, leaning against the door frame, his fingertips wiping the sleep from his eyes.

"Oh, Jesus!" She whipped around, startled, almost spilling her coffee at the kitchen counter.

He chuckled. "I didn't mean to startle you."

"It's okay, I didn't realize you were here."

"You didn't see me on the couch?"

"No, actually, I saw a heap of blankets but didn't see you

there. I thought maybe you were out in the barn with Sawyer if you were still here, or had slept in the spare room."

"I didn't make it that far."

She suddenly realized she was only in Sawyer's t-shirt and panties and that the shirt didn't quite cover her rear fully.

"Shit," she mumbled, almost spitting a mouthful of coffee out. He snickered and turned his head. "Um, go ahead and pour yourself some coffee while I go get dressed."

"Yes, ma'am." He passed her on his way to the coffee pot and she tried to avoid him seeing her rear, holding her shirt down as far as it would stretch.

"I didn't mean to offend you or anything," he said as the hot liquid filled his mug.

"Oh, no, I'm not offended. I apologize for not being appropriately dressed."

She entered the living room as he hollered, "I've seen you in less."

"Huh?"

"Your swimsuit."

"Oh, right. Well, still. Don't be looking at my ass, Jake," she said, walking to the bedroom. And he was, indeed, peeking around the corner at her, wearing a grin. She closed the bedroom door to get dressed, throwing on jean shorts and a t-shirt before opening the door to see Sawyer coming in the front door.

"Good mornin', darlin'." He gave her a smooch.

"Good mornin'."

"Oh, good, you're up. I could use your help outside," Sawyer told Jake as Jake entered the living room wearing the jeans and t-shirt he had on the night before.

"Yeah, sure." He slipped his boots on, coffee mug still in one hand, and followed Sawyer out the door. He looked back at Marina and smiled.

On their way out to the barn, Sawyer said, "Let me guess...my wife came out in my t-shirt this morning?"

"Uh, yeah." Jake was almost reluctant to admit he noticed.

Sawyer chuckled.

Jake just looked over at him then down at the dirt before his boots.

"Your cheeks blushed when I walked in."

"What?" Jake had an 'oh shit' look on his face. "No, they didn't." His brows wrinkled.

"Oh yeah, they did. I get it. She has that effect on me too when she wears my shirts. Hope you weren't checking her out."

"Of course not. At least she was wearing panties."

"You looked?" Sawyer stopped and lowered his brow.

"What? No." Jake didn't make eye contact and his heart started racing.

Sawyer laughed and slapped Jake's back. "I'm just screwin' with ya. Help me unload this wagon of hay before we jam."

Jake let out a sigh of relief before a chuckle.

CHAPTER 6
Cowboy in Training

The bell rang on the top of the front door at the western store in town.

"Hey there, Sawyer. What can I help ya with today?"

"Hey, Matthew. Just lookin' for a Stetson for a youngin'."

"Okay. Let's take a look over here on this wall." Matthew led the way and asked Sawyer, "So how did that wedding attire work out for you and your gentlemen?"

"Everything fit and looked great, thanks."

"This must be the blushing bride." He held out a hand for Marina to shake. She gladly accepted the greeting.

"Sure is. This is my wife, Marina."

"Lovely to meet you, ma'am. This guy mentions you every time he comes in here. Nice to put a name to a face."

"Well, thank you. Pleasure. I've been in here once to buy a black hat but it was a lady working that day."

"Yeah, Miss Barbara owns this place. Sweet lady. Now, how old is this youngin'?"

"Is he ten or eleven?" Sawyer asked Marina.

"I think he's turning ten," Marina answered, unsure herself.

"These here in this section should fit him. They're adjustable too," Matthew said, pointing to a youth section on the wall.

"Perfect." Sawyer stood looking at the choices.

"How about black? He liked yours," Marina suggested.

"Sounds good." Sawyer took it off the wall and carried it to the counter to pay. Matthew packed it carefully into a round hat box.

They arrived at Luke's party fashionably late. Luke's frown turned upside down when he saw them walk into the backyard.

"They came!" Luke shouted as he ran to greet them each with a hug. Sawyer handed him his gift.

"Are we allowed to hug him too? No wonder the kid was sad he hadn't shown up," said a mom attending the party to another mom.

"I wish. That man is going to age like fine wine I bet too," the other mom batted her eyes as they both checked Sawyer out. Marina noticed and heard their conversation but paid them no attention. She loved it, actually; she loved having the hot husband, the eye candy that caused all the ladies to have premature hot flashes. What she loved even more was that he was so completely devoted to her that she didn't have anything to worry about. They could drool and daydream all they wanted but her cowboy wasn't wandering off anywhere.

Luke was ready to open gifts and he chose to open Sawyer and Marina's first. Oh, the glimmer in his young eyes when he pulled that hat out. Luke put the hat on his head and asked, "How do I look?"

His cheeks turned a dark shade of pink when Sawyer told him, "Like a cowboy in training."

Everyone clapped and a loud whistle pierced the air. He continued to open the other gifts, wrapping paper and colored tissue paper flying everywhere.

Luke motioned for Sawyer to get closer so Sawyer hiked the thighs of his jeans and crouched down next to him.

"Think you could help make me a cowboy?" Luke asked.

"I don't see why not. Is that what you plan to wish for when you blow out your candles?"

"I'm not supposed to tell what I'm wishin' for," Luke whispered and shot Sawyer a harsh wink.

Sawyer chuckled and whispered, "Wish granted."

"Now I wanna be a cowgirl in training," the blunt mom nearby said and Sawyer overheard but pretended to be oblivious. Marina glanced over at her, surprised by the continued audacity.

"Why don't you come on over next weekend and we'll start that training?" Sawyer offered to Luke.

"Yeah?"

"Absolutely. The sooner the better. You'll wanna be a pro before you start wantin' to date the ladies." Sawyer winked at him, bumping shoulders. Luke smiled and nodded excitedly.

"This was my favorite gift," Luke whispered to Sawyer, adjusting his new hat.

"Well, you're a special kid. Now don't be forgettin' that hat when you come to ride the horses."

"Yes, sir. I won't forget. I'm not gonna take it off." Luke smiled proudly and thanked everyone.

Sawyer stood, clapped his hands together, and shouted, "Is it time for cake?"

CHAPTER 7
Still Taking the Reins

"Danielle is stopping by today to check out the therapy program. We may have to take in her overflow after she rehabilitates. She's out of room at the rescue facility." Marina approached Sawyer's desk, hands in her back pockets.

"Okay, sounds good."

"That okay? I should've asked you first."

"Absolutely, we have the room."

"Thanks, babe. I know she'll appreciate it. She still plans to foster them out, just doesn't have space."

"Perfect. She's welcome here anytime; she knows that."

"She does." Marina smiled with gratitude.

"How'd it go volunteering today?" he asked, pen set down to give her his undivided attention.

"It went well. She just got a few in that are in really bad shape so I'm going to share her donation request post to try to help."

"Good idea. Maybe this week we should donate half of our donations to her facility. We'll let our program attendees know ahead of time of course."

"I like that idea. I'm not gonna tell her either. We'll surprise her."

"Sounds good, darlin'. I haven't seen or talked to her in a while. She doin' okay?"

"Yeah, she seems to be. It was nice to get back out there, it's been a while. Many new furry faces there and I noticed the hay shed wasn't full. In fact, it's looking a bit low."

"Aww, I bet. Tell her if she needs anything to let us know… besides the hay that I'm about to order her."

"Will do." Marina gave her generous man a smooch before sitting at her desk to work on promoting their program along with Danielle's rescue and sent an email notice out to the attendees.

"I think Raquel and I might set up a book booth too so we can donate proceeds to Danielle."

"If Raquel is on board, that would be great."

"I might have already recruited her."

Sawyer chuckled. "I see you have things handled. Keep up the good work."

The next morning, the barn note read, "Adding to the herd". After chores, curiosity got the best of Marina so she went over to the stables. Danielle had just gotten there and Sawyer was out at her trailer, phone in his hand.

"I was just about to call ya." He smiled and hugged his woman.

"Hey, Danielle. You bring us new additions?" Marina shook Danielle's hand.

"I did. Just one. He's the most rehabilitated and is ready to foster. He's a good one so it shouldn't take long to find him a home. I think you met him yesterday."

Sawyer led the gelding down the ramp; a beautiful warmblood buckskin. Sawyer looked at Marina with a sideways grin, knowing buckskins are her favorite besides gypsies.

Marina said, "I agree. It'll take no time at all." She wore an excited smile.

Whiskey jumped at the buckskin, begging for attention, and the gelding reciprocated the play. Whiskey grabbed the loose end of the lead rope and started walking the horse across the driveway and into the yard.

"You gonna just let them take off?" Danielle asked.

Sawyer leaned against the side of the trailer and said, "Yeah, they're fine."

"It's adorable," Marina added cheerfully.

"Whiskey doesn't leave the yard so they won't go far."

"Well, looks like Bourbon made a friend already." Danielle was thrilled at the gelding's take on his new home.

"Oh, my goodness, the name fits right in around here," Marina commented. "It's a sign he has to be mine now. Those two are going to be good friends." The horse trotted right along behind barking, growling, rambunctious Whiskey.

Sawyer chuckled, shaking his head, knowing he couldn't argue.

Luke's mom dropped him off for a couple of hours for his first session of cowboy training as Danielle was leaving out the drive, empty horse trailer in tow. Luke was greeted by Whiskey, Bourbon following. All three took off running together, chasing each other around the yard. Bourbon was easy with his footing, careful not to trample.

"Hey, Luke! Come on back this way!" Sawyer hollered, knowing the critters would follow, as he walked toward the arena. Dust stirred as they grouped, entering the arena doors. Marina followed behind Bourbon.

"I'm gonna get Harley for ya, buddy." Sawyer continued to the stables at the other end. A few minutes later, he came galloping out on Kahlua, the silver flaxen, Harley galloping alongside all saddled up.

"Kahlua here used to be a wranglin' horse. Whiskey, well it's just in his blood. Hop on Harley. Marina, will you go get the alpacas?"

"Sure. Do I get to join in the wranglin' lesson?"

"Absolutely."

Only minutes later, Marina came back with both alpacas and the pony who wandered the arena. She hopped onto Bourbon's bare back and grabbed a fistful of mane. Luke used a step stool to mount Harley and adjusted his new favorite hat.

"I'm ready, Mr. Sawyer!"

"Corral 'em up!"

Luke went one way, trotting, while Marina went the other at a canter pace and Sawyer galloped, following up behind. They'd switch positions, teaching Luke the cowboy way. After that lesson, Sawyer had Luke stay on Harley and wrangle Kahlua with a lasso while standing still.

"I don't think I can do it, Mr. Sawyer," Luke said as he swung the hope above his head.

"Sure you can. No cowboy gets it on the first few tries. You're just new at it; ya need practice. You can take that rope home and practice today," Sawyer said, hands in his back pockets while he watched and instructed the cowboy in training. "Swing it in a wider circle. That's it. Little faster now. Hey, look at that!" It took Luke many tries but with much encouragement from Sawyer, he was finally able to lasso the horse. Sawyer had been so patient with him and gave great instructions. Luke never got frustrated and was so excited.

"Wow! I can't believe I did it! What else can I learn today?"

"I knew you could do it. Good job. Well, we could teach ya how to clean stalls and feed, stack hay and such one morning if you care to help with chores. You'd have to come early though. Cowboys have to do all that too. Today, we could do a quick health check on these horses. It's something we do daily, just a normal look-over to make sure nothin' is wrong. We'll check Cider's leg too and make sure it's healing up. You can help re-bandage it."

"Sure. I sure appreciate the lessons today, Mr. Sawyer. I'm having a blast."

"Glad to hear it. Next weekend will be tougher work though. Think you can handle it?"

"I'll be ready. Maybe in a few years, this place could be my first job." Luke walked on ahead of Sawyer and Marina toward the alpacas.

"Sure thing, kiddo."

Marina wrangled Sawyer's arm with hers and said, "It's so wonderful to see his energy level up."

"It sure is. He's a great kid. I'm glad he likes to hang around here."

Luke turned around to face them from several yards ahead and asked, "When are we doing guitar lessons?"

Sawyer chuckled. "One job at a time, cowboy."

CHAPTER 8

Practice Makes Perfect

The barn note read, "Have fun at your shoot today! I can't wait to see the photos!" Marina had finally cashed in that boudoir photo shoot session certificate that her friends got her as a wedding gift. She felt quite nervous going into the studio but was more comfortable seeing that the photographer was a woman.

"So are these photos for your husband?" the photographer asked as she screwed a lens onto her camera.

"Yes, ma'am." Marina changed her clothes behind a wall divider.

"I'd like for you to be as comfortable here as you are with him. Let him come to mind as you switch poses."

"Okay. That should be easy enough." Marina closed her eyes and relaxed her shoulders, taking in a deep breath before stepping out.

"Just let loose and have fun. It's just you and I here and your invisible husband," the photographer said as she spread a black silk sheet out onto the bed. Once Marina loosened up and was having fun, she was a natural; posing came easy at the thought of Sawyer being there and she came up with a few of her own ideas to experiment with. The photographer even offered her a modeling opportunity to advertise for her photography business.

Marina gladly accepted and together they decided to use a few of the pics taken that day. She let Marina see a select few, just the options for advertisement so Marina would have to wait to view the rest. A wine red velvet tufted sofa provided a perfect contrast to Marina's black lingerie and was one of the photos the photographer chose to use. Several wardrobe changes were a must and Marina became brave enough to shoot a few in the nude. Different backdrops and props were used, including a window with sheer curtains, and the perfect lighting illuminated Marina's sexuality. Shadows kept the mystery and light accentuated all the right body parts. She was excited to see how they turned out.

The following week, Marina received a text to check her email. She excitedly opened the laptop and sat on the couch with it. The photos turned out amazing; the lighting was perfect, her hair flowed with loose curls, and she rocked every outfit she wore. Even *she* was happy with how they turned out, which was a big deal to her since she was her own worst critic. She was thrilled and so excited to show Sawyer, who was strumming on his new electric guitar that the guys bought him. She hoped he was at a stopping point as she knocked on the music room door.

"Come on in, darlin'."

She turned the handle and pushed the door open to find him sitting on the chair with that pretty aqua guitar on his lap, jammin'.

"Sounds great!" She pulled up a chair next to him. Although she was anticipating his reaction to the photos, she loved the music he was creating.

"It's been a while since I played an electric. I guess I forgot how much I love it."

"Well, it sounds amazing and you look incredible with it."

"I guess it's like ridin' a bike." He smiled at her.

"You're a natural anyway."

"Thanks. You bored? You can hang out with me in here anytime, you know that."

"Well, actually, I'd love to, but if you're at a stopping point, I'd like to show you something." She stood and waited for him.

"Sure thing." He carefully set the guitar down, propping it against the chair, then followed her out to the couch, where they sat next to each other. She opened the laptop, but before clicking on the folder she turned to him and said, "The photographer sent my photos."

"Really? Let's see!"

"Be honest though. Okay?"

"I'm sure they're all fantastic. Open it!" He was so anxious it made her laugh; his brows were raised as he waved her on to hustle.

"Promise you'll be honest about what you think of them."

"Yeah, of course," he agreed sweetly, then rubbed his hands together with anticipation. She clicked the file and put it on a slide show so he couldn't see them all at once. By the second photo, he was biting his fist. By the fourth, his nostrils were flaring and his knee had started bouncing. He inhaled deeply through his nose then exhaled slowly through his mouth. With each new slide she'd look at the photo, then at him. She was smirking; she loved that he was obviously loving them but the nudes would be saved for last.

"Where'd you get those thigh highs?"

"I bought them for the shoot."

"You have them still?"

"Yeah."

"Go put 'em on."

"Right now?"

"Yep." He clicked pause as she stood. "I wanna feel them on you, against my skin while I look at the rest of these photos."

"Ooh, that sounds kinky." She ran for the bedroom and he chuckled.

"It's gonna be *hard* to choose which ones to hang on our bedroom wall," he hollered from the couch.

"On our wall?" she asked loudly as she slammed her dresser drawer shut in a hurry.

"Oh, yeah!" he hollered back as he adjusted the front of his joggers.

"Are you being serious right now?" She giggled.

"Dead serious. We might have to go through these photos several times because it's gonna be such a *hard* decision. I should put one on my desk at work too...or five."

"You wouldn't get any work done, babe."

"That's true." His lips arched into a slow smile.

"Besides, I can wear these to the office live, in person, anytime."

"Oh, that better happen."

She stepped into the doorway, chin tucked a bit at her shoulder, those wide, sparkling eyes looking at him. He leaned back and spread his knees farther apart, hands behind his head, offering himself.

"Oh, hell yeah." The bass in his voice was calling her. "We might not get through these until later." His eyes wandered up and down her body as she slowly walked to him, one foot in front of the other, up on her toes. He loved when she did that. Those black thigh-high stockings matched her black thong and corset; a set he hadn't yet seen. He cleared his throat.

"You were pretty quick at putting that on. It looks amazing."

"Then I guess you'll be quick to take it off."

"Nah, I think it's staying on." His teeth sunk into his bottom lip.

"Good thing I chose the crotchless thong then," she whispered into his ear as she sat on his leg and crossed hers. His soft touch up and down her leg was an instant turn-on. His eyes locked with hers as his fingers danced higher on her leg. He separated her knees, reaching between her thighs, then higher. She gasped before he grabbed the back of her head, keeping her still as he kissed the breath out of her. There it was, that body-tingling, butterfly-fluttering, heart-pounding sensation he gave her. She loved nothing more than how he made her feel when he showed his desire for her. Temperatures were rising quickly as their tongues swirled intensely around each other. She slid her hand down the front of his joggers, releasing him from his snug briefs. She pulled her lips away from his and slid down from his lap, positioning herself between his legs. He pulled his pants down below his ass and her nails dug into either thigh as his hand wrapped up in her hair. He watched her for a moment before his head leaned back against the couch, his chest rising and falling dramatically, his bare toes gripping the edge of the coffee table. He could barely contain himself so he pulled her hair and guided her back onto his lap. Her cleavage neared his face as she straddled him.

"You've made me so wet," she whispered, breathless and needy, as she lowered herself so slowly that it drove him crazy. He squeezed her ass in response; she may just bruise by morning.

"I can't promise I'll last long with you lookin' like this."

"I don't mind. We can go round two."

"One more photo and I'd be ready to roll again."

"We'll see about that," she whispered before he thrust into her harder.

Buried deep within her, he groaned, letting his beard brush her neck. She pulled his shirt up over his head and dropped it to the floor. Her knees pressed the back of the couch and into his sides as she told him, "Put your hands behind your head."

"Yes, ma'am."

She took hold of his biceps as she gyrated upon him, her movements smooth and steady. Occasionally, she'd break from kissing him to breathe hard upon his neck. It was killing him to not have his hands all over her, to not feel her soft skin, her every curve. She could tell by the way he was struggling to stay in the position that he wanted more control and she loved that he was willing to please her the way she desired. She threw her head back and moaned loudly as she climaxed. The moment she fell relaxed, trying to catch her breath with her forehead against his shoulder, he stood and flipped her onto her back. His joggers came off the rest of the way, then his briefs, and he lowered himself over her, his big shoulders towering above. The way his body moved...it was as if he were performing a horizontal lap dance. She felt his abs roll and he was absolutely gratifying.

"My God, Marina, you feel amazing." He ravished her with his mouth so completely that she didn't get a chance to respond. The tempo of his hips began slow, but once she clamped her legs around his back so tightly that her ass lifted when he did, he couldn't last any longer.

"You know that gets me every time, darlin'." He chuckled, shaking his head, partially disappointed it had ended so soon, but mostly astonished by the wonder that was his woman beneath him.

She lay her palm against his soft scruff and murmured with a wink, "Oh I know."

"You're naughty," he said, sitting his naked ass on the couch next to her. She sat up, closing her legs together, and curled up next to him. He stretched an arm around her and asked, "You did that on purpose, didn't you?"

"I like that it drives you crazy."

"Yeah, but then I finish too quickly."

"I don't see that as a bad thing."

"Oh? Why not?"

"Because I find it flattering."

"And that you should." His sexy sideways grin made her smile. "As long as you're satisfied—"

"Oh, you don't ever have to worry about that. I'm always satisfied with you. You're not gonna need another photo though. Not until later anyway." She gently tugged on his short beard, looking him in the eyes with passion still aflame. Her lips met his, softly and just barely, in a tease. His breaths became quicker and his nostrils started to flare again as her fingertips traced his defined pecs, trailing down his abdomen, below his navel...and he was ready for round two.

CHAPTER 9

Raisin' the Bar

"Bout time you showed up!" Chris hollered as Sawyer and Marina entered the bar.

"Yeah, yeah." Sawyer flopped his two guitar cases up on the stage as Marina went up to the bar to get drinks.

"It's supposed to be packed in here tonight," Trev said, straightening out tangled cords.

"Really?"

"Gladys advertised using us as bait," Trev bantered.

"Nice! Raising the bar up in here, I guess."

"Brought both tonight, huh?" Jake nodded at Sawyer's second guitar case.

"Yeah. Trev can fill in with the acoustic when I wanna play the electric."

"Sweet!" Trev accepted.

"I think she's trying to prep us for bigger crowds," Chris said, referring to Gladys.

"Nothin' wrong with that." Sawyer smiled and took the drink that Marina was handing him.

"Hey, Marina, is Becka coming tonight?" Jake asked.

Sawyer paused in the middle of putting the strap on his aqua guitar and looked over at Jake with a raised brow.

"Yeah, she should be. Last I knew, she planned to."

"Cool." Jake played it cool, but she assumed he'd asked for a reason. Sawyer looked at Marina and shrugged. She turned away to giggle incognito.

"You two need help tonight?" Marina asked Gladys as she took photos of the bar.

"Actually, we hired a young lady for the floor and a young man for the kitchen. I think we're set tonight, sweetie, so you just relax and have a good time." She flopped her dish towel at Marina's arm before slinging it over her shoulder.

"I'm glad y'all could hire more help. I feel bad not being able to work as much anymore with the program running on Saturdays."

"With the way things have worked out since Sawyer...well, since y'all bought this place, we were able to hire two. They're great and they work well together, so hopefully soon, Bob and I will be able to take a day or two off a week."

"That's great! I'm going to help you out with the bar's social media if that's ok. Take some pressure off you."

"Oh, thank goodness! That's not my cup of tea. You go for it, girl." Gladys was relieved that advertising was no longer her duty to maintain.

A few regulars were already drinking at tables and a few were finishing up their game of darts while the band fine tuned their instruments.

"Sounds like our kitchen help is back there now...and that's the floor help. She's still learning drinks but she's been great with everything else. She's a quick learner, much like you. She'll be bartending before long," Gladys told Marina as the new girl walked in the front door.

"I could help still if y'all need help. Just let me know."

"Nope. You need to keep that stress level down. We want little Sawyers and Marinas running around this joint."

Marina laughed. "Heard." She sat on a stool just in time to notice the new girl's walk slow as she gawked at the band.

"Good evenin', Lana." Gladys greeted her as she approached the bar, almost tripping on a stool leg because her attention was on the guys.

"Hi, Gladys. That's the band you were saying plays every Friday? Can I be scheduled every Friday, please?"

Marina snickered and turned her head away.

"Absolutely. It's our busiest night nowadays."

"Especially since you advertised this week," Marina chimed in.

"I sure did. I expect there to be quite a crowd. Can't wait to hear feedback after tonight."

The usual biker crew entered the bar, Justin trailing in behind them. He nodded at the guys and joined them in setting up for a few minutes before heading up to the bar. He sat on a stool next to Marina at the end and ordered a beer. Bob slid it down to him.

"I wasn't sure you were coming." Marina sipped her 'Marina Vodka', turning to Justin.

"I told Sawyer at the office today I would. Thanks, Bob. Danielle sent a card thanking y'all for the donation," he told Marina as his attention was turned.

"Aww that's sweet of her."

Behind the bar, the new girl smiled at Justin as she tied on her black waist apron. He paused, his lips against the bottle, before smiling back. She went into the kitchen and Justin quietly leaned in and asked Gladys, "So you hired a new chick? She's cute."

"She just turned twenty-one, Justin." Gladys pointed a finger at him.

"How old do you think I am?"

"Older than her."

"I'm twenty-five."

"Really?" Marina seemed surprised. "You're younger than the other guys?"

"Yeah."

"Hmm, imagine that." Bob shrugged.

"Do I look older?"

"No, I just assumed you all were the same age," Marina said.

"Chris is the oldest by a year, then Sawyer, then Trev and Jake are both a year younger, and I'm just a few years behind them."

"Y'all sure act the same age." Marina chuckled.

"I'm just more mature than they are." He slung back a chug.

"Mmm, I don't know about that." Gladys tipped her chin down with a head shake, making laughter ring from Marina and Bob.

Sawyer strolled up to the bar as the new girl came out of the kitchen's swinging double doors. She stopped in her tracks when she saw him and muttered, "Can I get you a drink?"

"Sure, I'll take another 'Sawyer'. Thanks." He handed her his empty glass then wrapped his arms around Marina from behind. Lana asked Bob to pour another for the "hot and obviously-taken cowboy."

"Another beer for you?" she asked Justin.

"Please."

She pulled a beer from the fridge and twisted the top off before handing it to Justin, shy eyes glancing up at him. His fingers lingered against hers *just* long enough to make it obvious that he was drawing out the exchange as he asked her name. After introducing himself, he introduced Sawyer and Marina just as Becka came in and the rest of the guys headed up to the bar for another round.

"Perfect timing. We're revvin' the music up here in a few." Jake met her in stride just before reaching the bar.

"Good. I was hoping I didn't miss anything."

"We knew you were comin'. We would've waited for ya." He flashed a suave smile.

"Aww, that's sweet." She playfully swatted his arm as he pulled a stool out for her.

"I'll buy ya a drink," Jake offered, standing next to Sawyer.

"Dude, I keep telling ya that we don't pay for drinks," Sawyer reminded.

"Shit, that's hard to get used to."

"Oh, you must be the bar owner," Lana said, realization dawning on her face.

"Yes, ma'am." He tipped his hat.

"So, these guys are on that no-pay list?" she asked, looking at a short list of names that Bob had written and taped to the register.

"Yep. The dirty dozen. The band and Justin and their ladies." Bob laughed.

"Good to put faces to names."

"You won't forget 'em. They're in here often." Bob polished a glass and stacked it.

"You make it sound like we're drunks, Bob." Jake laughed.

"Well, I've been working here every night for the last week and haven't had the pleasure of seeing any of you yet so that can't be the case. I surely would've remembered y'all," Lana pointed out.

"Yeah, see. You'll know them well enough by the end of the night for sure. Don't be afraid to give 'em hell too," Becka said.

Marina nodded in agreement and said with a smirk, "Don't worry, we still tip."

A larger-than-usual crowd began to trickle in. Gladys looked at the clock behind the bar after coming out of the kitchen with a tall stack of clean glasses for Bob to polish. "I put seven o'clock on the ad and it's about that time. Lana, get the guys another round so they can hit the stage."

Sawyer kissed Marina before gathering the guys with their drinks and heading to the stage. Guitar straps lassoed and drumsticks in hand, the guys made a little noise as the last few seats were filled and folks settled in against the back wall. She'd never seen the place full enough to be standing room only and it made her heart swell with pride.

"Wow, it's a full house tonight!" Sawyer greeted. "Gladys is raisin' the bar up in here so we're raisin' the roof!" The crowd shouted, ready for a jam session.

"Gladys and Bob really talk these guys up. I'm excited to finally hear them," Lana told Marina.

"They're worth the hype. Becka, you're still down for singing one with me tonight, right?"

"Sure! I'm down!"

"We're gonna show off Chris's low baritone voice tonight, and Jake's higher pitch too. You'll feel it in your soul," Sawyer announced before they jumped right into playing *Soul* by Lee Brice. What a surprise it was to hear the different tones up on the stage, all harmonizing perfectly together. The guys had a blast with it too.

"Jake's taking this next one, y'all. Get it!" Jake took the lead on *Catch* by Brett Young. He had his eyes on Becka for most of the song.

"Oh, snap! He's singing that for me, isn't he?" Becka asked Marina.

"It sure seems that way." They squealed like excited teens.

"While I'm up here at the lead mic, I'm gonna keep rollin'." Jake strummed that black sparkly electric guitar one note and the guys knew what to play, *All the Right Problems* by Chris Lane, and he seemed to be directing that one at Becka as well. The band blended the ending into a Morgan Wallen song, *Me to Me*. Sawyer switched Jake spots for a crowd cheering *Drinking Class* by Lee Brice. They had everyone up on their feet like they always did at least once every Friday. Beer sloshed as bottles were held in the air.

"Y'all are in for a treat tonight. These two beautiful ladies wanna do a fun number for ya, so I reckon we'll slide over and give them the stage. Give it up for Marina and Becka, everybody," Sawyer announced as he moved closer to Jake and let the girls take his place up front. He readjusted his black Stetson as he shot Marina a wink. *If You Go Down (I'm Going Down Too)* by Kelsea Ballerini had the crowd laughing. The girls sang perfectly together, Marina on lead. They acted it out like a skit, which took the band by surprise, not having a clue the girls had planned a fun display.

"We have another in mind. How about an acoustic version though? Trev?" Marina nodded and Trev jumped at the chance, the rest of the guys sitting where they could and settling in for the show. The girls sang *Leave the Pieces* by The Wreckers, it was one they sang car karaoke to on road trips together. The girls took a bow and Becka jumped down off the stage, Marina moving to follow, but Sawyer called her back before she could jump off.

"Hang on a minute, darlin'. I'm thirsty for some watermelon moonshine, how about you?"

"I'm feelin' it." She accepted the invitation back up to the microphone to sing *Watermelon Moonshine* by Lainey Wilson. The crowd didn't mind the slow-down, many couples danced, in fact. Lana was carrying pizzas to tables and serving drinks that Bob was pouring, barely keeping up with the crowd's demands.

"Since we've slowed down a minute, you care to sing a couple with me, darlin'?"

"Always."

Together they sang *To a T* by Ryan Hurd and, as always, sounded like a match made in Heaven.

"This next one is one I wrote with my lovely lady. That's right; we wrote it together. So now, we're singing it together."

"Tell That To The Stars" (Duet)

(Verse)
I've been throwing wishes up
From my pillow every night
Hoping someone like you
Would come into my life

(Chorus-both)
You're my shelter in the rain
You wash away my pain
You bring me happiness
Weathering storms through our scars
We were written in the sky
If they say that's a lie

Tell them all to go
Tell that to the stars

(Verse)
It was inevitable
It was fate we met that day
It would've happened
If not that way, then some other way

(Bridge)
Her:
Oh, your warm embrace
Provides me with a safe place

Him:
I want your hand in life
By my side as my wife

(Verse)
You lit a fire within my soul
We met when we were supposed to
You walked out of my dreams
I believe that to be true

(Chorus repeat-both)
You're my shelter in the rain
You wash away my pain
You bring me happiness
Weathering storms through our scars
We were written in the sky
If they say that's a lie
Tell them all to go
Tell that to the stars

(Verse)

I can't imagine life without you
You breathed life back into me
I wanna wake up in your arms
We'll never again be lonely

(Outro-Both)
We were written in the sky
Go and tell that to the stars

After the crowd settled down from their standing ovation, Jake mumbled into Trev's mic, "Show offs."

Sawyer hung his head, laughing as he stood and pulled his stool out of the way.

"Jake, you take this next one. You sound more like him anyways," Sawyer coaxed as Marina joined Becka and Justin back up at the bar.

"Is this because of that night you took me home after buying me drinks?" Jake asked before joining Sawyer at the front microphones.

"Well shoot, I guess it's no secret anymore." He patted Jake's back, making Jake crack up.

"Y'all don't wanna hear about that though." Jake strummed, the crowd yelling for him to explain, but he just laughed, shaking his head.

"Another night like that and he would've been sleeping in a barn," Sawyer joked with a strum.

"Or poolside." Jake shrugged and strummed harder, in competition. The guys all laughed as Jake turned the joking back on Sawyer.

"I love you." Sawyer blew a convincing air kiss to Jake who couldn't keep a straight face.

"I love you too," he mumbled into the mic, looking out over the full room.

Marina already knew what they were going to play based on their bantering. *AA* by Walker Hayes had the crowd roaring.

"I'm thinkin' *Last Rodeo* is a good fit for tonight. What do ya say? Wanna do Restless Road proud?" Jake knocked Sawyer's elbow with his own.

"Let's do it."

"I'm gonna like working here," Lana said as she passed by Justin at the end of the bar.

"I think I'm gonna like you working here too." He smiled at her, which made her blush. She was short in height and slim, brunette with brown eyes, and cute.

Sawyer and Jake both remained up front as Sawyer sang lead on *Hell of a View* by Eric Church then announced, "We have just one more for y'all tonight. You guys have been awesome! Follow the bar's pages on social media and feel free to come on out here to Backcountry when ya wanna party." With that, they blasted into *Every Little Thing* by Russell Dickerson. Sawyer killed it on the electric guitar while Jake tore it up on bass. They were high energy and the crowd went crazy over Sawyer's electric solo. He proved his lungs could belt out at full capacity, too. It was obvious that the crowd fully felt the band's presence, music rushing through them as they danced. The night ended with Sawyer and Marina dancing to *Dirty Looks* by Lainey Wilson playing on the jukebox. Marina was tipsy and giggly and Sawyer laughed at her as he carried her over his shoulder to the truck. Justin exchanged numbers with Lana and Jake was almost brave enough to steal a kiss from Becka...almost.

CHAPTER 10

His Cup Runneth Dry

Marina and Raquel sat on the couch, a laptop on the coffee table and a notebook on Raquel's lap. Marina balanced a throw pillow on her crossed legs with a magazine opened on top of it.

"Is Sawyer doing chores?" Raquel asked, not having been there long.

"No, I did them just before you came. We were watching a movie last night and he had to take meds for a bad headache. He's normally up before me but he's still sleeping. I checked to make sure he was breathing when I got up."

"Poor guy."

"Yeah, I'm thinking maybe he was dehydrated. He trained a couple of horses all day yesterday. He said he drank a lot of water but he was sweating a lot too. He seems more tired than usual lately. I actually forgot to tell him you were coming this morning." Marina took a sip of coffee then set her mug on the coffee table.

"I see that," Raquel whispered as she watched Sawyer walk from the bedroom to the kitchen. Marina looked up from her magazine just as he passed the doorway.

"Oh, shit!" She jumped up, tossed the pillow onto the couch, and made her way toward the doorway saying, "Sawyer. Babe." But as she reached the doorway, he stepped out in front of her... standing right in Raquel's view.

"Oh, shit!" Raquel mumbled to herself. He was wearing only black boxer briefs and Marina was thankful he wasn't completely nude.

Marina nervously smiled and said, "Morning, babe. I forgot to mention Raquel was coming over this morning. I'm sorry." She tried pushing him backward but he didn't budge.

"Good morning, ladies." He put a hand behind his head, stretching. Raquel's eyes widened at the sight of those biceps. "Hey, Raquel. You want coffee? Either of you?"

"We already have some, but thank you." Marina had given up on preserving his modesty at this point.

"Sure. Sorry, I didn't realize you were here. I'll go put clothes on." He nodded then went to the bedroom, his bare feet clunking on the wood floor, coffee mug in one hand. Marina sat and sipped her coffee as Raquel stared at her.

"I'm sorry," Marina said between sips.

"Don't be. I'm not. I love coming over here. He's never dressed. So...was he anglin' or danglin'?"

Marina spit her coffee out all over then covered her mouth. "That was just danglin'." She wiped the pillow with her hand.

"Damn! You're so petite though." Raquel was the straight-up bold type.

"I can handle him just fine." Marina laughed.

"I'm guessing it wasn't just training horses that had him worn out and dehydrated."

Marina smiled while looking up from her steaming mug. "Actually, now that you mention it..." She smirked. He came back out in jeans and pulled a t-shirt down over his torso.

"I did chores already, cowboy."

"Aww, you're sweet. Thank you, darlin'." He leaned down for his kiss good morning.

"How's your head?" she asked.

"Still hurts." He slid his boots on by the door.

"I'm sorry."

"Thanks. I'll be alright. I'm going over to the stables for a while. I have some office work to do."

"Okay. Tell Justin hi."

"Will do. Raquel." He tipped his head in her direction. "You ladies have a good day." He headed out the door and hollered, "Love you!"

She turned and tapped on the window as he stepped off the porch and hollered it back. The girls continued to work on Raquel's book. She needed honeymoon details for the sequel that she was writing about Sawyer and Marina. There were giggles involved in Marina's detailed story-telling.

Justin was parked at his desk, typing away, by the time Sawyer got into the office.

"Morning, Sleeping Beauty." Justin looked up at Sawyer as he walked by.

"Morning. Shit, I left my coffee in the truck." He leaned his elbows on his desk with a groan, his forehead resting in his hands.

"You alright?" Justin asked as he got up and poured a cup of coffee for Sawyer. He set it on Sawyer's desk.

"Nah, I have a headache from Hell. I'm dizzy, it's so bad. My head's not in the game today."

"Getting sick?"

"Nah, probably just dehydrated from yesterday."

"Working those horses did you in? You drank a lot of water though. What'd you do when you got home?"

Sawyer just looked up at him, sipping his hot coffee, and smirked.

"You work out at home? That could've been what took the cake."

"Uh...yeah," Sawyer replied, taking another sip, not even trying to avoid eye contact.

"Ah, so sexercise? Damn, dude, you must have really exerted yourself."

"I guess so." Sawyer rubbed his chin scruff.
"Now you get to have a migraine all day."
"So worth it." Sawyer chuckled. "Thanks for the coffee. Hey, if you wanna print that invoice out for Dave, I'll take it with me tomorrow morning. Payroll needs done today too."

"Yep, already on it. Hopefully your headache will go away by then."

"I hope so. Jake left a sports drink in the fridge here so I'll drink that after my coffee. That might help."

"You guys have been trying hard to get pregnant, huh?" Justin shuffled through papers on his messy desk.

"Yeah, we have."

"Trying *too* hard?"

"What do ya mean?" Sawyer flipped the laptop open.

"You're wearing yourself out and sometimes *not* trying so hard actually lets it happen."

"So, trying less gives better results? How's that?"

"I don't know. I've heard that when ya take a break from actively trying, ya end up pregnant."

"Hmmm, that doesn't make any sense."

Justin laughed. "Nah, you just don't wanna give it up."

"Why am I talking about this with you anyway?"

"Because I'm your office bitch, remember?"

Sawyer laughed. "Get back to work."

CHAPTER 11

When in Rome

"I'm loving this weather," Raquel said, taking in the cooler morning air from her perch upon Tango.

"I bet autumn comes early this year. Summer did, for sure." Marina slid down off Dixie's back.

"It sure did. I enjoyed helping out with chores this morning. It's been a while."

"I'm glad you were able to. It's nice, going for a ride this morning."

"It's been a while since I rode, too. It was nice of Sawyer to let me ride Tango. I know he's his pride and joy."

"Nah, that would be me." Marina giggled.

"True, but Tango's special. You gave him to him. That's why he chose him to gallop y'all off after your reception."

"Did he say that?"

"He did. He told me when I danced with him at the reception. He also said that the two of you would look the best on that big black beauty as you rode off dressed in your wedding attire. He was right. Those photos were beautiful."

"Aww, thank you. They did turn out great. He's having one printed to hang in the living room."

"Nice! It'll be hard to decide on a photo for the book cover."

Raquel dismounted and adjusted the shoulder straps of her backpack.

"Maybe I can help choose?" Marina asked as she sat on the ground beneath a big magnolia tree.

"Of course." Raquel fell quiet as she admired the quiet nature of the back field near the end of the trail. "It's so pretty back here." She let her backpack drop off her shoulders and swing around to her elbow.

"Sawyer widened the two-track a bit that goes around by the pond down there. It leads out by the old train tracks and to the property where the stables are. It's nice having our places connected so we don't have to drive down the road and around to the next."

"Yeah, nice shortcut." Raquel sat next to Marina and dug her notebook and pen out of her bag. "It'll be pretty this fall, with these maples back here, too."

"Yeah, these magnolias will stay green, which will be a nice pop of color against the reds and oranges." She leaned her head back against the tree trunk. "I remember the first time I came back here with Sawyer. We rode the horses to the end of the trail then cut through the field to head back to the barn. But that's not my favorite time out here with him. One day we rode four-wheelers back here to this very spot. It was the day he bought the new one. We flung mud on each other. He put a magnolia flower in my hair and we shared a beer."

"You hate beer." Raquel raised a brow in surprise.

"I know." Marina laughed. "We laid on our backs and watched the clouds roll by. I could tell he wanted to hang out. He would do that more often as time went on; making excuses to hang out with me instead of being at work. I loved it. He still does it. He's a quality time type of guy, which is so important."

"Yeah, it is. That's great." Raquel jotted down notes. "What's he like to live with?"

"What do you mean?" Marina looked over at her.

"Is he like most guys? Dirty, doesn't clean up after himself, stinky like a gym locker room?"

"Oh, no. No, he's clean and tidy. That house was immaculate before I moved in, too. His clothes get put into the hamper and he helps with house chores; whatever I don't get done during the day. He never complains about anything, which gives me nothing to complain about. He doesn't chew loudly or snore either. He's the perfect roommate. He even takes his boots off at the door, washes his hands before he eats, and doesn't leave the toilet seat up either. He's not afraid to show emotion and he treats me like a queen. He's as real as they get." She paused in thought. "I can't think of one single thing that irritates me about him."

"You sure? I mean, he's a man." Raquel waited a moment, staring at Marina. Marina pondered the question, ripping blades of grass apart, her elbows up on her knees as she stared ahead at the horses grazing nearby.

"Nope. Not one damn thing."

"Wow. You're lucky. At least so far."

"I sure am." She smiled wide. "I almost forget sometimes that he's mine. I still find myself shying my eyes away when he catches me watching him dress or undress or when he's working at his desk, or better yet, when he's working with the horses and unloading hay. I watch him all the time; I can't take my eyes off him for long." She was drifting off to daydream land and Raquel's hand was speed writing.

"Y'all are too cute."

The sun warmed their skin as they sat chatting and writing.

"I'll have this book done in no time. Then on to the next."

"Maybe I'll write a children's book about the therapy program. I can add pics of the horses in there like I did in the rescue book."

"Great idea!"

Cheeks flushed as the steamy honeymoon details were shared and the time flew by. It was the afternoon before they knew it and Sawyer came riding up on Foxtrot, leather crunching louder as he rode closer. The girls were all smiles watching that brawny man approach them. He tipped his hat and smiled.

"Good afternoon, ladies." He rolled up the sleeves of his half-unbuttoned flannel shirt.

"Good afternoon," Raquel greeted. Marina flashed a flirty smile.

"You ladies hungry?"

"I guess we have been out here a while," Marina said, looking up at him and shielding her eyes. The sun beamed overtop them, leaving his face shadowed until he tipped his chin up and let those baby blues sparkle under the brim of his white hat.

"I guess I am getting hungry." Raquel put the notebook in her bag and stood. Marina joined her friend and brushed the back of her jeans off before greeting Sawyer with a kiss as he bent down to her.

"You have a plan for lunch or you wantin' me to come make it?" Marina asked, smiling up at him.

He said, "I wanna treat the two of you to lunch in town if that's okay."

Marina looked at Raquel, who slung her bag onto her back, and said, "See? Not a damn thing."

"I agree." Raquel mounted Tango as Marina clicked for Dixie to come to her. She stood on a log to mount easier.

The café wasn't especially busy since true lunchtime had passed, so they got their food from the counter and Raquel chose a booth near the window.

"What are your plans for the rest of the day?" Marina asked Sawyer as he slid into the booth after her.

"Well, it's nice outside so I thought I'd go get some field stones from down by the pond."

"For landscaping?" Raquel asked.

"Yeah, at the stables. I think I need to work those newer horses a bit on sensory stuff so I'll probably do that first."

"They aren't scared of water are they?" Marina asked, remembering Smokie's sensory training.

"Nah, I don't think so. It's mainly that they don't like to be touched if they're being ridden, so I'll hop on and let Justin be the one to test 'em out." He laughed.

"I'm sure he'll appreciate that." Raquel giggled as Marina shook her head.

Sawyer asked for a book update and that became the topic of conversation for most of lunch. He could tell the girls were having fun with it.

"Oh, someone I know asked about using the stables as a wedding venue and asked for my help with planning."

"Yeah, go for it!" Sawyer insisted.

"You wanna help?" Marina asked Raquel.

"Of course! Sounds fun. Maybe the other girls will wanna help too."

"Let me get the pond, palms, and ferns in first, darlin'. I'm adding potted palms to the arena too. It'll look great."

"Perfect."

Sawyer dropped the girls off at the house before heading back to the stables. Raquel stayed much of the afternoon. Once they got on a roll with books, they lost track of time easily. As sundown was approaching, Marina wondered why Sawyer wasn't home yet. He didn't pick up his phone so she thought maybe she should go to the stables to check on him. She cut through the field, down the two-track, and as she neared the pond in the Jeep, she spotted his truck. Her tires slowed in the dirt and her eyes squinted. The sun's rays momentarily blinded her as the sun sank below the trees. Was she seeing what she thought she was seeing? Absolutely. His truck bed was loaded with field stones and there he was, sitting on his tailgate wearing only his underwear and hat. *What on Earth?* She thought to herself. He had just stripped his jeans off and flopped them behind him and his flannel shirt hung halfway out of his opened truck window. She rolled the Jeep to a stop and got out.

"Whatch doin', cowboy?" she asked as she joined him at the tailgate.

"Sweatin' my ass off, darlin'. It's been a long day."

She leaned her hip against the tailgate with her arms crossed and a smirk plastered across her face. "What's your plan?"

"Well, I reckon I was fixin' to get in that water."

"*That* water?"

"Yep." He removed his hat and placed it in the truck bed.

"We do have a pool."

"Where's the adventure in that? Nothin' wrong with nature, baby." He hopped off the tailgate and scooped her to him for a sweet kiss. "Come join me," he said as he walked to the water. She took a moment to take him in; the sight of that man blew her away. He looked like a Roman god the way he was sitting on that tailgate when she approached him and how he stood looking over the water before his toes touched it. That would be a view she'd never forget. If only she could sculpt a statue of him in that very moment. She watched that God-like man enter the water amidst the lily pads and sink until only his blue eyes were looking at her from above the water's surface.

After a few moments, he stood, letting water drip from his beard, those enticing wet lips parted, waiting for hers to join his. Now *that* could be a novel cover. How could she resist? She stripped her jeans and t-shirt off and slowly walked toward him, her bare feet sinking in the marshy water's edge, moss and mud sinking with them. He patiently invited her in further with his eyes. Orange sunlight danced upon her skin under the pink clouds, giving her a seductive glow. She stepped right up to him, water rippling, and he looked down upon her, directly into her eyes, into her soul. He embraced her face with his strong hands, his touch ever so gentle. His body screamed strength in every way, although everything about how he treated her painted him as the gentlest man she'd ever known. The perfect curved ridges of his sculpted pecs drew her attention and she reached out to trace her fingers down them, wet and rock hard. Her pulse quickened with every inch of his body her hands explored. Every time he looked at her so deeply, she fell in love with him all over again. The glow across his face made those eyes of his shine bright and she was once again lost in them. Wings fluttered in her stomach as his wet lips slowly met hers. Sensuality overtook them as that early fall sun sank behind the trees. He kept a tight rein on his control, but her persuasive tongue was eager. She held him to her tightly and with a calm, shuddering breath, he said, "Go get in the truck." Grabbing his arms, she leaned back, a brow raised in question.

"We're already parked, darlin'. This water's no place for what I'm about to do to you."

She smiled, not sure why she was surprised at his request, but she didn't move quickly enough for his urges. He hoisted her up and she clamped her legs around him. They kissed, absorbing each other, as he carried her out of the water and to the truck. Crickets chirped and bullfrogs bellowed. The windows were left down and they were left to the breeze, heating each other's bodies as the evening air cooled.

CHAPTER 12
Tailgate's Poppin'

Marina came outside to find Sawyer's truck facing the barn as he crouched in the truck bed under the exterior barn lights.

"Sawyer, what are you doing?"

"Settin' up."

"In the truck bed?"

"Why not? It's raised higher like a stage."

She smiled at his creativity.

"What are these shop lights for?" she asked as she turned one on and about blinded Sawyer.

"Damn, baby, that's bright!"

"Oops! Sorry!" She quickly shut it back off. It was one of those tripod construction site lights. He had one on each side of the truck out in front of the tailgate facing the truck.

"I think I'll need to adjust those."

"I thought it was movie night? Where are you hanging the screen?"

"Yeah, it is. I'm gonna hang it right here on the barn wall behind the truck."

"So y'all are jammin' first then moving the truck?"

"Yep. I figured since it's Friday night and Bob and Gladys are closing the bar early to come here for the movie, we'd jam out a few songs."

"Cool. It'll be fun."

"Kinda like a practice run for the fair."

"Except way less people watching, smaller stage, and less pressure."

"Jeez, thanks, baby." He chuckled as he adjusted the microphones.

"It's a good start. You have home-field advantage." She laughed.

"True. You choose a movie?" he asked, untangling extension cords.

"I picked out a few comedies to choose from. Think we should let everyone vote?"

"Nah, just ask the first couple that shows up."

"Sounds good."

"Becka bringing her popcorn machine?"

"Yep. She should be here any time."

"There's Chris and Stacy." Sawyer pointed down the driveway.

"Poor Jake's solo tonight I'm guessing?"

Sawyer gave her the let's-not-talk-about-it look. She nodded as Chris and Stacy got out of the truck.

"What the hell you doin'?" Chris hollered at Sawyer before shutting his truck door.

"Settin' up. You bring your drum set?"

"Yeah. We playing' up there?"

"Yeah." Sawyer jumped down to plug in a cord.

"Good thinkin' on putting the plywood down." Chris propped his arm up on the side of the truck.

"Needed a flat surface."

"What movie we watchin'?" Chris asked, brushing a strand of hair from his face that had fallen from his man bun.

"I don't know. Marina narrowed it down so y'all can pick."

"You streamin' it?"

"Yeah, we'll just hook her laptop up."

"Cool. Want help hangin' the screen?"

"Sure, thanks."

Trev and Trina arrived and backed up their truck next to Chris's so they could watch the movie from their truck bed. Sawyer and Chris were each up on ladders hanging the screen when they stepped out.

"Is that a blow-up pool?" Sawyer got a kick out of Trev's choice in movie-watching seating.

"Hell yeah! You've never watched a movie in a blow-up pool before?"

"Can't say I have but next summer that shit is happenin' in my pool. We'll put the screen out back."

"I'm game." Chris jumped on that bandwagon quickly.

"Pool lights on, hanging party lights…hell yeah." Trev was already excited. Becka pulled in with Jake right behind her. He backed in next to the other trucks by the barn.

"Well shoot, I don't have a truck bed to get all cozy in like you guys." Becka frowned, slapping her leg with her hand as she lifted her trunk.

"I'll share." Jake smiled and winked at her then helped her get the popcorn machine out of her trunk.

"Okay," she gladly accepted, flattered by his flirtation, then thanked him for his help.

"Girl, get that popcorn machine set up already, will ya?" Trina joked, walking over with a bucket of popcorn kernels.

Justin's arrival stirred up dust in the driveway as he whipped his truck around, flinging dirt and gravel everywhere. Cloudy headlight beams shone across the yard.

"Really, dude?" Jake threw his hands in the air when Justin exited his truck.

"Oh, relax. Like y'all don't play in the dirt every other day."

"That's true, we're always dirty." Chris laughed.

"Sawyer's been making me help out in the round pen sometimes. I didn't sign up for that shit. I miss working at the office in town, where he couldn't rope me into helping. I was happy just being a pencil pusher." He approached the growing group and added, "I'm glad I don't have to deal with cords when I play." The guys looked at each other, then at Justin.

"When you play what?" Chris smacked his gum in his mouth.

"My instrument."

"You read music?" Sawyer asked, a brow raised. "How did we not know this?" He climbed back down the ladder.

Becka started up the popcorn machine as Chris hammered a nail before climbing down.

Justin shrugged.

"So, you gonna tell us what you play or do we need to guess?" Trev asked sarcastically.

"Saxophone. Alto."

"Seriously?" Sawyer shifted his weight to one hip, hands in his pockets like he didn't believe him.

"Yeah, since like, sixth grade."

"So, are ya any good or you play as well as like...a middle schooler?" Chris smirked.

"Nah, I'm pretty damn good."

"Were you keeping this a secret for a reason?" Trev wondered aloud.

"No. Your band doesn't call for a sax."

Sawyer grinned.

"What?" Chris asked.

"I've been wanting to play a specific song that calls for a sax. That's why we haven't played it yet. You have it with you?"

"No. I don't carry the damn thing around like you do that guitar."

"Join in on our next rehearsal."

"Okay."

"I wanna play that song at the festival. We'll see whatcha got. I can't believe you've been holding out on us this whole time we've known you. Dipshit." Sawyer wore an excited grin.

"Deal, Dick."

Sawyer tossed his head back with a laugh.

"It would be a blast for you to play with us," Jake said, arms up on the side of the truck bed.

"It would be fun. Even if just in practice," Justin agreed.

"I still can't believe you play an instrument. Why haven't you ever said anything?" Sawyer was still dumbfounded.

"I guess I didn't figure y'all would care since it's not really a country-band-type instrument."

"That's bullshit," Chris teased, setting up his drums.

"Dude, it's something else we all have in common. Why would we not care?" Jake admonished.

"Okay, cool. My bad. Now ya know."

"Watch him totally jam out at rehearsal," Jake said as if Justin wasn't standing right there.

"I bet he does." Trev nodded.

"Don't be telling the girls. Let it be a surprise," Sawyer whispered as Becka was nearing.

"The girls ready for our little tailgate concert? I think it's dark enough and Bob and Gladys are here now." Chris pointed out, tossing drumsticks into the truck bed before jumping up into it.

"I'll go check." Becka walked back to the house to gather the girls while Trev set his keyboard up on its stand then hopped up on the tailgate. He and Chris lifted the keyboard then Trev plugged it in. Jake handed his guitar up to Chris before joining the guys.

"So, we'll have a live show before the screened one? Well, aren't y'all creative." Bob stood next to Trev's truck.

"I like that we'll still get to hear y'all play tonight." Gladys joined Bob at the back of Trev's truck. "It's a nice surprise."

"Glad you're cool with it." Sawyer hopped into the back of his truck. The guys tuned quickly as the girls all came out of the house with bowls for popcorn and liquor bottles.

Marina raised a vodka bottle into the air and hollered, "Wooo!"

Sawyer laughed, retying the plaid button-up around his waist.

"I didn't know Raquel was coming." Becka spotted her pulling in the drive.

"I was just on the phone to her a bit ago and told her she's welcome to join. She said she already had plans so I didn't expect her," Marina explained, meeting Raquel out at her car, liquor bottle still in her hand. Raquel was excited the guys were going to play and the girls put cushions and blankets on the tailgates, filled popcorn bowls, and got cozy. Marina turned on the "stadium lights", as Sawyer called them, when he asked her to. They weren't blinding but added just the right amount of light to their tailgate stage. Raquel and Marina sat on Justin's tailgate with him after he passed out beer from the cooler in his truck.

"I'm disappointed Sawyer's covering his ass with that shirt, to be honest," Raquel commented. Marina laughed and shook her head. Chris and Trev took to their stools and Sawyer and Jake strapped their guitars around them as they stepped to the microphones.

"This should be interesting, we're kinda cramped up here for room so don't be surprised if Jake or I fall off while jammin'." Sawyer chuckled and peered up at Jake from under the brim of his black Stetson.

"Speak for yourself. I'll push you off before I fall off." Jake said with a straight face as he tousled his hair.

The girls were hollering like they were front row at an actual concert. The guys jammed out to *All the Same Friends* by Russell Dickerson. It was the perfect song; about all the usual friends getting together on a Friday night, hanging out like they always do. Trev rocked out with Jake's bass guitar. They stuck with Russell Dickerson for *Big Wheels* and *Beauty and the Beach*, Sawyer singing lead, and Trev taking the featured Flo Rida part. The gang loved it, especially since Trev never sings anything more than background harmonies. Trina gave a standing ovation, blowing him a kiss.

"Here's an original we wrote last week during rehearsal. Let us know what y'all think." Sawyer slowed the tempo down a tad with one not even Marina had yet heard but he knew she'd love it.

"Sunlightin' & Moonshinin'"

(Verse)
It's a hot muggy day
Out there playin' in the hay
Simply melting over you
Who needs clothes anyway?

(Verse)
You gave my t-shirt a yank
Jeans stripped on the river bank
Holding you close to me
In the mud, our toes sank

(Chorus)
Soaking up the sunlight
Til stars in your eyes shine bright
Half the night has gone past
I want these memories to last
Time sure flies by
The moon lightin' up the sky
Oh, there's nothin' I rather do
Than sunlightin' & moonshinin' with you

(Verse)
Drivin' down a dirt road
Your hair flowin' out the window
Sun shinin' through the branches
Making your pretty hair glow

(Verse)
Moonshine on the tailgate swirls

Makes me wanna dance with you, girl
Grass under our bare feet
I'll give forever with you a whirl

(Chorus repeated)
Soaking up the sunlight
Til stars in your eyes shine bright
Half the night has gone past
I want these memories to last
Time sure flies by
The moon lightin' up the sky
Oh, there's nothin' I rather do
Than sunlightin' and moonshinin' with you

(Outro)
Wishin' on the stars forever more
Even though we already have what we're both wishin' for

Their small but mighty crowd stood clapping and Marina's squinty-eyed, cheeks-raised smile told him she loved it as much as he knew she would.

"What do ya think, ladies? Some Jake Owen?" Sawyer asked with a slow shrug. They hollered and whistled, clapping. The guys loved that their girls were their biggest fans. They played *Best Thing Since Backroads* and at the end of the song, Raquel hollered, "Wooo! Take it off, boys!"

Everyone was cracking up. She didn't drink often but when she did, she got the wild giggles, worse than Marina even.

"This truck bed isn't that kind of stage, ma'am," Sawyer stated in a low, sexy voice, making the girls laugh and holler.

"It could be though!" Raquel hollered in almost a desperate begging tone. The girls snickered as the guys found her comment amusing.

Sawyer turned to the guys as he covered the mic and said something then turned back to their friends, tipped his hat to them, and sported a slow-spreading sexy sideways grin. The fog was starting to roll in, settling low to the cooling ground.

"This one's for you, darlin'." He looked directly at Marina when he said that; like she was the only one in the little audience. They played *Black* by Dierks Bentley, which made it hard for Marina to concentrate on having fun with their friends. She wanted to jerk him off that "stage" and lead him to the bedroom. It's such a sexy song. He'd close his eyes once in a while and move his body slowly and seductively, his hips swaying with those ripped jeans; it was driving her crazy. He wore his desire for her across his face for everyone to see. His fingers on those guitar strings moved smoothly and with little effort. How was she supposed to lay with him in a truck bed, liquored up, through an entire movie without wanting him entirely? She looked at the other girls and their mouths were gaped open, their bodies still, just staring at him. That fog rolled as high as the top of the truck tires and floated in the light beams beneath the bright orange harvest moon. He was so goddamn sexy. She was glad she wore jeans, no easy access tempting their naughty urges amid their friends enjoying the movie. Even though they liked it a bit risky, it wasn't the time or the place. She knew if there was easy access, he would not be able to resist messing around and it would be impossible to hide her facial expressions that would give away her need for him in that very moment. He already struggled to control himself.

There was a brief pause after the band ended that song before everyone stood, cheering. It's as if they had to pick their jaws up off the fog-covered ground first.

"Good God!" Becka fanned herself.

"No shit!" Raquel agreed. "That performance was probably the best I've witnessed."

Sawyer put his guitar down and jumped off the tailgate. He walked over to Marina with swagger and melded his lips to hers.

"Let's take care of all this shit later and get watchin' the movie," Trev said as he jumped down from the bed of the truck.

"I'll pull my truck over here so it's not blocking the screen." Sawyer slapped Marina's rear and bit his lip with a groan before walking back to his truck.

"Jesus," Stacy muttered, hoping Chris didn't hear as he walked her way with Trev and Jake.

Sawyer turned his truck around to align with the others.

"We should take that equipment out of your truck bed now that we're done poppin' in it so y'all can have it to watch the movie in," Jake suggested.

"Yeah, we could do that. Moisture isn't good on this stuff anyway. Marina, darlin', you wanna get the movie ready?"

"Sure." She went inside for the laptop while the guys took their equipment down. The lights were turned off and moved to the side as Marina came out and set the computer on a hay bale next to the movie screen. Jake tossed her a tangled extension cord to plug the computer into on his way to hop onto his tailgate, where he offered a hand to Becka and pulled her up to join him. Sawyer was winding other cords up with his back to the screen when Marina hit play. She arranged her cushions and pillows and a blanket up near Sawyer when the song *Black* started playing and gasps echoed in the yard. She turned around quickly and was instantly horrified. She froze. Sawyer was none the wiser, not paying attention at all. Marina blurted, "Sawyer!" He knew in that moment exactly why that song was playing and why the gasps before silence.

He whipped around and leaped off the truck. "Oh, shit!" The guys were snickering as Sawyer ran for the outlet. There he was, on top of Marina, in their bed, silk sheet sliding off his backside. Yep, there it went as he was slowly grinding into her like a male stripper. His bulging shoulders bearing his weight, his tan ass cheeks clenching with each rolling thrust between her raised knees, her hair cascading off the side of the bed next to her as she gripped those strong shoulders of his. It was all right there on the big screen. He fumbled the extension cords, trying to find where they plugged into the computer.

"Baby, shut it off!" He unplugged it, not thinking about the computer being fully charged.

"I'm trying!"

Time wasn't on their side and it felt to Marina as if she were moving in slow motion as she tried to stop the video on the computer. When she finally managed it, she exhaled a burst of panicked air, looking at Sawyer, who dropped the cord he pulled from the outlet and hung his head, laughing silently. Their friends were quiet a moment, stunned into shock, before Justin hollered, "Oh, com'on! Ya might as well finish!"

"What?" Marina's eyes were huge.

"I've heard y'all going at it before, might as well watch it."

Sawyer and Marina both shook their heads no.

"Holy Hell!" Stacy gave Marina an envious raise of her brow and Trina cleared her throat, looking down, not able to make eye contact.

"I recant the comment I made earlier about him wearing that shirt to cover his ass. I'm satisfied now," Raquel joked.

"Whoops, sorry y'all. I guess we were poppin' in more than just the truck bed tonight." Sawyer walked over to Marina, who was once again frozen, her breathing rapid with panic and her eyes wide still.

"I'm sorry, baby." He chuckled and kissed her forehead.

"Oh my God, that did not just happen," she whispered, hiding her face in his chest.

He laughed with no shame. "Oh, but it did. At least it was my ass in the air and not yours."

She cupped her breasts in her hands, signaling that everyone saw them in the video, but Sawyer could only reply with a quick raise of his brows and a bottom lip bite.

Jake patted Sawyer's shoulder, laughing on his way to get popcorn from the machine.

"I'm so sorry y'all had to see that." Sawyer smirked, not embarrassed himself but he knew Marina was.

"Don't be sorry, shoot. We got *two* awesome shows tonight." Becka shrugged.

"Not like we haven't seen Sawyer's bare ass before," Chris reminded.

Marina hung her head, hiding her blushing face with the side of her hand as she tried to fix the issue on the laptop.

"Need help? I'm a computer guy," Justin offered, but Marina quickly answered with a head shake.

"How'd that happen?" Sawyer asked her, his voice quiet.

"I have no idea. Oh my God, this is so embarrassing."

"It'll be okay. We won't ever live it down though." He wrapped his arms around her, trying not to laugh.

Chris was drinking a beer as Trev popped one open and said, "You two gave me a chub." Chris spit his beer out in a wide spray then covered his mouth as he laughed so hard his squinting eyes watered.

"That's what I'm sayin'. Gonna be *hard* to concentrate on the movie now," Jake joked, joining Becka on the tailgate with a big popcorn bowl.

"You should be ashamed of yourselves. Good Heavens," Gladys told Sawyer with blushing cheeks.

"Yes, ma'am I should be, but I'm not. Can't smack me with a dishtowel either." He chuckled.

Marina looked at her and Bob and said, "I am so incredibly sorry. That was so disrespectful to y'all."

"Well... I don't think I could look at y'all the same way if it would've been y'all in some weird position," Bob said, arms crossed.

"I get that. Good thing we stopped it when we did then." Sawyer clapped his hands then said, "So, now that that's out of the way, shall we start the actual movie?"

"I almost rather keep watching that one." Chris chuckled and winked at Marina; he couldn't keep a straight face as he took a sip of his beer. Stacy elbowed his arm with a scowl and he shrugged.

"Oh, lord." Marina pushed play on the comedy and they all snuggled up cozy.

"Maybe with alcohol involved, we'll get to see the real thing happenin' over there in the back of Sawyer's truck," Justin joked, making Becka and Raquel laugh.

"Shut up, Justin!" Sawyer and Marina both shouted.

Jake managed to sneak an arm around Becka part-way through the movie like a teenager on a date.

It was a cool night, not too cold, but just cool enough to snuggle under a blanket, perfect movie-outside-type weather. Memorable for *so* many reasons.

CHAPTER 13

Sugar-Coated Ranch Hands

Sawyer had left the office door open for the fresh, colder air to breeze through. The morning was crisp enough, even with his fleece-lined jacket on, that he was thankful he had his coffee to warm his body from the inside. He stood from his desk and leaned in the office doorway, texting Marina to stop at the bakery for apple cinnamon and sugar donuts and coffee. The aroma of fallen autumn leaves filled the air. He was taking it all in when he heard the young ranch hands talking outside. He went around the corner to greet them but stopped when he heard the topic of conversation. He backed up to stay out of sight.

"So, let's make a bet then on what Miss. Marina wears today."

"Fine. I say cut-offs. I hope her ass cheeks show when she bends over too."

"Nah, it's chilly out this morning. I bet she wears jeans."

"Either way her ass will be bangin'."

"No joke. I gotta admit, I'm jealous of Big Boss Man. He gets to hit that."

"Ugh, I can only imagine how sweet it is."

Their voices quieted as they walked closer to the office door.

"You boys need help stackin' that hay?" Sawyer startled them as they passed the open office doorway where Sawyer stood, arms crossed as he leaned against the doorframe.

"Uh, no, sir. I think we got it. Thanks though."

Sawyer tipped his white hat to them with a smug look on his face. The guys neared the feed room and quietly spoke, although Sawyer could still hear them.

"Shit, you think he heard us?"

"I doubt it. Hope not anyway. We probably would've just been fired if so."

Sawyer grinned, walking back to his desk and taking his jacket off.

Justin pulled in the drive and Sawyer heard him talking to the guys when he got out of his truck but he couldn't make out what was being said. He was typing away on the laptop when Justin stomped dirt off his boots just outside the door before coming inside, Whiskey on his heels.

"Dipshits," he mumbled.

"Mornin'," Sawyer acknowledged his entrance.

"Mornin'."

"You grumpy today?" Sawyer asked, snickering.

"Nah, those two out there—"

"What about 'em?"

"They're looking to get their asses kicked."

Sawyer laughed. "Why? They still talking about my wife's ass?"

"You hear 'em? Jesus, it's not just her ass they're talking about. I just chewed their asses."

"Why?"

"Because I figured you would if you heard what they were sayin'. They weren't sugar-coating it."

"I don't wanna know what they were sayin' if it's worse than what I heard before you arrived."

"You'd fire their asses, I'm sure."

"They can say what they want, it's not like they can have her." He looked up from the screen with a sideways grin.

Justin chuckled. "Yeah, you don't have anything to worry about, man. That woman wouldn't do that to you. Not for those scrawny idiots, especially. The one wears a mullet for cryin' out loud."

"She wouldn't for anybody else, either. I wouldn't want her overhearing them being disrespectful though, so it's probably a good thing you said somethin' to them. Better you than me. She should be coming soon with donuts and fancy coffee."

"Oh, sweet. I didn't take the time to stop on my way here. I kinda miss the coffee shop being conveniently across the road and the bakery next door."

"I guess I'll just have to make extra trips to town then." Marina came into the office before her voice had finished echoing off the barn walls, her arms full. Sawyer jumped up to help her and set the big box of donuts on Justin's desk.

"Sorry, darlin', I didn't hear ya pull in."

"Aww, it's okay. Thanks."

"Thanks, Marina." Justin took his coffee from the drink carrier.

"You're welcome. I got a big box of all the same flavor of donuts. Thought maybe the guys out there would like one."

Justin was smirking as he grabbed a donut from the box.

"That was thoughtful. You can ask 'em." Sawyer pecked her lips with his sugar-coated cinnamon lips and his mouth full of donut. Marina stepped out to holler at the guys and Justin muttered, "We already know they want a sweet piece."

"Shut up, Justin." Sawyer sipped his coffee, smirking. She came back in and took her coffee from the carrier as she snatched a donut and sat at her desk. The ranch hands came in, one bumped the other's elbow and whispered, "Told ya." She was, indeed, wearing jeans with a snug aqua t-shirt which had a little horseshoe on the front left that read "Taking the Reins". It accentuated her busty chest and the ranch hands took notice. Sawyer just stared at the guys till they thanked them and headed back out to work.

"They weren't very talkative this morning," she observed out loud.

"Are they usually?" Sawyer asked, rubbing his jaw.

"Yeah. Hmm, weird." She shrugged.

Justin sank low behind his laptop, mouth full of donut so he couldn't laugh.

"They ever say things to you?" Sawyer asked her.

"Like what?"

"Like inappropriate things."

"No. They're always polite. Why?" She took a bite. Sawyer just shook his head and her eyes darted between Sawyer's and Justin's for a moment before Justin spoke up.

"They've got the hots for you."

"What? That's ridiculous. They're like, ten years younger than me."

"That doesn't matter," Sawyer said, then cleared his throat.

Her brows furrowed in confusion.

"We've heard what they think of you. You let me know if I need to jack their jaws."

"Oh, Sawyer, leave those boys alone." She laughed.

"They'd deserve it if ya asked me." Justin laughed, making Sawyer laugh too.

"I work with barbarians." Ice rattled in her latte as it swirled in her cup and the guys nodded in agreement.

CHAPTER 14

Horses, Bears, and Lanterns, Oh My!

"This is gonna be a fun weekend," Marina said, helping Sawyer unload the truck at the campsite.

"I'm looking forward to it. It'll be nice to have a stress-free weekend. Maybe without having to deal with work, we can get ya knocked up." He raised his brows.

"Oh my goodness, Sawyer."

"What? Did you really expect to sleep with me alone in a tent in the woods and not get it on? Baby, I thought you knew me better than that."

"Sawyer! Our friends will be right next to us. That would be rude."

"You just have to be real quiet about it. That's all. Then we wait till everyone has quieted down and it sounds like they're asleep." He winked then blew a bubble with his gum before letting it pop loudly. She wasn't surprised at his premeditated plans but still shook her head, laughing.

"Should we unload the horses?" she asked, carrying camping equipment to the cleared area.

"Nah, let's wait for the others to arrive because I don't know where we're hitchin' them up yet."

She tossed him a teasing salute before coming around the

truck to say, "This is a pretty area. I've never been up here before."

"It gets busy at certain times of the year. There's an equestrian camp a few miles from here and there's an RV park too. I'd rather be away from everyone and Chris is friends with the guy that owns this land so there won't be anyone around here but us."

"Perfect." She set her load of gear down next to his and grabbed him by the belt loops for a kiss.

"So...if you wanna get your yelp on, now's the time to be loud." He pressed his pelvis to hers and grabbed hold of her rear. She was about to accept that offer, laughing, when friends pulled in the long two-track drive, Justin first.

"Dammit! I swear that man needs to work on his timing."

She tapped his chest and said, "Let's go unload the rest of our stuff."

"Well, I'm walkin' behind ya. You know the drill," he said as he adjusted the crotch of his jeans.

"You bring me one to ride?" Justin hollered, setting his tailgate down to grab gear.

Sawyer looked confused for a moment then said, "Oh, you meant a horse! Yeah, I brought ya Athena."

"Seriously?" Justin flapped his arms down to his sides in disappointment as Marina giggled.

"No, I wouldn't do that to ya. You can ride Foxtrot."

"What did you mean, 'Oh a horse?' You two were about to force these trees and birds to be witnesses weren't ya."

"Pffft, no."

"Liar."

Sawyer laughed, opening the horse trailer side door. Justin helped him get saddles out and Marina grabbed halters and such.

"Sounds like Jake and I are solo this weekend." Justin tossed a saddle blanket over his arm.

"Y'all gonna share a tent?" Sawyer grinned.

"I offered." Justin shrugged.

Sawyer busted out laughing. "I was joking."

"I'm not. Less tents to put up and take down. You know what that son of a bitch said?"

"I can take a guess."

"He said he wasn't watching me pitch a tent out here in the middle of all this morning wood."

Sawyer's laughter rang out wide. Marina was laughing so hard she sounded as though she was crying.

She caught her breath enough to say, "If it gets chilly tonight, y'all could keep each other warm."

"Maybe with a pillow between us," Justin joked.

Chris and Stacy pulled in, coming up the two-track with their horse trailer in tow. Shortly after came Trev and Trina, then Jake. Sawyer let the horses down the ramp, handing Foxtrot off to Justin.

"You bring Dixie?" Trina asked.

"Nah, I didn't feel like brushing pickers out of all that fluff," Marina said.

"Oh, yeah, good point."

Hooves clunked and horse breaths whuffled as they were unloaded from trailers.

"We ridin' first?" Jake asked, tossing his tent into the pile of camping gear in the clearing.

"Sure. It's probably best we wear them out a bit before hitchin' 'em." Sawyer slapped a red buffalo plaid saddle blanket onto Tango's back.

"That's a beautiful horse, Jake." Marina petted down its muzzle.

"Thanks. I've had him a while. Sawyer found me this beauty right after we met. They're hard to come by." He saddled the Camarillo white horse, who was loving the attention from Marina. "Becka couldn't come, huh?" he asked as he cinched the strap.

"Nah, she has to work."

"Bummer."

Marina smiled, loving that they had been crushing on each other for a while.

"The weekend would be more fun with her here," Marina said, looking over at Jake to see his reaction.

"Sure would." He sported a smile. Stacy knocked elbows with Marina as she walked by, having heard about the blooming crush. "Speakin' of...Marina, can I borrow you for a second?" Jake gave her a side-nod and they walked off a few yards from everyone else.

"What's up?" she asked, hands in her back pockets.

"So, I want to...I guess ask for your permission to ask Becka out. I know Sawyer calls me a lady's man but—"

"Jake, I know you're not that way."

"I'm ready for a real relationship. Something serious that I think could last. I won't break her heart. That is, if she even accepts a date. I really like her so if you think she'd agree to a date with me, I'd like to ask her. Only if it's okay with you though, of course."

"Jake. I've gotten to know you well and I adore you. You'd be good for her and she'd be good for you. I'm sure she'd say yes and I'm completely fine with it. In fact, I'm excited. I appreciate you asking; it's so considerate of you."

"Thanks, I appreciate that. So, has she said something?"

Marina laughed. "Just ask her, Jake."

He chuckled with a nod. "Okay. Will Sawyer deck me if I give you a hug?"

"I won't let him." She laughed as Jake bear-hugged her. Sawyer wore a smirk as the two came walking back over to the group. He didn't ask what that was about but he had an idea. He already had Legend saddled up by the time Marina went over to do it.

"Sorry, babe."

He just smiled, not minding at all, as everyone else saddled up.

"Our stuff okay just tossed out here like this?" Trina asked.

"Yeah, of course. Nobody else is out here," Chris said, mounting Smokie.

"What about bears?" Trina asked.

The guys chuckled.

"If ya don't have snacks in your sleepin' bag, ya don't have to worry about bears," Trev told her.

"Um...give me a second then." She ran back to her sleeping bag to put snacks into the truck.

"Woman, are you serious?" Trev hollered and shook his head.

"Dude, your woman actually had snacks in her sleeping bag? That's hilarious." Chris laughed.

"Your woman chose to hang out with us for her birthday. She could've picked anything to do." Justin said, mounting Foxtrot and laughing.

"Yep. She said to surprise her with some sort of outdoor activity with friends. I figured we'd take the whole weekend. The rest of the girls were workin' though, so she's hanging with them next weekend. I even made her a cake." Sawyer waited on Tango over by the guys while waiting for the girls to join.

Chris stuck a long reed of grass in his mouth to chew on and said, "No way! You made a cake?"

"Hell yeah. I've watched her do it a few times. She's way more talented with it than I am but it turned out good. I cook and bake and stuff once in a great while. She sure was surprised when I brought it to her at the dining room table with a lit candle on it."

"I bet. We'll have to start calling ya Betty Crocker," Jake said.

"Or Suzy Homemaker since you do house chores too," Trev joked.

"Damn right, I do. I don't mind at all. She helps at the office so I help at home. That's the way it should be."

"And I love it," Marina confirmed as she trotted up alongside Sawyer.

"You girls comin'?" Chris steered Smokie back around in a circle and hollered to the girls who were mounted and headed toward them.

"Don't let Trev fool ya. He helps out with stuff around the house more these days," Trina praised.

"Is that so?" Marina asked, surprised.

"Yep. We had a chat about it a while back and he's stepped it up."

"Glad to hear it." Marina smiled.

"Chris was vacuuming when I got home from the store the other day," Stacy added, raking her strawberry blonde hair back into a hair tie. The guys all looked at Chris with raised brows.

"Alright, this subject needs to change." Chris clicked his heel into Smokie's side, going ahead of everyone else. The guys chuckled and the girls caught up.

"Chris, is that the Tennessee Walker you brought back from the road trip that Stacy is riding?" Marina asked.

"Sure is. He's been great."

"He looks great. Nice gait too. Smokie's better on the trail than last I recall too."

"Yeah, they're both good horses. It turns out that Smokie here is an Andalusian."

Stacy whispered, interrupting the conversation, "Hey" to Marina, who was riding next to her. Marina turned, Stacy and Trina both to her right as they followed next to each other behind the staggered guys. "So, you and Sawyer have been trying to conceive?"

Marina nodded, showing a little disappointment in her expression with slumped shoulders and a nose wrinkle.

"I'm really surprised it hasn't happened yet," Trina whispered.

"Me too," Marina said quietly.

"I'm sure it'll happen soon," Stacy assured.

"Yeah, it's always when ya least expect it, so I hear." Trina tossed her braids behind her shoulder.

"Thanks, I hope so."

"My sister stopped trying because she didn't wanna be hugely prego during summer, but that's when it happened," Trina shared.

"So, try less?" Marina asked, desperate for advice.

"Couldn't hurt to try that."

"Maybe going a while without altogether, ya know, because then it'll be explosive that next time. Know what I mean?" Stacy dramatized with her hands as she spoke softly.

"Nice theatrics." Trina laughed.

"I'll run that suggestion by Sawyer. I doubt he'll go for that." She snickered. "We've booked a romantic trip to Bali so hopefully that'll help. We need relaxation and stress-free time alone."

"Ooh, that sounds perfect," Stacy said, Trina nodding in agreement.

The trail was wide, trees lining either side. Rustling leaves brought a sense of calm and the chirping birds gave liveliness to the day as sunbeams shone through tree branches and across the dirt trail ahead. The sound of denim adjusting in creaking saddles was almost louder than the conversations. The trail led around a couple dozen wooded acres. The sandhill pines stood tall and gave much of the forest a cleanly groomed appeal. This time of year prompted pine needles to collect along the forest floor, providing a resource for wildlife.

"Did y'all know that these pines actually require fire every few years in order for their cones to drop?" Marina looked up at the towering trees.

"Really? They don't just drop like other pines?" Trina asked.

"Nope. Not generally. The heat from fire allows for release."

"Sounds familiar." Sawyer smirked, slowing down to ride alongside Marina. She swatted his arm playfully and added a giggle.

"Not sure why the cones don't fall in the summer then. This summer was a brutal one, didn't need a damn fire," Chris said, trading his chewed reed for a new one.

"It sure as hell was. Training horses, even early mornings or late evenings, was rough. Couldn't do that shit much during the middle of the day," Sawyer agreed.

"I'm looking forward to the cooler weather tonight," Stacy stated.

"Me too. Only having reached sixty-five degrees today, I bet it will be a great snuggle night." Marina hoped.

"Hoodie weather." Trina nodded.

"I hope you brought one of your own because you aren't stealing mine," Trev told her.

"Bitch, I brought one of my own so don't even start with me." Trina's head bobbed back and forth. She made everyone chuckle the way she talked back to Trev.

"Good because I only own two."

"I know. I brought your second one for myself." She turned her nose up. The girls were cracking up as Trev shook his head.

"Why do women always steal our hoodies?" Trev asked sincerely. Justin shrugged and Chris shook his head. Sawyer said, "I don't mind Marina wearing my stuff."

"Shut up," Trev dismissed Sawyer's comment.

"She always gives them back."

"They smell like you, that's why I wear your shirts." Marina reached out for his hand, which he gladly took hold of.

"You did bring one though, right?" Sawyer asked her. "Because I only packed one. Of course, I'll give it to you if you didn't."

She giggled, "You're sweet. Yes, I brought my own."

"Good girl." He grinned that sexy sideways grin that made her bite her bottom lip. Stacy and Trina just stared at him, their jaws loose with envy. Marina was already looking forward to the cooler snuggle weather with him later on.

After a two-hour ride, saddles were hung over a downed log as the hitched horses grazed green grass that stuck up between fallen leaves in the tree line. Justin and Trev put a couple of water buckets out for the horses while Sawyer and Jake started a campfire in the clearing and the others started setting up tents. Sunset hues spread their mark upon the Earth.

"Hope somebody brought lanterns for tonight, otherwise we'll have to leave the fire going if y'all want enough light to piss behind the bushes," Chris mentioned.

"I brought one," Sawyer said as an orange glow flared in the pit.

"I packed one too." Justin dug it out of a tote.

"Perfect. That should be enough." Chris let down the flap on the front of his tent after Stacy hauled their blankets inside. Sawyer and Jake set up their tents while the girls gathered food from the coolers to cook dinner over the fire.

"I brought cards for poker if anyone wants to play after we eat," Jake offered as he shook out his sleeping bag.

"Sounds good." Sawyer nodded.

"Bring your guitar?" Trev asked Sawyer. Sawyer looked at him with a lowered brow.

"Sweet." Trev tossed another log on the fire, sparks flying into the air.

"That might have to be a quick poker game. It's getting darker out sooner the last few nights," Chris said, joining the guys at the fire.

"It will be. Jake always wins anyway," Sawyer teased.

Marina put olive oil and chicken breasts in the big cast iron skillet over the fire. Stacy broke out a tub of pasta noodles to dump into a pot of boiling water and set a fruit bowl on a stump.

"What's for dinner, ladies?" Justin asked as he wandered over to help.

"Bruschetta chicken. Wanna chop the tomatoes and basil?"

"Sure." He took a knife from Marina and the cutting board from Trina. "Fancy for campin', don't ya think?"

"Nah, this is an easy dish. Two pans and done."

"It's a great idea. Something everyone likes too. Hey, who was in charge of bringing beer?" Justin asked loudly.

"That'd be me," Chris hollered, snatching the reed from his teeth. "I threw some Ciderboys in there for you girls too."

"Thanks!" Marina gave a thumbs up.

Sawyer snagged a beer and cider from the drink cooler, leaves crunching as he stepped over a log and handed Marina her cold brown bottle. He wiped his wet hand on his denimed thigh then planted a smooch upon her cheek as he popped the top off his own beer.

"Thanks, babe."

"Smells great. I'm starvin'." Sawyer unwrapped the flannel shirt that hugged his waist and slipped one arm through, then the other. He pulled the front straight but didn't bother buttoning it. Marina caught herself staring and pulled him to her with her arms wrapped around him between shirt layers, feeling the curvature of his strong back. He set his beer on a tailgate next to them, which they'd used as a countertop, and tucked her hair back behind her shoulder before cradling her face in his hands and connecting his lips to hers.

"You're warm." She smiled, looking up at those glacier blues.

"And you're getting chilly. I'll go to the tent and grab you a long-sleeved shirt."

"Thank you."

"Of course, darlin'." He kissed her forehead before going across the clearing to their tent.

"Food ready?" Chris asked, approaching Stacy.

"I think so." She handed out plates as Sawyer came back over and handed Marina her shirt, which she pulled down overtop of her t-shirt.

"It's definitely going to be snuggle weather tonight," she said with a smile, taking a plate from him.

"I'm looking forward to keeping you warm." He smiled and winked.

"We know what you mean by that and we don't wanna hear it. Not again." Justin laughed, plopping garlic sauce and noodles onto his plate. Sawyer chuckled and looked at Marina who then popped a tomato chunk into his mouth.

"We aren't really going to hear them, are we?" Stacy asked Chris. Justin laughed and nodded.

"Well, I mean, I guess it *is* her birthday weekend." Trina shrugged. "Would you be surprised?"

"That wouldn't matter," Justin and Jake said simultaneously.

Everyone sat around the fire in folding chairs, eating and chatting, then broke out the poker cards after cleaning up dinner. Two hands in, a car pulled in and Becka got out.

"Oh, my goodness! What a great surprise!" Marina hustled to her for a hug.

"I wasn't gonna miss out on all the fun," Becka said.

"You had to work though."

"Yeah, I just came from work and I'll call out sick tomorrow."

"Aww, thanks for coming to join us!"

"Sure thing, boo."

Jake was standing, smiling, cards still in his hand as everyone else sat, watching Jake's reaction to Becka showing up. His face was lit up and there was a glimmer in his brown eyes that was undeniable.

"Glad I brought a blanket," she said as she and Marina joined everyone. Jake put out an extra chair next to his and patted the seat for her to sit.

"Thanks."

"Hey, Becka." Jake smiled as she sat.

"Hey. Good to see you guys."

"You too. I'm glad you decided to come. You have a tent?" he asked.

"Shoot! No."

"Hmm…I guess you'll have to bunk with me." He turned to her to see her smirk.

"Okay, yeah, I could do that. Thanks for the offer."

"Of course." His white teeth peered through his half-cracked smile.

"So now I'm the only one flying solo tonight?" Justin asked, bummed.

"Yep. Looks like you're pitchin' your own tent tonight," Trev told him, making everyone snicker.

"I really need a girlfriend."

"You need to actively look for one then. You work and hang out with us. You waiting for some random chick to run into you with her car on the way?" Chris asked.

"Good point."

"Grab that guitar, Sawyer, since we can never play poker without Jake winning." Chris grabbed the cooler and plunked it down closer to them by the fire then passed out a round of bottles.

"I can't help it if I'm just that good at the game."

"Maybe it's the poker face." Stacy shrugged.

"When it comes to being around Becka, he doesn't have a strong poker face though." Trina bumped elbows with Stacy as Sawyer got his guitar out of the truck and took his seat, propping his guitar on his thigh. The sun had pretty much sunk so Chris lit the lanterns then took his seat next to Sawyer.

"What are we strummin' to?" Sawyer asked.

"Why don't ya do that four-chord thing?" Trev asked, sippin' his beer.

"I love it when y'all do that." Marina got excited.

"What is it?" Becka asked.

"It's where ya start with a song that plays four main chords then blend it into a different song that shares the same chords and just keep it going. Genre doesn't matter."

"Cool. Let's hear it."

They had a fun pickin' party, singing along to every song he sang. Sawyer and Chris both drank more than usual and were showing the effects of the alcohol. They were cracking up, leaning on each other in tears over stuff that wasn't even that funny. The girls were giggling at them.

Out of songs and half the crew too drunk to follow along, Sawyer set the guitar down and they started sharing stories.

"I haven't seen Sawyer this wasted since the lawn mower races." Jake laughed.

"The what?" Trina did a sideways head bob.

"Trev hasn't ever told you about that?"

"Nah, spill it."

"So, I think it was two years ago, Sawyer fixed up a lawn mower and Chris had just bought a new one and stopped to show it to Sawyer on his way home with it. Justin and I got a phone call telling us to bring our lawn mowers over for a race. It was too hilarious to pass up. There was definitely alcohol involved."

"Definitely." Justin laughed.

"Sawyer had a few glasses of whiskey before we got there and was on his third beer by the time we started racing. We lined up like it was a damn horse race. Chris somehow almost fell off while pissin' around but still won with Sawyer right on his ass."

"Wow. That sounds hilarious." Trina laughed.

"I was told about these guys riding horses through a drive-thru," Marina added, grinning.

"What the? Trev, what the hell?" Trina swatted Trev's arm as he was cracking up.

"Sawyer walked me up to the door one night after we were out drinkin' and I fell into the bushes." Jake laughed.

"Wow." Stacy was half amused, shaking her head.

"The guys were laughing so hard they left me there till they could gather themselves. Apparently, it took all night because I woke up to Sawyer dragging me across the yard the next morning."

"Just face-planted it?" Stacy asked.

"Yep, pretty much. I think I passed out as I was falling. Took a good branch beating. That was the night before a wedding I was supposed to be in."

"Supposed to be?" Marina asked, intrigued.

"The bride didn't show up. I didn't have to look like shit in photos after all."

"Oh my God, Jake! Who was the bride?" Trina wasn't even laughing anymore.

"Who cares?" Trev asked her.

"I care." She scowled at him.

"My cousin." Jake laughed. "She always was a bitch so it didn't matter to me either way. I congratulated the groom."

"Sounds like Justin's next girlfriend." Sawyer couldn't contain his cackling.

"You're a dick." Justin rolled his eyes, which just made Sawyer and Chris cackle even harder. They were about to fall out of their chairs.

"Am I missing something or...?" Stacy asked with furrowed brows. Marina shrugged, giggling at Sawyer.

"They're just extremely drunk." Marina got her hoodie from the passenger seat of the truck and put it on over her head then handed Sawyer his.

"He was wasted way worse than this when y'all had that little, ya know...when you left that time before the wedding. It was a bad drunk though, not a fun drunk," Trev said, choking on the bug spray clouding around him as he sprayed.

"Yeah, again, I'm really sorry about that," Marina said, still ashamed about causing chaos.

"We laugh about it now. Well, not about y'all, but about how drunk he was. He fell asleep against a horse in the stables, fell asleep drunk and drugged up with a sedative poolside in a thunderstorm, wandered the house naked after we practically had to drag him back inside to sleep it off... we laugh now about those round ass cheeks making us turn our heads away."

"He does the naked thing when he's sober too but I don't turn my head." Marina scooped her arm up with Sawyer's.

"They don't like being confined," Sawyer said, still chugging and chuckling. Marina took his beer away and set it in the grass on the other side of her chair.

"Why'd you take that away? I can't get any drunker. It's getting chilly now." Sawyer put his hoodie on and scooched Marina's chair close to his so they could snuggle more easily. Hoodies and blankets were keeping everyone warm around the fire, the crackling flames growing taller, sparks floating into the air as the crew became tired over their last drink.

"I think I'm turning in, y'all." Chris stood and took Stacy's hand.

"He even smells drunk. Goodnight," she said, waving over her shoulder to everyone as she followed him to their tent.

"I'm cold. I'm goin' to bed too." Trina stood and side-nodded for Trev to follow.

"Goodnight." Jake stood and offered Becka a hand. She was surprised but gladly accepted. Jake seemed excited to be sharing a tent.

"I gotta warm up my lady too." Sawyer and Marina stood and he slapped her rear with a moan. "Giddy up." He raised his brows and bit his bottom lip.

"Ooh, okay. Happy birthday to me." She giggled and hopped onto his back.

"Yee-haw! Hope y'all brought earplugs!" he hollered as he hustled to their tent.

"Aww shit," Justin mumbled, the last to leave the fire. "Should we put this out?" he asked loudly, but he was the only one still out there. He kicked dirt over the fire and gray smoke rolled above the tents as he positioned the lanterns on either side of the pit before entering his tent. Between the giggles and squeals coming from Sawyer's tent, there was an alarming, high-pitched howl. Justin dashed from his tent and hollered, "What the hell was that?"

"Wasn't me." Sawyer spoke up.

"Snakes, gators, and bears, oh my!" Chris hollered then laughed.

"Just a coyote, Justin. You need somebody to cuddle with ya till ya go to sleep?" Jake teased.

"You volunteerin'?" Justin joked.

"Nah, I'm cozy right now."

"Yep, and I'm not movin'," Becka hollered.

"Ooh," Trina teased.

"I'll be fine. If I'm missin' in the morning, that coyote probably drug me off. No biggie," Justin joked, ducking back into his tent.

"Shit, I left my guitar out there. I can't have it getting damp." Sawyer ran out to get it and put it in his truck. He was freezing, wearing nothing but jeans, unbuttoned.

"You'll go out for your guitar but not for a strange wild animal noise? You suck." Justin zipped his tent as Sawyer laughed, tip-toe hustling his bare feet across the cold ground. Upon entering the tent backward to zip it up behind him, the lighting was but a faint glow from the lantern outside. He turned to see Marina lying nude on top of her favorite cozy blanket.

"Oh, hell yeah!" He wore an eager wrinkle on his nose as he pulled his jeans off and crawled over top of her in just his white boxer briefs.

"I don't wanna be taking advantage of your intoxicated state." She smirked slyly.

"You're funny, Miss Marina."

"As much as I love you calling me that, It's Mrs. Brandton now."

"Oh, excuse me, ma'am. I beg your pardon."

"There's no need to beg." Her tongue moistened her lips as she glided her soft, chilled hands up his chest and shoulders then grabbed his shoulder blades, pulling him down to twist her lips with his. A dancing lantern glow lightened his beard as she admired his handsome face and pushed the front of his briefs down, releasing him like a spring.

"I love that you stripped naked with all our friends close by."

"Yeah?"

"Yeah, risky is sexy," he whispered in her ear, the warmth of his breath upon her cheek. Her eyes closed as he kissed her neck, holding her hands in his above her head, their fingers intertwined as he penetrated her. She gasped a sharp breath and looked him in the eyes. His fingers released from hers and ran through her hair alongside her face. Her sudden grip on his ass forced a deep thrust.

"I'm not gonna last long if you do that again."

"You never go *that* fast." She grinned, accepting the challenge.

"I'm never this drunk either." He snickered.

"Well, then maybe I should be on top so I'm not tempted to keep grabbing your ass." She pushed his chest and he gladly rolled over, taking her with him. Wavy honey hair brushed across him as she sat up, straddling his body. The way she moved drove him crazy and he took her to a higher state of mind. He kneaded her breasts and she was fully receptive to his skilled hands. His collarbones protruded with his deep breaths, her own shuddering as she took all of him in. The raw energy she felt when with him was electrifying and her quiet moans got louder. She felt his current, which caused her body to tense up as her back arched. He felt her clench around him, pulsating, claimed by a surge of ecstacy. He quickly covered her mouth to muffle the sound, which she didn't seem in complete control of. She relaxed and lowered to his chest. He tipped her chin up and pressed his lips to hers. She rolled, lying next to him, wrapped in his arms and that plush blanket the rest of the night.

The next morning, half of the group was up shortly after the sun. Justin started the fire as the crisp morning air proved to be still hoodie weather. Jake was up and had started boiling water for coffee by the time Trev and Chris woke and tended to the horses.

"Sawyer is always up early. It's weird that he's still sleeping." Justin poked around in the fire with a stick to allow oxygen to quicken the flames.

"He was pretty wasted though." Jake yawned. Stacy came out of the tent and wrapped up in a blanket by the fire, still not quite awake, and Trina joined her shortly after.

"I see you survived the coyote," Trina teased.

"I sure did." Justin laughed.

"They getting up today?" Chris asked, pointing to Sawyer's tent.

"Who knows?" Trev shrugged, breaking up a hay bale to distribute amongst hooves.

"Should I wake Becka or let her sleep?" Jake asked.

"I'd let her sleep. Never know if she's a real bear in the mornings." Justin and Jake sat in chairs near the fire, hands in their hoodie pockets.

"You must have worn her out," Justin said without making eye contact.

"Nah, I was a gentleman. We snuggled but that was it. It was nice."

"Wow, you really like her, huh?"

"Yeah, I do."

"You gonna ask her out?"

"I wanted to last night but thought I'd see how the night went first."

Becka came out of the tent with her messy bun on the verge of unraveling, wrapping herself in a blanket, and sat by Jake.

"Sleep good?" he asked her.

"I slept like a rock. Thanks for keeping me warm." She smiled a big, thankful smile, as did he as he patted her knee. Chris and Trev joined everyone around the fire and took notice of Jake's good morning mood. Marina unzipped their tent and started to step out but seemed as though she was trying to get Sawyer to his feet.

"He awake yet?" Becka hollered. "Good grief, even I'm up."

"Well, I'm trying to get him up," Marina hollered back. "Sawyer, you have to put pants on," Marina said quietly, but everyone heard and snickered. She came out and sat in a chair, hands in her hoodie pockets. He stumbled out right after, trying to put his hoodie on, his brows turned in as though he was blinded by sunlight.

"You scowly or got a hangover?" Trev asked, pouring a coffee for Sawyer and handing it to him.

"Thanks. Hangover."

"Well, you're no stranger to those," Chris said, blowing on his hot coffee between his hands.

"Yeah, yeah."

Trev handed out coffee mugs.

"I figure after breakfast we'll get another trail ride in before we load up," Chris said.

"I'll have to wake up a bit more first." Sawyer rubbed his eyes with his palm.

"A ride sounds nice," Marina said, sipping her coffee, steam clouding her face.

"Didn't have your fill of ridin' last night?" Chris asked with a smirk.

"Hmmm?" Her wide eyes looked over at him.

"You realize that with our tent across from y'alls, we could see y'alls silhouettes in the tent?"

She looked at Sawyer then back at Chris.

"Are you being serious?" she asked.

"Were y'all watchin' the show?" Sawyer chuckled.

"There was no point in him covering your mouth, sweetie." Stacy couldn't resist a smirk.

Marina spit her coffee out in a spray. "Oh my God. The stupid lanterns."

She looked at Sawyer, who just shrugged, laughing.

CHAPTER 15

Refraining from Frustration

Dr. Chen welcomed Marina and Sawyer into her office, shook their hands, and gestured for them to have a seat across from her at her desk. Her less-than-wide smile gave the uneasy feeling they were about to receive undesirable news. They were both nervous as hell, Sawyer rubbing his palms back and forth on his jeans. He could feel his deodorant was having a hard time keeping up with his nerves. Marina sat with one leg crossed over the other, her foot wiggling with anticipation.

"I have your blood work results back, Sawyer. But before I forget, Marina, I'd like you to increase your vitamin B intake a little bit. I'd also like you to start on a prenatal vitamin, even just over the counter for now would be fine and I can prescribe one down the road. Sawyer..." She flipped her folder open and shuffled through paperwork in an organized fashion then said, "I think you should take a multivitamin if you aren't already. Your iron is slightly low so I'll give you a script for that."

"That explains feeling lazy lately," he said.

"Yes, that will do it. Marina, your hormone levels still look good. Sawyer, there doesn't seem to be an issue with your little soldiers either. For now, I recommend less stress for both of you. Now, there are options such as fertility treatments we could try but they're costly. Let's start with new blood work in a month after the vitamins have had a chance to do their jobs. Oh, and it may seem silly, but you could research holistic at-home remedies. Some could be a myth but may be worth a try."

"Are we going to have to consider more extreme measures later down the road? Honest opinion." Marina was worried, her concern shining clearly in her eyes.

"As in?" Dr. Chen asked, closing the folder.

"As in artificial insemination, adoption, surrogacy? I'm starting to worry." Marina took Sawyer's hand.

"They are options, but I feel we should begin with less extreme and less invasive. The options you mentioned are financially and emotionally costly. They may have to be considered later on, but again, I suggest starting small and working our way up."

Sawyer leaned his elbow on the arm of the chair, his chin resting on his fist, deep in thought. He gazed off, just staring at the doctor's bookshelf behind her.

"Sawyer?" Marina wanted his attention.

"Hmm?" He looked at her and rubbed his chin.

"What are you thinking right now?"

He let out an emotional exhale. She could see his eyes becoming misty as he scratched his head and looked around the room.

"So, we'd see you for blood work in a month then for results a couple of weeks after?" he asked.

"Yes."

He nodded with his head down. "We'll take your advice and talk things over at home."

"Of course. If it's any consolation to either of you, couples have been successful in getting pregnant after some time being abstinent."

"Abstinence?" Sawyer shook his head no.

"Sawyer." Marina wanted him to hear the doctor out.

"Sure, the stress from trying so hard sometimes doesn't allow it to happen. Several of my patients have had success after a few weeks of abstaining. You may not have to wait that long though. We could check a sample again for you at the end of each week."

"Weeks? I'm sorry, did you say weeks?" Sawyer looked dumbfounded.

"Yes, sir, I did."

Sawyer looked at Marina with wide eyes and raised brows.

"That shouldn't be too difficult," the doctor noted, but Marina raised her brows and pursed her lips.

Sawyer spoke up. "For who?"

The doctor smiled at him, then at Marina.

"Thank you." Marina stood and shook the doctor's hand as Sawyer remained seated, arms crossed and brows furrowed in silent defiance.

"Sawyer, you ready to go?" She took her purse from the chair and waited a moment for him, looking at him, then at the doctor with a smile, then back at him. He stood slowly, pulling his shirt down and clearing his throat.

"Grab your hat, love." Marina pointed to his hat, which he had laid on the corner of the desk when they entered.

"Oh, right...thanks." He put his hat on and exited, Marina right behind him.

They stopped for lunch on the go and took it back to the office at the stables. Not a word was mentioned on the topic until they entered the office. She sat at her desk and opened the food containers from the deli café and set aside the container they had brought back for Justin.

"How'd the appointment go?" Justin asked, taking his container to his desk. "Thanks for lunch by the way."

"You're welcome. It went okay, thanks," she answered.

Sawyer just looked down as he wheeled his chair over to her desk to eat next to her.

"You okay, man?" Justin asked Sawyer, noticing the tension .

Sawyer chewed on the inside of his cheek for a moment before saying, "That woman is bat-shit crazy if she thinks I'm going weeks without making love to you. We're getting a second opinion." He looked at Marina, not having touched his food yet.

"Yep. Told you." Justin laughed.

"Um, babe, if I were to get pregnant, we'd have to go six weeks after I give birth before we could make love."

"What?" He gasped.

She giggled and nodded.

"Oh, you're joking." He relaxed in the chair.

"No, I'm not. Sorry, babe."

"Why? How?" He sat up straight again.

"It'll take that long for me to heal. Doctors say six weeks."

"Holy shit," he said, perplexed.

Justin was trying to contain his laughter, turning his chair away as he bit into his sandwich.

"What are you snickering about?" Sawyer asked, his tone grumpy.

"You won't die from holding off, Sawyer." Justin laughed.

"Says who? And *you* might."

"Okay..." Justin put his sandwich down. "How long have you two 'held off'?"

"How long is your period usually? Five days, tops?" Sawyer asked Marina.

"Yeah, basically. Most times you can't even wait that long."

Justin stopped chewing as if he were disgusted.

"See? How am I supposed to go six weeks while you heal? I'm already freaking out about a couple of weeks. I didn't realize it takes that long to heal but I suppose it makes sense."

Marina shrugged as she took a bite of salad.

"There's other ways of...ya know." Justin mentioned before chugging water.

"Of what?" Sawyer was so distraught he couldn't think clearly.

"Of satisfying you, babe."

Justin was smirking, waiting for it to dawn on Sawyer what they were referring to. Sawyer looked back and forth at them until

Marina said, "We can get a babysitter and take your truck through a car wash." His confused look turned into an *Ahh ha!* look.

Justin choked on his water and turned away again.

"You told him about that, didn't you?" Marina asked, not surprised the least bit.

Justin was nodding when Sawyer answered, "Maybe. That wouldn't be satisfying you though, so how's that fair?"

"I'll be okay, babe. It will be really difficult but I'll be sore and exhausted anyway, I'm sure. Just being close to you and making sure you're taken care of in that aspect is all I need...until that six weeks is up, then you're all mine."

"It's not the same. I don't like it."

"Sawyer, dear, you'll survive. You won't have a choice. As far as what the doctor said about abstinence, maybe we *are* trying too hard." She giggled then continued to eat her salad as she finished updating Justin on what the "bat-shit crazy" doctor suggested based on their results. Sawyer just sat there and rolled his eyes.

"Once you two have kids, it'll be hard to squeeze in your 'getting-it-on' time, anyway," Justin said with a mouthful.

"Nah. Even if I have to corner her in the laundry room for five minutes, it's happening. She won't ever have to worry about that being an issue."

Justin laughed as Marina's cheeks turned a brighter shade of pink.

CHAPTER 16
Stress Relief

Settling in bed after a long day, Sawyer began gently massaging Marina's shoulder beneath his firm touch as she lay on her side.

"Mmm, that feels good."

"Roll over." That low demanding voice sent a tingle up her spine. She rolled to her stomach, and he moved her hair off to the side, draping it across the pillow. The pressure he applied to all the right spots made her not want him to stop. He didn't miss a spot either. Her back, shoulders, neck, scalp; he covered all the bases. She fell asleep during the massage, tired from working hard that day.

The next morning, she entered the barn, pulling her sweater closed in the front, to see that he left her a barn note that read "Today, we're relieving that stress."

"Good morning." She peeked around the doorway to the feed room where Sawyer was restacking hay.

"Good mornin', darlin'."

"What's the note about?"

"I booked you a massage for today."

"Did you?" Her grin widened as she leaned against the doorway.

"Deep tissue, too. I figure they could do better than I can."

"Nah, I'm perfectly happy with your hands being the ones all over me. This is thoughtful of you though. Thank you."

"You're welcome. If they don't do a good enough job, you let me know as soon as you're back home." He winked with a sideways grin.

"You know I will. You want help?"

He slung a bale up onto a pile.

"Nah, I'm about done but thanks for offerin'. Have you eaten?"

"Not yet. Have you?"

"Nope. I'll come in and get cleaned up and take you to breakfast at the café. Sound good?"

"Sure. That sounds nice."

"Then I'll hang out in the truck or get some stuff I need at the hardware store while you're getting your massage." He wiped the sweat from his brow with the back of his gloved hand before tossing up the last bale with a grunt.

"Okay." She loved watching him work and stood there watching him for longer than was entirely necessary. He removed his gloves after he threw that last bale and flopped them down onto the countertop as they walked out together. The breeze outside made the crisp morning air feel even more brisk but hard work didn't require more than a t-shirt for him.

"I'll be quick in the shower."

"Showering to go to the hardware store?" She giggled.

"Can't be givin' Shanda anything to be runnin' her mouth to Gabby about," he bantered and threw in a chuckle. "Besides, I can't take you on a breakfast date smelling like the barn and sweat."

After enjoying each other's company at breakfast, Sawyer pulled up to the spa on the other side of town and walked Marina in.

"Relax and enjoy, darlin'. I'll be back here before the hour is up."

"Thank you, Sawyer." They exchanged a kiss before he left.

She stripped from a white robe and lay face down on the massage table as instructed by the masseuse, then spread a towel to cover her bare backside. A wall of live bamboo and a trickling waterfall over smooth black pebbles lined one wall of the dimly lit room. Essential oil fragrance of sweet orange and lemongrass filled the air and the zen meditation music was at low volume. She heard the masseuse enter the room and a few moments later, a warm liquid covered Marina's back before hands began spreading the oil. They didn't feel as dainty as she had imagined they would; they certainly didn't belong to the petite masseuse she met upon arrival. These strong hands found the knots within Marina's tense muscles with ease. She anticipated them working on the muscles just beneath her shoulder blades and was not disappointed when they finally got there then drifted to her lower back, a thumb on either side of her spine. Just the right amount of pressure was applied to the tender areas.

The touch strayed lower; her hips and upper-glute region. Marina squirmed a bit, feeling a tad uneasy as she had never had a masseuse wander so low. Warm oil heated the backs of her legs; a trickle the full length. She didn't realize this was intended to be a full-body massage but it might prove to be relaxing for her muscles—until the insides of her upper thighs were reached. She clamped her thighs together with possessive denial, tensing up as a man's voice whispered, "Just relax." Her eyes popped open and she squeezed her thighs together even tighter, extremely uneasy now, knowing it was a male masseuse. She wouldn't have felt comfortable with another man's hands on her in that way, not so intimately, and she had been assigned a female so what the hell was going on? Her heart rate was increasing, skipping a beat, and she wanted to stop him. She was quickly questioning herself on how to go about this when she suddenly stiffened, frozen. This couldn't have been the type of massage Sawyer intended for her to get. Those oiled hands slid higher on the backs of her thighs until they reached about an inch from the massage turning erotic. She tensed up more, her stomach churning at the invasion of his touch, and cleared her throat nervously.

The man suddenly had both hands full of ass cheeks when she finally shrieked, "Excuse me, sir. I don't feel comfortable with you touching me there." She panicked and his hands respectfully retreated, albeit slowly.

A scream clawed its way into her throat when he crawled over the top of her, but he growled in her ear before she could let it out. "I'm sorry. I was under the impression you were mine for this hour." Familiar lips kissed her neck seductively. The panic and an unexpected spine tingle rushed through her as she swallowed hard, grabbed the edge of the towel, and flipped over, wrapping the towel around her front side. She was shocked and relieved.

"Sawyer? What the—?"

"Shhh." He pressed an oiled finger to her lips then leaned down, gently and slowly kissing her. He tasted of the caramel apple pastry they shared at the café. Delicious. Her modesty instantly dissipated and she found that line he said about being his for the next hour hot. She wanted to ask what was going on but was so turned on by his surprise that she didn't care how he got into the room. He must have paid off the masseuse and took her place.

In hindsight, she should have known those were familiar hands—his touch was unmistakable in the way it made her spine tingle. She only got that feeling with him. She didn't want to ruin the moment by asking questions, she could do that later. In that moment, she was going to savor every drop of oil rubbed into her skin. From her fingers to her shoulders, his kisses trailed down her neck as he slowly uncovered more of her relaxed naked body, his lips making their way down her chest. He straddled her legs, having already stripped down to his black briefs, his chest shiny and coated in oil. The temptation was too much, she couldn't just lay there soaking it all in, she wanted her hands on him. She reached for his chest, only her fingertips copping a feel before he grabbed her wrists, "Not yet. I'm not done with you." She bit her lip, finding it difficult to lie still. He was irresistible. His glistening abs tightened along with his powerful thighs as he held himself above her, massaging her groin. He'd look at her with sultry eyes, a mystery in them that was igniting her insides and spreading like wildfire. She felt the heat in the apples of her cheeks as the massage turned completely erotic. She was about to lose control. He knew how to keep a relationship spicy for sure. It turned him on that she wouldn't have been comfortable with another man's touch. Between that and her sun-kissed, oiled skin beneath his grip, his briefs were stretched to the max. He was practically busting out of them. She couldn't relax, not like she would've with a regular massage. She was yearning for him, every oiled inch of his body. He drove her crazy; the anticipation of where his touch would wander next was almost too much to bear. His hands were occupied, so she took the opportunity and grabbed hold of his pecs. His skin was slippery, enticingly so. Her palms slid down his ripped torso and he didn't have it in him to stop her.

"I can't turn you down any longer when you turn me on so fucking much."

He took it slow, too slow for her taste. She wanted his briefs off, for him to be as naked as she was. She was thoroughly enjoying the massage, although, at this point it wasn't so much about the actual massage. The adrenaline rush of the pseudo massage was fading, replaced by a bone-deep need to have him inside her. He captured her nipple between his lips then worked his way down to her navel, crawling backwards down her beautiful form. He was relentless in making her lose her mind.

"Close your eyes," he whispered as he crawled off the table. She followed his instruction and he massaged her legs, then arms, one at a time. He'd plant a barely-there kiss on her lips, the last time slipping her a little tongue, tantalizing her. She could barely relax; she wanted him so badly. Her breathing became even more rapid when he kneaded her breasts gingerly, stimulating her senses, the scent of warm vanilla coconut oil filling her nostrils strongly every time he dripped it onto her body. He straddled her again, bare this time, nipping at and sucking her neck. Her eyes couldn't stay closed any longer. She grabbed his face and looked him in the eyes before tasting his sweet lips. She felt his bareness against her and she couldn't resist looking. All of his strength above her made her feel dominated and his oiled, throbbing length slowly slipped inside her; oh, was she ever ready for him. His abs rippled and their eyes connected as he satisfied her in every way. Their slippery bodies moved against each other fluidly, releasing all tension and stress for the rest of that hour.

CHAPTER 17
Nashville

"I reckon we need to come up with a band name. Darlin', you're good at naming things. Any ideas?" He leaned on the gate, watching her think it over.

"What about naming yourselves after the bar where you play? That's kinda where it all started. Y'all should be the ones to decide though."

"That's a great idea, thanks. I'll run it by the guys once I pick them all up." He watched her finish brushing Dixie.

"You all packed?" she asked, picking horse hair out of the brush.

"Yeah, just the last-minute stuff left." He opened the gate for Tango to enter the pasture.

"You don't sound too thrilled. Are you changing your mind about making the album?" She walked alongside Dixie.

"Nah, I just don't wanna leave you. You sure you don't wanna come along?"

"You guys should go. I'll stay to take care of the animals. Becka said she would help." She let Dixie into the adjacent pasture as Sawyer walked over to her.

"I wish you'd come along."

"This is something that you and the guys should go do together."

"They wouldn't mind if you came along, darlin'."

"I know, and I appreciate that. I love that you always want me with you but maybe it'll do us good to be apart for the three days."

His brows turned in. "How do you figure?"

"Well, we've been trying really hard, ya know?"

He turned his gaze over to the horses, hands on his hips. "I'd still rather share a room with you than the guys though."

"I'm sure. I rather have you snuggled up next to me in our bed too, but this trip is something you should do. You'd regret not taking the opportunity for this experience. We can video call." She took his hands in hers and he sighed.

"I know I should and I'll be rushing home to taste love on your lips."

"Aww, good. To be honest, it's been a rough week for 'her' so she could use the break."

"You liked it though." He grinned.

"Oh, I know I did. She just needs the next few days off."

"She better be ready when I get the green light."

Marina shook her head laughing. "Oh, Sawyer. What am I gonna do with you?"

"Is that a rhetorical question?" He was serious but Marina turned and walked away.

"I'm gettin' some before I leave today though, right?" he hollered.

She turned around, walking backward as she said, "Yes, Sawyer. Of course." She turned back around, heading to the house.

"Yes!" He ran to catch up, slapping her rear when he reached her.

∽

Once the guys settled in at the hotel in Nashville, they met Todd and Anna at the studio.

"How do you boys want this contract written up?" Anna asked, eager to make a deal right there in the recording studio.

Sawyer rubbed his clammy palms on the thighs of his jeans and said, "Well, um...I think we've all agreed on keepin' it small; at least for now. We'd like to make an album, play at venues like fairs and bars and such. This is mainly for us to have fun and do something on our bucket list, so to speak. We all love what we do daily and it takes up most of our time so we aren't lookin' to get rich and famous. Our private lives are too important. Is that how you guys still feel about all this?" The guys all nodded and verbally agreed.

"Well, I'm glad we're in the position to make this happen for you gentlemen." Todd handed Sawyer a pen. "I'm certain you guys will do well and progress quickly if you decide to roll with the punches. Stars need names so we do need to add a band name to this contract before printing it out for you to sign. Do y'all have one picked out?" he asked, leaning on the back of Anna's chair. Sawyer nodded and looked around at the guys who looked excited. "Backroad to Backcountry."

Anna nodded, impressed with the idea. "After listening to *Love Drunk,* that makes complete sense."

"That song was inspired by true events." Chris laughed and nudged Sawyer's elbow with his.

"Isn't that bar you guys play at called Backcountry?" Todd asked.

"Yep. Sawyer owns the place now," Chris said.

"The band promoting the bar and vice versa...smart move, cowboy." Todd nodded. Anna printed the contract and the guys looked it over before scratching their signatures across the paper. Justin did too, since he would be handling the accounting as their manager.

"How does it feel to be signed with a producer, boys?" Anna asked as she handed Sawyer their copy.

"Pretty damn good."

CHAPTER 18
Batting in the Outfield

"You do know I know nothing about baseball, right?" Marina asked Sawyer, tucking her pants into her calf-high socks.

"It's okay. I'll tell ya what to do." He tucked in just part of his jersey to keep it from flapping when running. She stared at him as he flipped his ball cap around backward, a tuft of spiky hair sticking forth from the hat hole on his forehead. She secured her wavy blonde ponytail before putting her own ball cap on.

"Think the other team is any good?" she asked as teammates joined in the pit.

"I hope not." Sawyer chuckled.

"I don't know, I heard they were pretty good last year." Trev picked out a bat from the rack with a shrug.

"Well, I reckon we need to be even better then." Sawyer slapped Trev's shoulder as he walked past him to pick up Chris's hair tie he had dropped and was looking for.

"Thanks. Can't be havin' this shit flying around in my face," Chris said, putting his hair up into his usual man-bun. He dropped his voice so only they would hear the next part. "So how's that abstinence thing goin'?"

"We tried that; we really did. It only lasted six days."

"What happened?" Chris snickered.

"Somethin' got in the way."

"What did?"

"This thing in my pants. It's got a mind of its own."

Chris laughed loudly, slapping Sawyer's back.

"Tell me you girls are good at baseball," Marina said as Stacy and Trina joined them in the dugout.

"Hell nah." Trina lowered a brow but then shot the girls a wink.

"We're relying on the guys to do all the work," Stacy admitted.

"Yikes." Marina seemed worried.

"Cars are still pulling in. I think I saw Becka parking." Justin buttoned up his jersey as he stepped down into the pit.

"Where the hell is Jake?" Chris asked, looking around.

"He'd better show up, we don't have any extra bodies," Sawyer said, repeatedly tossing a ball into the air and catching it as he leaned against the little building.

"There they are. I was getting worried; Becka's never late," Marina opened a bottle of water she had taken from the cooler. Jake and Becka looked chummy as they approached the dugout together from the direction of the parking lot. Jake was all smiles.

"Nice of you two to join us," Chris bantered.

"Oh, we're not *that* late," Becka bantered back.

"Any idea who's playing what position?" Justin asked.

"I guess we better figure that out." Sawyer started drawing a baseball diamond on the chalkboard.

"Who wants outfield? Girls?"

"We'll do whatever," Marina spoke for all of them.

"Trev?" Sawyer pointed at him with chalk.

"I should be shortstop, huh?"

"Yup." Sawyer nodded. "Jake, watchya want?"

"I'll take any base."

"Okay how about you take third and Trina takes first. You used to play softball, right?" Sawyer asked her.

"Damn right I did." Trina tossed her braids behind her shoulders with confidence.

"Chris, you take second. Justin, you cool with catchin'?"

"Yup." Justin gave a nod with his arms crossed.

"Who's pitchin? Jake, how about you and I take turns with that and third base?" Sawyer set the chalk down and brushed his hands together.

"Sure."

"We'll all be battin'." Sawyer swirled a finger in the air.

"I like that," Chris agreed.

"We don't need a batting order, do we? Fuck it. Let's mix it up. Who's battin' first?" Sawyer asked.

"I will. I feel like beatin' somethin'," Trina volunteered. The girls snickered but Trina's face remained stoic.

"I kept pulling her covers off last night so she's a bit pissed at me," Trev mumbled out the side of his mouth.

"Damn," Chris whispered with raised brows.

"They've only got two chicks on their team," Stacy pointed out as the opposing team took the other dugout.

"Maybe that's why they were good last year." Marina shrugged.

"We'll be alright." Sawyer smooched her cheek.

"We're gonna have fun no matter what." She nodded.

"Look at 'em. Whispering while lookin' over here like high school mean girls. Makes me wanna give 'em' somethin' to whisper about." Trina beat her fist into her other hand.

"Damn! Somebody's feisty today. She's definitely batting first." Jake laughed, his foot on the bench while tying his cleats.

"Maybe they're thinking we're gonna suck having as many girls as boys on our team," Stacy said.

"Or they're starin' at my man. I would be." Marina winked at Sawyer and slapped his butt. He laughed and shook his head then pulled her to him for a good kiss.

"Well, they just turned around so that's probably what it was." Becka cackled.

Marina whispered to Sawyer, "Easy, cowboy, we can't be getting all riled up."

"These uniforms look snazzy, Sawyer. You two picked out cool colors," Chris said.

"They're the nonprofit's logo colors."

The whole ballgame was for charity; the opposing team playing for a local church.

"Teal and yellow? I didn't realize y'all had a logo yet." Chris said as the others just stared at him.

"Honey. They've been wearing the t-shirts for months." Stacy pointed to the logo sprawled across Justin's back.

"Oh! No shit? Huh."

Stacy rolled her eyes and laughed at her man's airhead moment.

The umpire took the field, ready to start the game, and the players took their positions. The opposing team batted first. Sawyer pitched two up, two down before the third batter hit a long one. Trev took off and leaped, catching the ball in his leather glove, the team cheering as they ran for the dugout to switch positions. The opposing pitcher looked serious but he didn't realize how serious Trina was about having lost sleep. She wiggled that bat against her shoulder, kicked a little dirt up behind her, and whacked that ball for a home run on their first bat of the game. The metal bleachers roared as town folk cheered for Taking the Reins.

"Either the crowd doesn't care for that team's attitude or they think our charity is more important." Sawyer chuckled, nudging Jake as they stood, ready to bat.

The first inning proved difficult for the girls to keep up and that big one on the scoreboard wasn't sitting well with any of them.

Marina puckered her bottom lip out and said, "I'm sorry, babe. Us girls are dragging y'all down."

"Don't be silly, darlin', we're out here to have fun anyway. We proved we weren't messin' around when Trina hit a home run on the first bat so they stepped up their game."

The game ran a close score until the last inning. Their white uniforms were stained red with clay and green from grass; sweat marks ran down their chests, backs, and under their arms; and hair was falling from hair ties as they entered the bottom of the ninth, but they were still having fun. The teamwork on the field between the guys was just as effortless as on the stage. Quick communication and signals allowed for the ball to be caught and thrown from outfield to the basemen quickly, tagging many outs. The team had played hard the entire game. Sawyer called for a pit huddle.

"We're tied now and have this last chance to come back. We can do it. They're pretty damn good and the fact that we're keeping up now with no problem tells me we got this. Let's kick their asses."

Hands clapped and game faces were worn like war paint. On the last hit; when Sawyer's bat connected with the ball on a fast pitch, he put all his weight and strength behind it. Those muscles took off running and Jake, Justin, and Becka hauled ass from the bases. That ball was long gone. Jake slid into home just for the hell of it, forcing Justin to leap over him and they got out of the way just before Becka made it home, Sawyer almost plowing her over. The scoreboard changed, touting their win, and the crowd roared. The rest of the Taking the Reins team was jumping up and down and screaming in the pit. They ran out onto the field to join the team in celebration.

"Drinks on me at Backcountry!" Sawyer laughed and hoisted Marina onto his back.

"I'll stick with water," she whispered in his ear.

"Really? Why?" He twisted to look up at her, his arms supporting her legs. She smiled and raised her brows.

"No way!"

"Maybe. I'm not certain yet. Just in case, I shouldn't drink. Don't say anything in case I'm not."

"You got it, baby. This day just got even better." Their lips connected before they all rushed off the field.

CHAPTER 19
Another Disappointment

After a round of drinks at Backcountry, Sawyer excused himself and Marina, in a rush to leave. Sawyer hustled Marina into the house once they got home, practically dragging her by the hand as he ran to the bathroom and started digging under the bathroom sink. She asked, "What are you doing?"

"Where are the pregnancy tests?"

She took a box off of her side of the vanity and handed it to him.

"Oh." He stood after taking it from her and fumbled to take it out of the box before handing her the stick.

"In a rush?" she asked with a snicker.

"Yep." He kissed her forehead and peeled off his filthy jersey before shutting her in the bathroom. He ran his dirty uniform to the laundry room then ran back to the bedroom.

"Okay, now we wait." She exited the bathroom and he darted in.

"It takes three minutes, babe."

"I know, it'll only take me two to shower real quick."

"Don't be peeking at it." She rested a hand on her hip as she stood in the doorway.

"Wouldn't dream of it, darlin'. Wanna jump in with me to make sure I don't peek?" He winked.

"Sure." She giggled, stripping her clothes quickly to join him. It was the fastest shower they'd ever taken together; a quick wash and out, no messing around. She threw on leggings and a t-shirt as he put on jeans and a three-quarter-sleeved baseball tee.

"Oh...oh that shirt."

"What?" he asked, looking down as he pulled it down over his stomach. "Is it all wrong?"

"Oh, yeah...but in all the right ways."

He smirked and put a ball cap on backward.

"I believe it's time to peek at that test." He held a hand out and she took it as they entered the bathroom together to look at the test result. The excitement practically fell off his face as they saw a negative result. He just stared at it for a moment and let out a sigh before framing her face in his hands. With a soft kiss left upon her forehead, he said, "I guess we keep tryin'. I mean, stop tryin'."

"I'm so sorry." She struggled to meet his disappointed eyes.

"Don't apologize."

"I got your hopes up just for you to be let down. You were so excited."

"It's okay. We both knew there was a chance of it being negative."

"Yeah." She looked down but he tipped her chin up.

"Darlin', look at me. We'll just keep tryin'. It'll be okay. I have you and you're everything to me."

"You're everything to me too. Maybe we'll have to resort to a more extreme method after all. I don't want to, but—"

"Let's think about that tomorrow. This was enough for our emotions for one day. Okay?" He scooped her to him by her lower back and wrapped his arms around her. She saw that glimmer of hope leave his eyes and that was harder on her emotions than the negative test result was.

"Let's go for a horseback ride, do chores, and then just watch a movie or somethin'; take our minds off it for a bit." He took her hand and led her to the living room, snagging her cozy blanket off the foot of the bed on their way out. He tossed it onto the couch before they slipped into boots and headed out the door.

They took a stroll on Tango through the field, Sawyer's comforting arms around her the whole ride. Not many chores needed to be done, the bare minimum since most could wait until morning. They were both eager to cuddle on the couch, wrapped in each other's warmth, refraining from trying again.

CHAPTER 20
Don't Leave Me Hangin'

Marina rubbed her eyes as she blindly shuffled out of the bedroom and into the living room, then through to the kitchen. Sawyer was leaning with his hip against the kitchen counter, wearing only a tucked towel that rode low on his hips. Steam rolled above his held coffee mug and he cut her a half smile as she entered.

"Good mornin', darlin'." He cupped his mug with both hands.

"Good morning, handsome." She stretched her arms above her head before stepping close to him and lowering them around his neck. She rose to her toes to give him a silent good morning kiss. His mug clunked onto the countertop as his arms wrapped around her and a groan rumbled in his chest as he nibbled at her neck.

"I thought we're supposed to be refraining," she stated, struggling to keep her hands locked together behind his neck.

"We are, although it's extremely difficult with you in just my t-shirt." His grin widened as his eyes wandered her body and a hand slid down to her rear, but she slid it back up.

"Why are you in just a towel then?"

"Well, see...the shower wasn't enough to wake me up so I needed coffee right away, no time to put clothes on."

"Mmhmm." Her lips pressed together.

"I didn't wanna wake you getting clothes out either."

"Is that so?" She wasn't convinced.

"Maybe." He shrugged then smiled wide, his pearly whites flashing.

"I think you're a tease, Mr. Brandton," she whispered in his ear, making him bite his lip amidst the smile. Batting eyes looking back, she walked over to pour a cup of coffee. He remained leaning against the counter, watching her. She walked back through, passing him, to the living room and bent over to grab her book off the coffee table. A purple thong stole the show, as did her dainty eyeglasses as she sat on the couch and crossed one leg over the other. He was fighting the urge to march over to her and fling those glasses from her face before attacking her with powerful lust. Thinking a few deep breaths might help calm him down, he held his coffee and closed his eyes for a moment. It had been seven days since they had made love and they had been sleeping with a body pillow between them.

"What's on the agenda today?" she asked as she flipped to the page she had previously left off on. He came around the corner, holding his towel where it tucked at his hip with one hand and his coffee mug in the other. He took his time walking toward her, taking a sip, his eyes above his steaming mug, stripping her with his sultry gaze as he stopped on the other side of the coffee table. Her heart started beating rapidly. Good God, he was a sight. So often she thought this but it was different now that she couldn't have him; different from how it was back when he was just her boss, even. She tried to not look at him with desire in her eyes but she was sure her face showed every thought that was going through her head. Her book tilted, nearly falling from her fingers. The bookmark fell out onto her lap and she didn't seem to notice; her attention was fully on him.

"Well, I was plannin' on listening to leather creak as I

whipped horses into shape, but I'd rather hear you moan while I—"

"Sawyer!" She quickly stood to her feet, dropping the book to the floor. Pulling down at the bottom of her shirt, she cleared her throat. He set his mug on the coffee table, walked around it, and stepped right up to her, bare toes to bare toes, grabbing hold of her hips and pressing himself against her.

"Oh, God," she whimpered. He said nothing, just looked down at her while keeping his tight grip. Her palm upon his chest, she swallowed hard and asked, "You know what you're doing to me right now, don't you?"

"I'm pretty sure I know what's going on inside that purple thong you're wearin'."

She stared up at him, lips parted, chest rising and falling rapidly. The butterflies were fluttering too, out of control and in a frenzy, swarming her. She felt what he had going on under that towel, hell, she saw it when he was walking toward her, that bulge, at attention and begging for her attention. With a headshake, she said, "We can't."

"Why not?" The back of his middle finger ran the length of her arm.

"We're not supposed to be...we can't." She gave him a weak shove but he held her there. She felt him pulsate against her groin and she wanted to give in. He was being so persuasive. How would they ever get through this abstinence ordeal? She had to stick to her guns, someone had to and she could rely on him for anything—except this. He gave the towel a slight yank and it fell to the floor. *Don't look down! Don't look down!* she thought to herself, but dammit she looked.

"Whoops." He raised a brow and looked at her, his invitation blatant and brazen.

"Fuck," she whispered, all flustered. "We can't. I'm going to go take a cold shower. You should be dressed when I come out."

"It's sexy when you cuss." Oh, his southern accent struck a chord when he said that. She was practically panting as she turned and walked toward the bedroom. He flapped his arms down to his sides and said, "Baby, tell me you're gonna finish what you started. Are you really just gonna leave me hangin'? Please don't leave me hangin'."

She hollered from the bedroom, "Oh, honey, you're not hangin'." He stood there for a moment, right there in the living room, naked. The shower turned on so he picked up the towel and marched to the bathroom. He said, "Your shower's about to get hotter because I'm not gonna get stiffed."

She laughed and said, "I guess we'll try again tomorrow." He shut the bathroom door behind him.

CHAPTER 21
Last Resort

After having left Dr. Chen's office hand in hand, silence fell upon them on the truck ride home. As tires slowly pulled into the drive and dust settled, he took Marina's hand then shut off the truck and turned to her. He sighed a defeated exhale before saying, "Maybe we'll have to think about a surrogate."

"You think so? There isn't any proof that there's an issue with either one of us though. Maybe what we're trying with the vitamins and such just hasn't had enough time to make a difference. We've only been trying a few months."

"You heard her, baby. Something should be working by now."

"I started eating a lot of raw organic honey and I've been trying every other remedy I've read about too. I bought you bee pollen because I read it's supposed to help male fertility. I've adjusted my diet, I'm drinking fertility tea...I'm hoping something will work because I don't want to have to do something as extreme as ask someone else to carry our child. Who would we ask about being a surrogate even? My sister? Becka? I don't think I could ask that of them. That's too big of a favor. Then they'd get attached, seeing the baby often. That could be heartbreaking for them. Not to mention too many things could go wrong. I couldn't trust a stranger either."

"If it's me...we could consider Jake."

"I'm not sleeping with Jake, Sawyer." Marina seemed surprised he would have even suggested such an idea.

"I'm not saying sleep with him, he'd get too attached." He winked. "But artificially, ya know. Maybe we'll have to try that ourselves first and if we still aren't successful—."

"I don't want Jake's baby, Sawyer. I want yours. Nothing against Jake, but he's not my husband. He's not the one I'm in love with. I don't want anyone else to carry the baby either. I want to do it myself. I want to experience pregnancy. I want to have a life growing inside me that is half you and half me." She started tearing up and put her forehead against his shoulder. He swept her hair away from her face, feeling defeated.

"I know, darlin'. That's what I want too. I don't know what to do. I feel bad I can't give this to you."

"Oh, Sawyer. I'm sorry my body isn't cooperating. We've been trying so hard; I just don't get it."

"I know, me neither. We just keep trying then." They got out of the truck and walked up to the porch, taking a seat on the swing together. He put an arm around her, taking in the fresh autumn air and watching colorful leaves fall from the deciduous trees.

"Or...or we stop trying. The doctor and many people we've talked to have said that, often, that's when it happens," she reminded.

"That should be a last resort."

"I disagree. I think having a child that isn't both of ours would be the last resort." She looked up at him, damp mascara sticking her lashes together. Her misty eyes were breaking his heart.

With a nod, he said, "Okay. You're right. I gotta take one for the team. Abstinence it is."

"Yeah?"

"Yeah. It'll be tough but we have to try; try harder than we have been, I mean."

"We have to be serious about this. You're going to have to start wearing clothes," she bantered as she wiped her wet cheek.

"Deal."

"Some couples try for years and spend so much money on fertility drugs and hormone therapy, artificial insemination and in vitro too. The doctor said today that we shouldn't need any of that, so that's a good thing. The odds are more in our favor than we thought. We have to believe it will happen if it's meant to." She fiddled with his black wristbands and relaxed against him.

"I'd love to promise that it'll happen, I just don't want to make a promise to you that I can't keep."

"I know. It's okay." Her wide eyes met his, full of hope.

"We'll be okay, no matter what, right?" he asked, nodding for her to agree.

"Always." She believed it too.

CHAPTER 22
Playing Hard to Get

Darkness had settled on the Brandton Ranch. With a laundry basket under one arm, Marina pulled out a dresser drawer and put clothes in it. She set the basket on the bed, took out a few items, and put some of them in a different drawer.

"I'm not sure how to go about this abstinence thing, Sawyer."

He was in the living room shutting off the TV, closing the blinds, and folding the couch blanket.

"Me neither. I don't think it's in my blood." He chuckled. "I seriously think your doctor is full of shit though so I'm tellin' ya right now, darlin', it's not gonna be weeks. I've been reading the opposite of what she's sayin' by the way." Whiskey wandered in and plunked down on his bed.

"Well, maybe we should wait until our vacation to make love and if it doesn't do the trick we'll just keep trying the way we want to."

"I can go along with that. It'll be difficult to wait, but if that's still what you wanna do, I'll roll with it."

"Well, when you look like that, you make it really difficult. I'm trying to keep myself distracted."

"You sayin' you want me to put a shirt on?" His smirk could light up a room.

"That would help. Maybe wear something ugly and baggy. Not sure if *that* would even help."

He chuckled. "I don't think I own anything fitting that description."

"You don't. I've already looked. Not sure how I resisted you back in the day."

"What do you mean? Like when we first started dating?" he asked.

"Yeah, but no, I mean from that first time I came here for you to show me the ropes."

He smiled. "Trust me, it was hard for me too."

"Sometimes I pretend we're still just boss and employee. Daydreaming." Her bottom lip curled in with a bite. He walked toward her, slowly, stopping in the bedroom doorway, a grin spreading slowly.

"Really? Why?" He leaned against the frame, arms crossed.

"I don't know. I guess I loved that feeling of seeing you but not quite being able to have you, then imagining what it would be like if you approached me while looking deep into my eyes with passion and kissing me so sensually, feeling for me what I felt for you. Everything we experienced all over again. It was the most intense feeling in the world and I just wish I could relive it a million times over. You still give me butterflies and all of that, but getting to put my hands all over you for the first time was amazing. Exhilarating. You know what I'm trying to say."

He swaggered into the bedroom as she dropped the small stack of folded clothes she was attempting to put away. He stopped a few feet from her, his washboard abs and that *V* that shied away down the front of his tight low-rise jeans, bare chest shining in lamplight and she just stared at him with her lips parted, looking him up and down.

"You're already driving me crazy, Sawyer." Her voice almost trembled as she was about to crouch down for the now-unfolded clothes, but he gently grabbed her arm. She paused, looking up into his blue eyes.

"You wanna role play?" His deep voice rumbled.

"What?" She stood up straight and he let loose her arm.

"Wanna role play? I'll be your boss again, make it feel like old times. Just for a little while." He picked the clothes up off the floor and handed them to her then inched his face close to hers. She could feel his breath upon her cheek. Her eyes clenched shut as she curled her fingers into fists so her hands didn't magnetize to his chest of steel. They were both taking in the moment the most they could.

"You're smirking so I'm taking that as a yes." He grinned, his beard brushing against her face, which felt as though it were on fire. She nodded yes as her eyes connected again with his.

"I'll sleep in the spare room tonight," he said, turning loose his belt from his jeans.

"Why?"

"Well because, darlin', you can't have me. Remember?"

She about melted right there, her legs feeling instantly weak. It was suddenly difficult to swallow, or breathe, for that matter. His thumb touched her lips as he tipped her chin up high. He got closer, almost touching his lips to hers, but instead backed up and tossed his belt over near the hamper, then said on his way out of the bedroom, "Goodnight, Miss Marina."

She inhaled a deep breath and said, "Yes, sir. Goodnight."

He stopped for a brief moment, refraining from turning around, then continued. She admired him from head to bare toes then closed the door. She had to, otherwise, she would've gone running after him.

"Holy shit!" she whispered, her heart pounding loud enough to ring through her ears. There it was; that feeling all over again; the feeling of wanting him but not being able to have him, the tingling up her spine too. It was different from the butterflies that fluttered every time he kissed her. She wasn't sure it was possible to be able to feel this way again with him, but he never ceased to amaze her.

The barn note read "Thought about you last night" and she smiled as she poured coffee, almost missing the cup in an early-morning daydream. Sawyer entered the barn as Marina was putting down fresh straw in the stalls and sipping her own coffee, trying to wake up.

"How'd you sleep, Miss Marina?" He wore a sly smirk. She thought to herself that he's committed to this role-play thing and it's hot!

"I slept okay, thanks. It felt like something was missing though. And you?"

"You walked out of every man's dream and into mine." His hand grazed the small of her back as he walked by. His touch awakened something within her, like a love potion, spilling over and absorbing into her flesh.

"You saying I was on your mind?"

"Maybe." He winked. Were his jeans fitting even tighter today or was it her imagination? That white t-shirt too. It already had a little dirt smudged on the front of it and the way he adjusted his hat after having been bent over to grab a bale of hay...she stared, surprised that those jeans hadn't yet ripped out. Assuming he was going to do everything in his power to seduce her, only to leave her sulking in regret about the abstinence decision, she anticipated his masculinity being extra. Of course, he did exactly that, all day long. Her libido was in overdrive. She was trying to push it out of her mind that she already had him, all of him. In her mind she was starting over, just for the time being because, of course, she didn't want to forget any moment they'd shared, but for the sake of attempting abstinence to conceive a child, creativity was mandatory.

Thunder rumbled as she finished pitching straw in the stalls. Sawyer came in, his shirt damp, and said, "Well, it's starting to storm and I don't have any wood that needs choppin', so you wanna sit on the porch swing with me and watch it roll in?"

"Sure, boss, I'd like that." She flashed a flirty smile, which made him look at her as though he was about to kiss her like he did on the tailgate the first time they kissed, or on the tree stump in the electric rain storm. He put his arm around behind her on the porch swing but rested it on the swing itself. The rain came down harder and the thunder grew louder. They were quiet more than they participated in conversation. Whiskey lay at their feet, snoozing through the storm.

"I enjoy moments like this with you." He looked over at her, staring into her pretty eyes.

"I do too. Maybe after the sky clears, we could go for a ride down the trail."

"Yes, ma'am. Sounds good."

A few days later was Halloween. Sawyer brought pumpkins home, which they carved under the sweet tea olive tree together. Tiny white blooms fell with the breeze. He set up hay bales, pumpkins, and various colored mums by the barn for cute couples' photos. Apple cider and their favorite donuts were enjoyed while passing out candy from the front porch. Sawyer had painted white skeleton bones on Tango's coat and he and Marina dressed up in Dia de los Muertos costumes. They enjoyed seeing the creative costumes of the kids who stopped by; many being program participants. Luke stopped by, of course, dressed as a cowboy.

After a busy next few days at work, Sawyer took Marina hunting. Dressed in camo, they sat together in cozy fold-out chairs in a blind. The weather was cool and rainy and they spoke in whispers as he shared hunting stories with her, mainly of muddy wooded adventures with Jake.

"I'm so excited for our trip next week." She sat back and relaxed in the chair.

"Oh, me too!" He leaned forward, elbows on his knees. "Makes me wonder...besides work, is screwing all we ever do or does it just seem that way right now since we can't? I mean, it's as though we have to really work at spending quality time together doing other things lately. It used to come so easily."

She laughed. "I guess now that you point it out...we do other stuff though."

"We do?" He leaned back, a smirk sprouting.

"Yes. We go out to eat, we ride horses, we work, you rehearse, I go out with the girls, we go to the bar on Friday nights, we make meals together, we watch movies, we have the program, too... you've got brain fog or something." She giggled.

"Lack of sex will do that." He nodded.

"Is that what it is?" She was still giggling.

"Shh, you'll scare away the deer, darlin'."

"What deer?" she asked.

"Shh." He stood from the chair with a finger to his lips and leaned down over Marina. He kissed her and their bodies quickly grew heated, but they were interrupted by the sound of a twig breaking just outside of the blind. He paused, his lips against hers, and his eyes popped open and he stood. She remained still and quiet as he stepped to the small window and motioned for Marina to join him.

"You wanna shoot it?" he whispered. She shook her head no and said, "Let it live."

"But I want jerky," he whispered. She covered her mouth to laugh and gave him a pointed look. He dropped his head.

They watched the deer wander around the area, thankful it broke the heat that was building between them. "Today's its lucky day. If you weren't out here with me, that son of a bitch would be jerky by tonight."

"I'll go buy you some jerky." She laughed.

"What's the point in hunting if not for killin' and eatin' somethin'?"

"To enjoy the outdoors, the quiet, and quality time with each other."

"I can't argue with that."

They called it a day and packed up after the deer wandered off.

CHAPTER 23
Last Hope

Sawyer was trying to keep himself busy, doing everything to distract himself from caving. It had been nearly two weeks since they last made love. He worked out harder, because he said it helped relieve sexual frustration, and was writing songs, spending a lot of time in the music room, even just jamming out to cover songs. Marina noticed the distance between them but understood the reasoning. He had been forthcoming about not being able to resist her. He'd go for horseback rides alone and work with the horses at the stables more. He worked training horses at a nearby stud farm for a few days; things he had been putting off for a while. He even went to Dave's to help him out for a long day's work. The band played at Backcountry Friday night then Saturday morning after chores, Marina asked, "Do you have plans today? I feel like we haven't spent much time together lately. I know you're keeping your distance so we don't slip up, but I really miss you."

He stopped in the barn doorway next to her and cupped her face in his hands.

"I am so sorry, darlin'."

"It's okay, I understand."

"It's not because I don't want to spend time with you. That

could never be the case. I just have a hard time keeping my hands off you. I don't trust myself. I thought if I was around you less, it might be easier to deal but I miss you too. I didn't mean to push you away. We *should* be enjoying this alone time together."

"Think we can be around each other today?" she asked, hopeful.

"You have a chastity belt?"

She laughed loudly. "Oh, Sawyer."

"I'll do my best to behave."

"Coffee in town?"

"Sounds good. Out in public would be easier. Go hop in the Jeep."

They sat outside at the patio table at Chillax-A-Latte Café, sipping on their coffee and chatting.

"I'm so glad you had coffee with me that day, back when I was just your boss."

"Me too. Pretty sure I fell in love with you that day." She batted her eyes.

"Really?" His foot dropped down from the adjacent patio chair he was propping it on. She had his attention.

"Yep. How sweet you were, such a gentleman. The way you looked and smelled and talked to me; you wanted to know me. I noticed the way you looked at me although at the time I thought I was imagining things."

"You weren't just imagining it. I saw you for you and I loved what I saw."

"You made me melt that day and every day after."

He took her hand as they played a people-watching game. They liked to guess people's names and life stories, just making up stuff. Before heading home, he told her to get in the Jeep and he'd be right back. He walked across to the flower shop and, after several minutes, came out with two armfuls of potted bamboo.

"What's this?" She laughed as he set them in the back seat and on the floor.

"Bamboo for our bedroom."

She leaned her head back against the headrest, laughing.

The yellow sun peered through the branches of the live oaks across the dirt road; bright enough to cast a blinding glow across the windshield. When they got home, they took a bike ride down the road around to the property and through the trail back home. It was a good cardio workout to replace their usual. A horseback ride together followed, along the train tracks and around the pond, then they raced back. They were enjoying each other's company so much that they accidentally skipped lunch.

"I hate that the sun sinks so early this time of year." She dismounted Legend as he dismounted Foxtrot.

"Shit! I didn't make sure you ate lunch!"

"Oh, Sawyer, I'm a big girl. I guess I wasn't hungry, just enjoying time with you."

"I'm sorry, darlin'." He took her saddle and hung it up before his own.

"It's okay, really. You feeling hungry now?"

"Yeah, let's wash our hands and go to town after we put these two out to pasture."

Their favorite taco truck never disappointed; that's where Marina chose to go for dinner. It was where they had their first date, just before their first kiss on the tailgate. On their drive home, he pulled off onto the shoulder of the dirt road. After the dust settled, he told her to stay put and got out then walked the ditch, picking flowers in the headlight beams, which he arranged in a bouquet on his walk back to the Jeep. He got in and handed it to her.

"For my beautiful lady. They screamed your name."

"Aww, thank you. They're beautiful. I love that you do things like this. Too bad you can't scream my name later." She put the hair tie from her wrist around the stems to hold the bouquet together as he laughed.

"Thanks for thinking of me."

"My mind's always on you, darlin'."

"Are we drinkin' moonshine on the tailgate again?" she asked, grabbing hold of his hand.

"Nah, I don't wanna recreate our memory of that night. It was too perfect. Plus, when you drink you get frisky. Can't be havin' that now." He winked.

When they got home, he dropped his keys on the end table and petted Whiskey as he went to the kitchen to fetch a vase. She put her bouquet in it and filled it with water while he turned on some music. He took her hand and danced with her to *Forever for a Little While* by Russell Dickerson before kissing her on the cheek and telling her, "Goodnight, Miss Marina." He smiled sweetly.

"We aren't even gonna snuggle? I sleep best with your arm around me from behind."

"Baby, you know why we can't spoon so we'll save the spoonin' for the kitchen." He chuckled and walked to the spare room and closed the door, avoiding the temptation of taking her into his arms and kissing her the way that leads to heart-racing lust.

CHAPTER 24
Bali

"This has been the longest few weeks of my life." Sawyer tossed their luggage into Marina's SUV.

"Well, the waiting is about over. Thank goodness."

"I'm so excited for this trip." He opened her door and shut it when she got in. He let Whiskey jump in before hopping in himself.

Bob and Gladys were happy to welcome Whiskey once again for a doggy bar-life vacation when he was dropped off at their front door.

"I'm so glad we chose to go on an adventure together. I'm excited to go exploring while we hike and snorkel. I love that you love to do this stuff with me, Sawyer."

"Of course, I do, darlin'." He took her hand on the console and looked over at her, mischief in his eyes. She knew exactly what he was thinking; that look told all. "I'm looking forward to a lot of things." He looked ahead at the road.

"Me too, like hanging out together in the private plunge pool and in our awesome room that's completely open to the elements." She knew he meant one thing in particular but wanted to see how long it would take him to actually say it.

He nodded. "Yep, all of that and more." He turned back to

her and leered a big, wide smile; teeth shining bright. He sure could be stubborn. She smiled back, of course, it was an uncontrollable response, but she still wasn't going to be the one to say it. She'd continue to act oblivious.

∼

His knee was bouncing fast as they waited at the terminal gate. He kept looking at the time on his phone.

"We'll board in a few minutes. Why do you seem so anxious? Everything okay, Sawyer?"

"I'm a ticking time bomb, Marina! I'm about to fucking explode!"

"Shh, I know, I know, it's been a really hard few weeks for me too." She looked around, her eyes big.

"I bet it's been *harder* for me...if ya know what I'm sayin'." His brows were raised high.

"How did you manage before I came around?" She bit the inside of her cheek to keep from laughing.

"It was easier *because* you weren't around. I haven't always been a sexual animal like I am with you. I see you or think of you and...*it* gets harder."

She giggled.

"I'm seriously struggling with this. I don't know what my problem is."

"I know and I'm so sorry."

"It's not your fault, darlin', and hopefully the strugglin' will be worth it, but I'm telling ya right now, as soon as we make it into our resort room, your ass is mine."

The gate agent announced it was time to board and Sawyer was the first out of his seat.

"Row twenty-three? Did you plan that?" she asked as she found their seats on the plane.

"Sure didn't. You go ahead and take the window seat."

Marina scooted in the row and into the window seat. Sawyer paused for a moment after putting one of their bags up above.

"Won't it fit?" she asked of the puzzled look on his face. He shut the overhead door and cleared his throat before hiking the thighs of his jeans up a bit and sitting in the seat next to her.

He leaned close to Marina and whispered, "Someone just touched my ass."

She smirked. "What?"

"I'm serious."

"Who? Maybe they just bumped you."

"When I was putting our bag up there...someone grabbed a handful of ass cheek. It was intentional."

"I don't know how with your jeans being so tight." She giggled.

"Marina, I'm...I'm serious. I'm afraid to look over next to us." He took the backpack from Marina and unzipped it on his lap. She looked over and smiled at a middle-aged woman who wasn't being discreet about checking Sawyer out.

"Oh, my," Marina said quietly. The woman had no shame; she was quite bold, still staring him up and down.

"It's gonna be a long flight," he mumbled as he took his small laptop out of the bag.

"Working on vacation? Sawyer, we need this trip to, ya know...relax."

"I know. How else am I going to distract myself?"

"Are you bowing out of the mile-high club?" She giggled and squeezed his arm with hers.

"For this flight I am. After weeks of being abstinent, it's gonna happen somewhere better than a lavatory."

Marina looked past Sawyer at the flight attendant and the middle-aged woman, both of whose jaws were loose as they stared at him.

"Did I not whisper that?" he whispered to Marina and she shook her head no. A lady in the row behind the middle-aged woman tapped the woman's shoulder and showed her the book she was reading. It was Raquel's book. Sawyer and Marina were recognized and became the talk of the cabin. What an experience that was! He smiled and nodded at the ladies then dove into working on the laptop, showing Marina loving affection often throughout the flight.

The long flight was worth it. The scenery landing in Bali, Indonesia was breathtaking. Their resort was like something out of a dream vacation magazine. A thatched roof suite on a cliff in the jungle with a private plunge pool on the edge and bright flowers blooming everywhere. It felt like being in a giant bird's nest. The remote location was exactly what the two of them needed; just them alone, away from the everyday, away from schedules and to-do-lists.

"Sawyer, come look! We can see a waterfall from here!"

"We should go explore where it flows to." He set their bags down at the foot of the canopy bed.

"Yes!"

A steep trek up the mountain path led them to roaring waters. The terrain was all over the place. Who knew there could be lagoon pools hidden up in the cliffs beneath a waterfall, smaller falls cascading into smaller pools? The lush greenery surrounding the falls was beautiful. The air seemed cooler with much of the lagoon area being shaded and they could feel the mist upon their skin as they dipped their bare toes into the lagoon pool.

"It's not too cold." Marina tossed her flip-flops onto a rock. Sawyer's joined them a moment later. He looked around; they were completely alone.

"We should've worn our swimsuits." Marina stepped into the water, ankle deep. Sawyer was stripping down to his briefs already.

"Sawyer." Marina looked around.

"Nobody else is out here, darlin', and nobody around here knows us anyway. We'd never see 'em again." He flopped his clothes up onto the rock with their shoes and stepped into the water, sinking to his shoulders right away.

"I've heard that before." She hesitated a moment, sporting a cheeky grin before stripping down to her bra and panties. He stood and held a hand out, which she took hold of.

"Careful, it's a bit of a drop-off." Just as he said that, her foot slipped and he caught her with an arm around her waist. She braced herself, holding onto his broad shoulders until her feet were steady. They held each other close for a picture-perfect kiss in front of the waterfall. Running his fingers through her half-wet hair, he looked into her teal-ish eyes, lust reflecting back at him. He broke that amplified intensity by taking a step back and splashing water at her. Sinking, he swam backward, teasing as she splashed him back. She swam toward him until she met him at the bottom of the falls, water falling around them in a thunderous cascade, creating bubbly waves around them.

"Someone's coming!" she whispered in a panic as branches rustled in the direction of the path.

"Hold your breath," he hollered then pulled her along by her hand through the falls and to the other side. The air felt even more chilly, damp, and misty. There was green moss growing on the slippery rocks beneath their feet and up the natural wall. She took in the fresh earthy scent before wiping water from her face. He pulled her close against him, the warm skin of his chest heating her chilled palm.

"You're cold," he noted, wrapping his arms around her body. She hugged him tightly, absorbing his body heat.

"I'm certain you'll warm me up." She looked up into his blue eyes and could tell he was holding back; his nostrils were flared and there was a hunger in his eyes like a lion stalking its prey.

"Think they're gone?" she asked, trying not to shiver.

"I don't know and I don't care." His lips smashed against hers and she felt her body temperature rise immediately. His hand wrapped up in her hair at the back of her head, holding her in place. Their pent-up urges were forcing a loss of control. Reclaiming her in the way he kissed her was invigorating and she was melting with his touch as they kindled an inferno between them.

"I don't want to waste any more time but you're too cold for this here and it's slippery."

"What do you suggest?" she asked, running her hand down his carved pec.

"I think I should take you back to our room and lay you down on that bed."

"I think that sounds perfect."

They stared at each other a moment more, letting the anticipation linger, not wanting to let go of each other, as if it would be forever before they held one another again.

"Those eyes of yours..." His thumb ran down her lips before his tongue tangled with hers, softly but heatedly.

Her lips slowly retreated and she looked up at him through hooded lashes and said, "You're warming me up."

"That's because we go together like fire and oxygen, baby. We're lightin' it up!" He pulled her hips against him as she admired him with a smile.

"Mmm, I do believe somebody else is warmed up too." She looked down at his firmness, her tongue tracing along her upper teeth.

"He sure is. We better get back to that room." He took her by the hand and led her through the falls, across the small lagoon open to the dimming sapphire sky, and to their clothes at the water's edge. They hadn't taken towels to dry off with, so dressed still wet.

"I don't know about you, but I don't feel like wasting the energy hiking all the way back. I noticed a shortcut right through here," he said, leading her through walls of vines and other flora.

"How is it a shortcut?" she asked as he suddenly stopped.

"You trust me?" he asked with a smirk.

"Of course I do."

He moved aside a tangled mess of vines and said, "Jump."

Hand-in-hand they jumped, Marina screaming most of the way down the cliff's edge. They splashed into the turquoise water below. She popped up first, smoothing her hair back and looking around for Sawyer.

"Sawyer? Sawyer!"

He popped up a few feet from her.

"Woooo!" He shook water from his hair and laughed.

"Oh my God, I can't believe we just did that!" she yelled.

"That was amazing!" He swam to her for a kiss.

"That had to be a good sixty-foot drop. You're crazy!"

"But you have to admit, that was awesome!"

"It was! It was scary though, too. It could've been shallow water."

"Nah, I saw this online as a feature near the resort and saw a sign for it on our way to the falls. I knew we'd be okay. I wouldn't risk getting you hurt."

"Glad you did your research. I trust you...even still after that adventure." She laughed as he grabbed her to pull her close. "What an adrenaline rush!" She wiped water from her eyes and said, "I'm ready for another."

"You ready to get back to the room?"

"I am. This view is amazing though."

"I can think of another view that's amazing and I've been missin' it something fierce."

"Hopefully our room isn't far away then."

She noticed a colorful wooden multi-destination sign outside of the resort and commented on how much she liked it.

"I'll make you one to put out by our pool. We'll list all the places we've traveled together on it."

"I'd love that."

Upon returning to their room unscathed, he told her, "Take your clothes back off," then locked the door, water dripping everywhere. A smirk dazzled her face as she replied, "Yes, sir." Her tank top came up over her head then fell to the floor as he walked barefoot over to her, his skin still wet and glowing.

"Allow me," he said in a deep growl as he unbuttoned her jean shorts and shimmied them, and her panties, down off her hips.

He pushed her wet hair back behind her shoulders. She watched him, appreciating that his attention was fully on her. She unbuttoned his jeans and peeled off his tank top, grabbing a bicep as his arm was still raised above his head. She was practically salivating, she had missed the strength of him more than she realized. She missed being this close to him, undressing, his breath upon her neck. He dropped his jeans, his briefs along with them, stepping out of them one foot at a time. She felt his short beard against her hand, once again looking into his eyes.

She whispered, "I'm obsessed with you." She had that innocent, nervous, first-time-together look in her eyes and he was ready to ravish her, just as he had that first stormy night when sparks flew. Her bra hit the floor and he pulled her nude body close against his.

"You're flawless," he whispered into her ear, sending a tingle throughout her body. She felt the ridge of his stiffened length against the inside of her thigh and heard the desperation in his voice when he said, "I'm gonna be inside you all night long." Her fingers ran through his hair as she ran her other hand down his back, then further to his ass cheek. "This is it, Marina. I'm about to get you pregnant. It's happening tonight."

"Is that so, cowboy?"

"Yes, ma'am, it is."

Oh, that seductive, pouty look on her face did it for him. He looked at her possessively, that strong jaw fierce, and kissed the breath completely out of her. Lip-locked, the two of them almost had to fight for oxygen.

He carried her sideways, like he had the night of their wedding when he carried her over the threshold, then gently laid her down on the bed. He crawled on top of her, the strength of his body towering above her. He was thirsty for her, just as she was for him. The anticipation of feeling him inside her had become too intense to bear. Her nails dug into his ass cheeks as she tried pulling him down to her.

"I've waited too long to not enjoy every single second of this. I'm going to take it slow so I can savor you."

She wasn't sure how he was restraining himself but she was enjoying the teasing no matter how badly she wanted him inside her. He entered slowly and moaned, feeling her sweet, deep heat within.

"Oh, baby, I've missed you. All of you."

She nodded in agreement. "Mmhmm. God, I've missed you too, so much." Kisses trailed down her neck but didn't leave her lips long, returning to quench a mutual thirst. "You feel so good, Sawyer." She could feel his muscles tense and flex at the sound of her moans.

"Mmm, I don't know how long I can last."

"We've got all night." She bit her lip with a devilish grin then bit his lip. He drove a harsh thrust, forcing her to crescendo into a screaming tremor just before he erupted. She held onto his triceps as he framed his hands around her face, leaning his forehead onto hers as he held himself above her on his elbows. He let out a deep exhale.

"I just need five minutes."

She smiled, knowing that was seriously all he needed before hitting round two. She pulled him down next to her and he held her in his arms. His chin rested on top of her head as he played with her hair, her cheek pressed against his pec. Her fingertips traced up his vein-bulging arm, his shoulder, down his back, lightly, almost a tickle. Her palm ran over his hip and down the side of his beastly thigh and his breathing became more rapid. When she couldn't reach any further, her light touch trailed up the front of his thigh and to his groin. Her toes rubbed up and down his lower leg, her wide eyes looking up at his baby blues, which were locked on her.

"You're so beautiful. I'm the luckiest man alive."

"Aww, no, I'm the lucky one. You're perfect."

"You're everything to me. I hope you know that." He stroked the side of her face with the back of his hand ever so gently.

"As you are to me." She smiled, her fingers running down his chest.

She felt the warmth of his breath upon her face as he said, "I want to do so many naughty things to you. I'm craving every inch of your body. But tonight, we're making love. Tomorrow night, expect naughty." He snatched her lips with his as he began groping her body.

She grabbed hold of him and replied, "Go ahead. Spank me. I deserve it."

A grin spread across his face before he was suddenly upon her, kissing her so passionately, holding her close against him. She let him take control, she loved all that muscle surrounding her. He spoiled her in every way, especially intimately. He reveled in making her feel thrilling waves of ecstasy. Not only did they read each other's body language well, but she found it immensely comforting to know he could read the depths of her soul. He knew exactly what she liked, how she liked it, when to do it, and always found new ways to excite her. The things this man did to her—to her body and her mind—there was nobody else on Earth that could make her feel that way.

The next morning, during twilight hours, she lay awake, head on his arm and his other wrapped around her. She must have been moving a bit, not realizing she was restless. He rubbed her hip and kissed her shoulder then asked if she was okay, all while his eyes were still closed.

"I am. I didn't mean to wake you." She rolled over, facing him, but he couldn't keep his eyes open. His arm now heavy on her other rib, she gently rolled him to his back. He murmured something as he adjusted to a more comfortable position, obviously still sleeping.

"Sawyer," she whispered, but no answer. Rubbing his chest didn't wake him and she was feeling frisky. Lying next to him and with a watchful eye waiting for a reaction, her hand wandered all over his body; above and below the covers. He'd squirm a little and let out a deep exhale every so often. She felt bad waking him since he was obviously wiped out but she couldn't keep her hands off him. Merely seconds after reaching down and fondling him, he was alert...well, part of him. His eyes were still closed but he turned his face and moaned, his chest rising and falling faster. Never having awakened him this way before, she thought he might enjoy the impulsive behavior so she crawled on top of him and took advantage of his erection. Oh, this felt so naughty, but she was enjoying having her way with him without his recognition. His eyelids cracked open and he slowly came to realize what was happening.

"Hey, baby." He smiled. "So, it wasn't just a dream. Whatcha doin'?"

"You."

"Yeah, you are." He grabbed hold of her hips.

"Sorry, I had to wake you this way."

"Don't be sorry. Hell, I'm not. This is the best way to wake up. I wake you up by sticking it into you sometimes."

"So, it's okay?" She hadn't stopped grinding on him.

"Oh, it's more than okay. I love it."

"Good. Because you're just so sexy, I couldn't help it." She leaned down, kissing him fiercely, a fist full of his hair, nails digging into his collarbone, which eventually led them both to bliss. They burned like twin flames of eternal love throughout the whole day.

CHAPTER 25
What A Nightmare!

The air in Backcountry was thick with smoke and an unusual fog lingered throughout town, blanketing everything in mist for days. The band had begun playing before Marina arrived. The lighting was dim, just strung Christmas lights glowing in the corners. Marina choked on the smoke that filled her virgin lungs as she sat at the bar.

"Are people allowed to smoke in here now?" she asked Gladys as she nodded at Bob.

"People in this town do what they want, sweetie, you know that. This place is no different. You want pizza?" Gladys shouted over the music as she walked toward the other end of the bar.

"Yes, please. I'm starvin'. Thanks."

"Here's your rum," Bob said as he slid a drink down the bar to Marina.

"Rum? What the hell is going on in here tonight?" Marina mumbled to herself.

Three college girls were serving busy tables, the three college girls that hit on Sawyer back before he started dating Marina. She recognized them right away.

"Great. That's all we need; more drama," Marina grumbled, rolling her eyes. She waved to Sawyer, who acknowledged her with a sexy grin while singing. He paid the girls no attention but why would Gladys hire them, knowing they had been hitting on Sawyer?

"Ya know, if y'all were that desperate for help around here, I could've come back to work more often," Marina said, sliding her full drink back down to Bob, a little sloshing out along the way.

"We weren't desperate, I wouldn't say. They came in here asking about working on the busy nights so they could listen to the band play and Lana was having a hard time keeping up by herself."

"They're doing more staring and flirting with the band than they are serving." Marina had a less-than-impressed look on her face as she watched the girls dancing around up front by the stage. "They're about to piss me off."

"Oh, Marina." Gladys slapped her with her dish towel before heading to the kitchen to get Marina's pizza. She came back out moments later with a supreme topping pizza.

"Um...Gladys?" Marina was confused, staring at a pizza that wasn't her usual request.

The front door opened and a silhouette strutted in and approached the stage. Lights switched on, brightening the whole place. It was Derrick! His arm raised and instruments paused. One loud gunshot turned Sawyer's white t-shirt red-splattered as Sawyer collapsed to the stage floor with a thud, his hat and guitar landing nearby.

"Noooooo! Sawyer!" Marina screamed, running for the stage at a speed that felt like slow motion. Jake jumped off the stage and tackled Derrick to the wood floor, kicking the pistol from Derrick's reach. Marina scooped Sawyer's head onto her lap, he was so limp and heavy. She applied pressure to the gunshot wound in his chest while screaming for help. Gladys dialed 9-1-1 as patrons scattered and ran for the door. Trev helped Jake restrain Derrick while Chris tried helping Marina. Sawyer wasn't conscious, nor was his chest rising, so Chris felt for a pulse. He shook his head at Marina and said, "He's gone, Marina. I'm so sorry."

"Noooooo! Sawyer, don't leave me! Sawyer!" She was sobbing, her head down on his chest. Blood pooled beneath and around him on the stage, seeping down into cracks between wood planks.

∽

Sawyer was awakened by a loud, shrill scream. He sat up in a panic and quickly turned to Marina. She was screaming and crying but he could tell she wasn't awake. He switched the lamp on as he tried to calm her down. He flung the covers back and scrambled closer. He took her into his arms and shushed her, letting her know he was there.

"Marina, Marina, baby, wake up. Shhh, it's okay. I'm right here."

She was downright sobbing hysterically. He held her face in his hands, his forehead against hers. Her eyes were open but looked glazed over.

"Why aren't you waking up? Marina, you're freaking me out. Baby, wake up!" He shouted and she quieted down. His eyes stared into hers. She was trembling fiercely and grabbed his hands beside her face, and at that point, he could tell she had woken.

"Sawyer!" She flung her arms around his neck and held him tightly.

"Hey, hey, you okay? You were having a nightmare. What were you dreaming about, love?" She was quiet for a moment, catching her breath and trying to wake up enough to snap back to reality. He held her against his chest.

"It's okay, everything's okay. I'm right here." He slid himself up against the headboard and pulled her to him. She sat between his legs, snuggled to his chest. Her heart was racing incredibly fast. She had a death grip on his arm as she lay sideways against him. His knees were up on either side of her, providing a protective barrier; she felt comforted with his arms wrapped around her tightly. He played with her hair because he knew it was relaxing for her. She felt his chest as it rose and sank.

"You're really here? You're okay?" She turned and looked up at him, her wet eyes looked so vulnerable to the Hell she had just experienced.

"Baby, I'm right here. I'm fine."

She laid her head against his chest again, listening to his heart beat.

"Take a few slow, deep breaths with me. You gotta calm that heart down. It's about to beat right out of your chest." She breathed slowly with him. He wiped her flowing tears from her face then leaned forward, shoving a pillow behind his back.

"Don't let go," she panicked.

"It's okay. I got you. I'll hold you all night."

"Promise? I need to feel your heart beating."

"I promise, darlin'." He held her, consoling her, breathing the same rhythm, hearts beating together, all night. Even when he eventually fell asleep sitting up, he held on to her as she lay in front of him, against his warm bare skin. The sun peered through the window at the curtain's edge a few hours later, the rays beaming in across his face. He woke to her looking up at him.

"Good mornin', darlin'."

"Good morning. You didn't break your promise."

"What promise is that?"

"That you'd hold me all night."

He smiled at her. "Did you go back to sleep?"

"I did. It was long after you had fallen asleep though. Thanks for snuggling."

"Of course. I wouldn't have been anywhere else." He moved her hair away from her eyelashes. "Want me to go make us some coffee?"

"Sure, that would be nice. Can we drink it in bed together?" she asked.

He smiled as he crawled off the bed.

"I was plannin' on it." He kissed her forehead before going to the kitchen. She got comfortable up against the headboard and patiently waited for him to come back in, coffee mugs in hand. His bare feet slapped and clunked on the wood floor. He handed her a mug and got back into bed next to her. She moved up against him as he put his arm around her.

"Do you wanna talk about it?" He sipped his hot coffee cautiously. She was quiet for a moment.

He said, "Only if you want to, of course."

"It was horrible, Sawyer."

"Yeah, you were really shaken up. You were kinda freaking me out."

"I'm sorry. I don't know why I had such a hellacious dream. It was an absolute nightmare."

"Seemed like you were in a sleepwalking episode or something. You were almost hyperventilating."

"It felt so real."

"Traumatic for sure."

"I dreamed that we were at Backcountry on a Friday night but nothing was right. It was smokey, my pizza order wasn't right, I definitely don't drink rum, and you don't wanna know who was serving drinks. You and the band were on stage, which was the *only* normal part of the whole situation. The band was playing like usual when Derrick came in and shot you. There was screaming and the band tried to help. I was leaning over you, applying pressure, but then you died moments later in my arms. I had never been so terrified in my life. I don't ever want to experience losing you."

"I'm so sorry, baby. That sounds horrible. I hope we never have to experience losing each other." He squeezed her tightly.

"My entire world ended in that moment, Sawyer. I don't know what I'd do without you."

"I don't know what I'd do without you, either. I don't think I could survive that kind of loss."

"I wouldn't want to survive it." She leaned over and sat her mug on her nightstand so she could feel his handsome face in her hands. They became lost in each other's eyes for a moment before hers became dampened with emotions again. He softly caressed her back, those strong hands gliding up and down and she pressed her lips to his, her eyes releasing tears as they clenched shut. She had to make sure he was truly there in that moment, as real as she was.

"It's cool outside this morning. Wanna go sit on the swing and watch clouds change shape?" he asked.

"I'd love that. Think the horses will be getting hungry?"

"They can wait."

A week had passed and Marina continued to have night terrors. As before, he'd console her and hold her all night. He was making breakfast Sunday morning when she woke and joined him in the kitchen.

"Good morning." She wrapped her arms around him from behind.

"Good mornin', darlin'." He took her hand and spun her around as if in the middle of a dance then pulled her to him for a kiss. "I did hold you all night, just so ya know. I got kinda hungry though."

She laughed. "Thank you. You wanna know what the dream last night was about?"

"Only if you wanna tell me." He kissed her forehead and stepped to the side to pour her a cup of coffee.

"I dreamed that Gabby was back in town and I was at the coffee shop with Becka when you came in arm-in-arm with Gabby and kissed her in front of me. I dropped my coffee to the floor, in shock as to why you'd be with her."

"Was that why you were crying or was it because you spilled your coffee?" he joked, his head tilted and a brow raised. She smiled and said, "I appreciate you trying to make me smile."

"It worked."

"It did." She took the steaming mug he handed her.

"You know you never have to worry about that though."

"I know. I don't know why I've been having nightmares." She leaned against the counter.

"Last night wasn't as bad as the first one you had. The way you were so upset was scary that night."

"Yeah. Maybe I should see a doctor if they continue."

He nodded and kissed her lips before making her plate and handing it to her.

"Maybe I'm not wearing you out good enough at night before you go to sleep." He snickered as they sat at the table.

"You wear me out just fine. Too much almost sometimes. Maybe that's the problem."

He looked at her with a wrinkled nose, pausing, then said, "Nah," with a shake of his head, making her giggle.

CHAPTER 26
Another Star

The exhaustion had gotten to Marina quickly one evening. She started chores but couldn't finish. She didn't realize she had left the hose on in the trough, overflowing the water onto the ground until Sawyer found it when he got home from work late. He finished chores then brushed the horses, since their winter fluff was starting to come in, before going into the house with the sun still sinking to the horizon, only to find her in bed and asleep already. He assumed the week of nightmares keeping her up had finally caught up to her.

The next morning, he had finished the chores at home and was over at the stables before she rolled out of bed. She called him when she woke to let him know she wasn't feeling well so would be staying put for the day. He came back to the house at lunchtime to check on her but she was napping peacefully in bed. He finished work early that afternoon and she seemed to be feeling better but said she was still fatigued. They decided it would probably be best to try and get in to see the doctor the next morning.

The next day, Marina went to see her doctor, promising she'd bring up the nightmares. Sawyer had put in a long day training a horse at Dave's, returning home later than usual, well after dark.

She left a barn note for Sawyer that night so he would see it as soon as he got out to the barn the next morning. It read "It's time to decide what we're naming the next star in our galaxy." She lay in bed, sleeping soundly until Sawyer busted through the back door and ran through the house, his boots thumping the wooden floor loudly and Whiskey running in to catch up. When he reached the bedroom doorway, he stopped for a moment. Having run from the barn, he was slightly winded. The adrenalin rush of the surprise may have played a part in that. He braced the door frame as if to keep from falling forward.

"Marina, does that barn note mean what I think it means?" he asked, wide-eyed, feet frozen to the floor.

Still groggy, she nodded and smiled.

"Seriously? For real?"

"Mmmhmm."

"Woo hoo!" He leaped and smacked the doorframe with his hand. "You sure?"

"I'm sure." She laughed and sat up, excited about his reaction. He ran and leaped onto the bed, crawling to her. She was attacked with a sweet kiss upon her lips as he sat on his knees and cradled her face in his hands.

"I can't believe this."

"I know, me neither. It's finally happening!" She smiled and sounded awake enough to be just as excited as he was.

"You're having a baby! We're gonna be parents!"

"I know!" Her eyes misted with joy.

"When? When did you take another test?"

"Yesterday morning. I didn't have you sit and wait on it with me because I didn't want you to feel disappointed again if it was negative. It was positive though so when I went to see the doctor, I had her test me to make sure so I didn't give you false hope again. I'm sorry I didn't include you."

"Oh, no, don't be. Honestly, I love that you did it that way because I'm going to forever cherish that barn note."

"Yeah?"

"Yeah. It's perfect. The excitement I just felt reading that note...everything's perfect, you're perfect." He kissed her forehead and looked at her with gratitude in his blue eyes. "I couldn't be happier right now. God, I love you so much."

"Aww, Sawyer, I love you too, so very much. We finally made it happen." She took hold of his shoulders.

"One hundred percent ours, too."

"I'm so glad we were patient and believed that this could happen for us." She took his hand.

"We were patient? I'm kidding. I'm so glad too, darlin'. I can't believe you were able to hide your excitement from me."

"It was tough. We have to call our parents."

"Yes! Let's do that right now. I'm calling your mom first." He pulled his phone from his back pocket and dialed Aliza, putting her on speakerphone as he kicked his boots off onto the floor.

"Good morning," Aliza answered.

"Good mornin'," Sawyer and Marina said in sync.

"So, we have some news for ya." Sawyer sounded excited; he couldn't contain it.

"Okay, what's that?"

"I'm pregnant!" Marina shouted, grabbing Sawyer's arm.

"What? Are you serious?" Aliza was screaming with excitement.

"Yes!"

"Oh, my God! Are you really? You're sure?"

"I'm sure, Mom. It's actually happening."

"Finally, we did it!" Sawyer joined in on the shouting.

"I'm so happy for you both!"

"Mom, are you crying?"

"Yeah." She sniffled.

"Aww." Sawyer sat up next to Marina against the headboard, holding the phone between them.

"Good things come to those who wait. It was just timing. Must be the universe wanted y'all to have more time together, just the two of you. Y'all needed that relaxing vacation. It was meant to happen this way."

"Must be, Mom."

"Ahhh! I'm so happy!" Aliza screamed. "I'm gonna be a grandma! Don't forget to call your sister," she added, making Marina and Sawyer both laugh. He wrapped his arm around her and showed a smile that could light ice on fire.

"We're absolutely thrilled," Marina said before suddenly becoming emotional and burying her face into Sawyer's chest. She was crying tears of joy and relief, sobbing actually. The hormone changes were taking hold already.

"Aliza, we're gonna let ya go so we can call my parents real quick after my girl gathers herself." Sawyer kissed the top of Marina's head.

"I was your first call?"

"Yes, ma'am."

"Aww, I feel so privileged. Thank you both for sharing the most wonderful news. I love you both. Congratulations!"

"Thank you."

"We love you too!" Marina blubbered.

Sawyer chuckled. "We love you too, Aliza."

Before dialing his parents, he took a moment letting the reality hit him all over again. He dropped his phone onto the bed and bear-hugged Marina. Her happiness brought tears to his eyes. They sat holding each other and crying together for several minutes. Whiskey wandered into the bedroom and whined and whimpered, sitting on the floor at the foot of the bed.

"We just had to have hope. Can you believe it?" He held her face in his hands.

"I'm so happy that this is going to happen naturally for us after all."

"Me too. It's a relief."

"I can't believe I'm carrying and growing a precious life, one that's half you."

"And half you. Whether it's a girl or boy, it'll be perfect."

"I feel biased already too. I don't care which it is, as long as it's healthy."

"Me too. Life couldn't get any more perfect." He gently swiped hair from her face as she rested her head against his chest again.

"I couldn't agree more. I love you more than anything, Sawyer. Thank you for this gift." Her wide, glassy eyes looked up at him as he looked down at her.

"No, thank you, darlin'. I love you too, more than anything." He caressed her cheek softly. "You ready to call my parents?" he asked excitedly as they wiped tear trails off of each other's faces. She nodded yes so he grabbed his phone and once again put it on speaker.

"Hey, sweetie, whatcha up to?" Caroline answered.

"Well, Mom, Marina and I have something to tell you. Dad with you?"

"Yeah, just a sec." Caroline covered the phone and hollered for Tom. "He's comin'. Everything okay?"

"Oh, yeah, Mom. Everything is great." Sawyer tried to conceal his excitement, at least lower it, careful not to give it away.

"Hey, son."

"Hey, Dad. You two on speakerphone?"

"Yep. Shoot."

Sawyer looked at Marina and nodded.

"We're pregnant!" they both announced together.

"What?" Tom asked excitedly while Caroline just plain screamed. With a chuckle, Sawyer held the phone away farther until Caroline calmed enough to speak. Marina took Sawyer's hand, squeezing it hard.

"I love that y'all are so excited," Marina said into the phone.

"Oh my gosh! I can't believe this! It's a miracle! Tom, we're going to be grandparents!"

"We sure are! Congratulations to both of you."

"Thank you, both of you," Sawyer said with a sniffle.

"It's been a difficult road. Could've been tougher, of course, but we did it somehow," Marina said proudly.

"Oh, I know how," Sawyer mumbled in a low bass tone. "Persistence paid off." He smiled before kissing Marina so passionately that he forgot they were still on the phone.

The rest of the day was spent snuggling while making phone call after phone call.

CHAPTER 27
Attentive

Sawyer woke to Marina bailing out of bed quickly and running to the bathroom. She had shut the door most of the way but Sawyer could hear her vomiting. He jumped up and ran in. She was on her knees in front of the toilet, heaving, and waved behind her, signaling for him to leave the bathroom. Instead of leaving, he held her hair while rubbing her back.

"I'm so sorry, darlin'."

She took a ragged breath and sniffled before saying, "It's okay, babe. I'll be okay. You don't need to be in here for this." She even had the decency to courtesy flush.

"I got you. I just wish I could take the sucky parts of pregnancy for you."

"You're sweet, but I don't wish it on you either. Not that pregnancy is a bad thing, of course, I feel blessed, but I really hate puking."

"I hate it for you, baby. You know I appreciate what you're going through."

She rested her head on her arm on the toilet seat.

"Thank you for saying that. We both want this."

"I see the toll it's taking on you already."

"Aww, this is nothin' compared to birth, I'm sure." She smiled. "I'm glad I cleaned the toilets yesterday."

He laughed. "Well, I'll do that from now on. You don't need to be around any chemicals."

She nodded slowly, exhausted.

"You good to come back to bed?"

"I think so."

"Take your time. I'm here when you're ready."

"I better brush my teeth first." She stood from her knees, Sawyer taking her by the arm to help her up, and brushed her teeth as he waited in the doorway.

"I'm okay, babe."

"You're still white as a ghost." He took her arm in his and walked her back to bed, where she tucked her legs under the covers and he pulled them up for her before bending over to kiss her on the head.

"Can I get you anything, darlin'?"

"Maybe some water, if you don't mind."

"Sure. I'll be right back." He scooted quickly out of the bedroom, Whiskey standing from his bed and stretching before following. Marina sank deeper, bunching the pillow under her neck and tucking the covers under her arm. Sawyer returned with a glass of water only a few moments later but found Marina asleep. He quietly set her water glass on the nightstand and smiled as he watched her sleep a moment before ushering Whiskey out of the room and quietly closing the door behind them. He did chores and went to the office to retrieve his laptop then hustled back; he didn't want to be gone long in case she needed him. Upon returning, he peeked in on her. Her sleeping position had changed but she was still asleep so he poured himself a steaming cup of coffee and sat on the porch swing with Whiskey and his laptop, wearing just his jogger sweats. After working for about an hour, he peeked back in on her. She was still sleeping so he worked out for about forty-five minutes and was making himself a protein shake when there was a knock on the front door. Whiskey barked once and beat Sawyer to the door, nails scraping. Sawyer slid Whiskey back and opened the door to find Raquel wearing a big smile.

"Good morning," she said cheerfully, a bag slung over her shoulder.

"Mornin'." Sawyer looked confused. "Come on in."

"Marina and I are supposed to work on some book stuff. Where's she at?"

"Um. Sleeping still, actually."

"Babe, are you talking to someone?" Marina came down the hallway to the living room, itching her nose with the back of her hand as she stretched her other arm in the air.

"How are you feelin', darlin'?"

"Better, thank you. I guess I fell back asleep."

"It's okay, you needed it."

"Hey, Raquel. What are you doing here so early?"

"Um, I'm late." Raquel looked at the wall clock.

"What time is it?" Marina squinted at the clock, her eyes not focusing.

"Almost eleven." He kissed her on the forehead before heading to the kitchen to finish his shake.

"Wow, it's almost lunchtime! I'm so sorry I slept so long."

Raquel waved her hand like it was no big deal while Sawyer came back in chugging his shake, sweat still running down his shiny skin.

"You needed it, baby. You had a rough start to the day." He offered his shake but she politely declined.

"Looks like you had a good workout." Her eyes wandered to his torso.

"Yeah, but you're my favorite cardio, darlin'." He tossed her a wink and Raquel about slid out of the chair. "Can I make you something to eat?" He offered as he had her get comfy on the couch.

"Maybe a dry piece of toast would do me good."

"You got it." He gave her a smooch before heading back to the kitchen.

"Have a rough night?" Raquel asked as she sat next to Marina on the couch.

"Yeah, I woke up around four having to puke."

"Eww. Feeling better now after you slept more?" Raquel asked, taking her notebook out of her book bag.

"Yeah. So far, anyway. Sawyer held my hair back, which was so sweet but I didn't want him to see me like that."

"He's your husband, he's *gonna* see you at your worst. Plus, men should see what their lady goes through. They have more appreciation that way." She chuckled.

"Well, I still don't want him to."

"I'm sure. Do you feel like doing book stuff today or you wanna save it for a different day?"

"We can do it today, sure. I plan to just lounge around anyway."

Sawyer brought her toast to her with a fresh glass of water. He put the footstool up for her and went to fetch her favorite cozy blanket from the bedroom.

"He's so attentive. It's adorable," Raquel said with a wrinkle of her nose.

"He is. It's so sweet. Thank you, Sawyer."

He laid the blanket over her legs and asked Raquel if she wanted anything. She politely passed but was practically drooling watching him walk away to the bedroom.

"Boy, he sure makes it hard to concentrate, doesn't he?" Raquel admitted her distraction as she flipped open her notebook.

"He sure does, no matter what he is or isn't wearing. Even his voice from another room is distracting."

"I agree. It was a nice surprise when he opened the front door, not gonna lie."

They giggled as they heard the shower turn on.

"Is it just me, or is he bulking up?" Raquel asked, opening her laptop.

"He is. He works out harder and longer when he's stressed. I thought he'd slack off a bit once I got pregnant but he mentioned the other day that he's worried about something happening."

"What do you mean?"

"Like me not carrying to term, but everything is fine so far."

"Aww, he's just worried because it took a lot of effort for you to get pregnant."

"Maybe. He told me to be extra careful because he couldn't shake a bad feeling and he doesn't want to scare me but he wanted to let me know he's terrified of something bad happening."

"That's a bit unsettling."

"Right? I'm glad he felt he could tell me though. Maybe me sharing my nightmare details didn't help. He's just been spending more time in the workout room than usual. He did the same thing when we went through the whole abstinence thing too. Big time. Not that I mind at all, he looks amazing and is as healthy as a horse now that his iron level is back up to normal, I just don't want him stressing."

"Maybe getting the nursery ready would help ease his mind a bit. Have you been thinking of a theme and colors?"

"Yeah. I think it's a parental instinct to start thinking of stuff like that right away when seeing a positive test."

"Absolutely! That's exciting stuff." Raquel was excited for her.

Sawyer came out of the bathroom, wrapped in a towel, moments after they began writing down notes, but shut himself in the bedroom to get dressed.

"Well darn." Raquel watched the door shut and giggled, Marina joining her. He came out dressed in dark-washed jeans and was pulling his gray t-shirt down. He sat in the chair to put socks and boots on and they watched him as they discussed book cover options.

"Darlin', I'm going to the office for a while to work. You have

Raquel here but call me if you need me. I'll give y'all girl time." He then looked at Raquel and nodded, she returned the nod.

"Okay, babe. You care if we use an actual photo of us for the cover like the first book?"

"Nah, I don't mind at all. It's a cool idea. The first one turned out great."

"Thank you!" Raquel smiled proudly.

"It's just too hard to choose one." Marina turned to look at a few hanging on the wall.

"Let me know if we need to take a new one." He tugged his pant legs down over his boots.

"Sure thing."

He stood and walked over to her, bending to give her a sweet kiss before telling the girls bye and leaving. Marina waited for the door to shut behind him before saying, "He had to buy new jeans last weekend because his thighs won't fit in most of his old ones."

"Uh oh. Even your favorite light-wash ripped pair?"

"He's about to bust out of those too. He found some just like it in a bigger size Sunday though. I was relieved." She giggled.

"*Pheew*, yeah, those look nice."

"So, there were these skinny jeans...I don't know what made him try them on, I guess he saw something online perhaps, but oh my God, Raquel..." She started laughing.

"Did they look hot? I'm sure they did."

"Oh, yeah totally! But he could barely move and was pulling at the crotch of them as he walked out of the dressing room. Chicks stopped dead in their tracks. He said, 'How the hell do dudes wear these damn things?' like, really loud." Marina was laughing so hard she could barely speak, which was making Raquel cackle. "I snuck a photo as he was walking around in front of the mirror." Marina showed her the photo on her phone and Raquel's eyes grew huge.

"He looked in the mirror and turned around a few times then asked me to help him pull them off." At this point, Marina was about in tears from laughing so hard.

"Did you help him?" Raquel asked between laughing breaths, but Marina could only nod.

"I'm kinda surprised he would stray that far from the bootcut look," Raquel said.

"Me too. Needless to say, he did not buy them."

"You'll have to buy bigger clothes soon, too." Raquel rubbed Marina's still tiny belly.

"Yep, before ya know it. Time flies. Seems like yesterday I started working for him and he was flirting something fierce. Then we shared our first kiss on the tailgate...and there was that day out on the tree stump in the storm, which led to our first time making love...the adventures we'd take on, even the small ones, were amazing. The nights we spent at the bar were so much fun and he was so protective of me. Proposing in the barn loft, wedding planning, starting the nonprofit and getting married, the once-in-a-lifetime romantic honeymoon, our recent vacation, and now I'm pregnant. So much has happened in such a short time. Life goes by too quickly to rush things like that but we don't want to miss opportunities either. I have felt so many emotions with all of it. I can't imagine having experienced them with anyone else."

Raquel took notes as she listened, then put her pen down on her notebook and turned to Marina.

"You found the perfect man. Not just perfect for you but just seriously perfect, and you're experiencing perfect moments. I'm so happy for you. It's a beautiful thing. There's no way y'all could have ugly babies, either." They busted out laughing. "Oh, and it's sweet that you're dedicating your new children's book to the baby. Sawyer's gonna love that."

"Thanks. I'm excited to read this sequel you're writing. Hopefully, we can give you enough material for a third soon. Everyone loves a good trilogy."

"They sure do, especially about you two."

CHAPTER 28
A Mess She Was

There was a note next to the decaf coffee Sawyer had brewed for Marina in the kitchen. It read "You relax today, darlin'." She smiled, pouring a cup. Decaf wasn't the same and she was missing having her fancy iced latte, but the taste of decaf had a placebo effect and allowed her to sleep. Caffeine isn't good for a fetus, especially in the first trimester. She had been up sick half the night and here it was, lunchtime, and she was just now waking. She put a jacket and her boots on and Whiskey followed her out to the barn. That dog was stuck to her like glue, sensing something was different in a good way. As they approached the barn, Sawyer came around the corner and said, "Look at you. You look a mess." He turned and walked back into the barn and Marina stopped walking, brows raised, surprised by his comment, even though her hair wasn't combed and her leggings didn't match her shirt. He came back out with a brush and sat on the bench then clapped his leg, calling Whiskey to him.

Looking down at herself, she said, "Well, I haven't showered yet."

"Oh, baby." He chuckled. "I didn't mean you. This furball needs a brushin'. Darlin', you know better than that. Come sit."

She sat on the bench and he wrapped an arm around her, giving her a smooch.

"I do look a mess though."

"No, you don't. You never do. You couldn't if you tried."

She rested her head on his shoulder a moment, Sawyer's finger under Whiskey's collar to keep him there.

"I'm sorry you had a rough night. Feeling any better?"

"A little. I'm sure I'll take a nap later. I'm just so tired all the time."

"It's okay to nap, you're growing a human." He flashed a smile.

"You're not going to the office to work today?"

"Nah, I have stuff here I can do."

"Are you not going because I don't feel well?"

"Yep."

"The office isn't far."

"I know, but I figure the closer the better. I have a load of hay comin' here shortly. It's a big one so it'll take a while."

"You're so sweet. Wish I could help ya with the hay."

"You come first, always will. Justin is headed over in a few. Thank you, though."

She gave him a big hug, which he returned, accidentally setting Whiskey free in the process.

"Shit! Come here!" He hollered in a gruff tone and Whiskey came back to him with his head down and bobbed tail tucked downward. "Nice try. Sit." Whiskey sat on the ground between Sawyer's legs as Sawyer started brushing him. Normally, Whiskey didn't mind being brushed, but he had knots behind his ears and didn't have the patience for Sawyer to detangle them.

"You need me to do that? I'm sure you have other things to do," she offered.

"Nah, thank you though."

"I think I'll go in and read a book then."

"Sounds good. Promise you'll relax today?"

"I promise."

"We need milk so I'll go to the store in a bit too. Anything else we need?"

"We still have milk." She tilted her head in confusion.

"Not anymore. You put it away in the cereal cabinet instead of the fridge yesterday, darlin'."

"No way."

"Yes, way." He laughed.

"Oh no...the pregnancy brain thing is starting already."

"It's okay. Don't worry about it. Just send me a list. We're supposed to go to dinner tonight with Jake and Becka so we'll see how you feel later."

"Okay, sounds fun." She smooched his cheek and said, "Sorry about the milk," before heading to the house.

Justin came over and helped Sawyer unload the trailer of hay and stack it in the barn, then Sawyer went into the house to shower about the time the sun was barely above the treeline. He came out of the bathroom but Marina wasn't on the couch where she was when he got home.

"Marina?" He buttoned his jeans and grabbed a t-shirt from the basket on the bed that Marina felt too shitty to put away. He reached the spare bathroom doorway as she was splashing cold water on her face.

"You okay?"

"Better now. I had to throw up again."

"Aww, baby."

"I'm okay." She patted his chest as she passed him in the doorway.

"I'm going to brush my teeth. Would it be okay if—"

"I'm calling Jake to cancel right now."

"Please tell him I'm sorry."

"You don't need to apologize, darlin'."

After brushing her teeth, she crawled back into bed.

"You hungry at all?" he asked, entering the bedroom. She shook her head no with her cheeks puffed as though she might puke at just the thought of food.

He chuckled. "Okay. I'm gonna grab somethin' real quick and I'll come in to chill with ya."

He came in with his guitar not long after and sat on the edge of the bed.

"I won't puke on you; you can sit next to me."

He laughed. "Okay. I thought I'd play y'all a song." He sat next to her, leaning against the headboard.

"We'd love that."

With a rub and a kiss on her belly, he sang *Beers to the Summer* by Russell Dickerson.

"This little one is going to love you singing and playing at bedtime every night," she told him, her hand on his thigh.

"Hope so. I'm sure Mama will be a great book reader, too."

"We're gonna crush this whole parenting thing." She snuggled up to him.

"Yeah, we are. I'm so thankful I get to do it all with you."

"Me too." Her lips met his for a sweet, lingering kiss before he propped his guitar up against the wall and stripped his jeans off to lay with her. She got comfortable with his bicep as her pillow, snug against him. He planted a kiss on her forehead as she thought of how lucky she was to have this heavenly man by her side. She had grown tired easily; creating another life within her was draining. His heartbeat and the feel of him stroking her hair never failed to soothe her to sleep.

CHAPTER 29
Trampled

The barn note read "Went to the hardware and feed stores. Be right back. I'll do chores." Becka had already come to help Marina out though. While the trough was filling in the first pasture, Becka cleaned out stalls and Marina stuffed hay in feed bags. She took them out to the pastures to hang them on the posts and Dixie followed like she does most mornings, pulling hay out through the mesh as they walked. Marina hung up the bag in the first pasture then continued to the second. Dixie was to be put out into the third, and as Marina was about to enter the gate to the second, Athena came up to the fence. Sawyer pulled into the drive and got out of his truck as Becka came out of the barn. Athena nipped at Dixie over the fence. Dixie reared up, almost kicking Marina, and pushing her into the fence with her massive shoulder as a flair of dirt kicked up behind fluffy hooves. Sawyer ran for her with Becka hot on his heels. Dixie ran for her pasture while Marina yelled at Athena.

"Marina!" Sawyer shouted as he hauled ass across the dirt. He reached her just before Becka did and gently took her by the shoulders. "Are you okay? Are you hurt?"

"I'm fine. I'm good. Really. Might have a few bruises

tomorrow from hitting the fence but I'm okay." She coughed after having inhaled dirt before it could settle.

"Oh my God. That scared the shit out of me." He held her tight, her head pressed against his chest.

"You okay?" Becka asked.

"I'm good."

"You got lucky," Becka stated.

"Damn right, you did. That can't happen again. I think it would be best if you stayed away from the horses."

"What?"

"Just while you're pregnant."

"The whole nine months? Sawyer, that's ridiculous." Marina played it off as no big deal but Sawyer's heart sure was racing.

"Marina, I'm serious. This could've been bad. Anything can happen around all that muscle." He pointed at the horses grazing peacefully in the green pasture.

"Anything can happen around all this muscle too." She tapped his chest and smiled.

He took her face in his hands and said, "Darlin', we can't take the risk of anything happening to our little one. We've worked so hard for this. I don't know why I didn't consider your safety around the horses more seriously before now. I am so sorry."

"Sawyer, it's okay, you have nothing to apologize for. I'm fine. I'm always careful around them. I'll just have to be extra careful from now on."

"No. I don't want you to be around them. I want you to be on the outside of the fences and stalls, not *with* them."

"I can't ride either, can I?"

"No, ma'am. I'm sorry, love, but it's just the way it needs to be."

She looked at him like her world was falling apart then dropped her head before he scooped her up for a hug.

"He's right. He didn't joke back when you joked so ya know he's serious. Don't want anything happening to that little one," Becka agreed.

"I understand. I want to protect our little one too. I'm honored and excited to be carrying a part of you within me. I'll do my best to protect this little life, it's just going to be so hard to not be able to do what I do every day." She could feel his racing heart as his chest rose. "It scared me a little but it *really* scared you, didn't it?"

"Absolutely." He rubbed her belly.

"I'm sorry I was careless."

"You weren't, baby, you were just doin' what you do every day. This is why I said in the note I'd do chores though."

"I'll have to make sure I'm more careful. I'm glad you've reminded me. I'm sorry."

He let out a long exhale. "You let me do the work. You just worry about taking care of yourself and our baby. That's a big enough job. I don't know what I'd do if I lost either one of you." He kissed her lips and stroked her hair.

"Okay."

"I don't normally tell you what to do, you know that. But this...this I'm putting my foot down on. Ya hear me, darlin'?"

"I hear you." She smiled at him while thinking of how caring and protective he was.

"Aww, it's great that he's so protective of you. I love it," Becka told Marina. "You got a good one, boo."

"I love it too. I sure do. I completely understand where you're coming from, Sawyer." She lifted to her toes to kiss him again.

"I'll go put Dixie inside the gate." Becka left them alone to love on each other, him thankful for her safety.

CHAPTER 30
Playin' Your Cards Right

Marina read the barn note that morning and hefted a sigh into her decaf. "Working late tonight. Love you." She ran her errands throughout the day and caught up on house chores since there wasn't any work for her to do at the office. She texted Sawyer, asking, "You want dinner?" He texted back, "So sorry. Lost track of time. Go ahead and eat, I'll grab a snack when I get home. Should be less than an hour." She ate leftovers out of the fridge from the night before then settled on the couch watching TV until he got home.

"Hey, darlin', sorry I'm so late." He came through the front door, took his boots off, hung his hat, and leaned over the arm of the couch for a kiss.

"Hey, babe, you had a long day, huh?" She set the remote on the end table.

"Yeah, I got it done though, so we have the rest of the weekend to spend together."

"Aww. Is it chilly outside?"

"It's cooled off quite a bit, yeah. I'm gonna grab a shower real quick." He pulled his shirt up over his head and flung it into the hamper.

"You want me to make you something to eat?" she hollered as

he entered the bathroom. He stopped in the doorway, hand on the doorframe, and asked, "What did you have?"

"I just ate the leftover tacos from last night. I should've saved you some."

"Nah, it's okay, baby. You're eating for two now." He chuckled. "I'll just grab something when I get out. Thanks though." He hustled in the shower and came out to the living room in just a pair of loose workout pants. He raided the fridge but didn't find anything that sounded good so he ate an apple while waiting for popcorn to pop.

"You're making popcorn?" Marina hollered from the living room, the buttery aroma hitting her nose before the popping even began.

"Yeah, I'll share. Your senses sure are on point."

"They are, yeah, so if you wouldn't mind taking the trash out in the morning, that would be great. I tried but I started gagging."

"Deal." He laughed, his cheek full of apple. "I'll run it outside right now."

He took the trash out and when the popcorn was finished popping, he poured it into a large bowl and brought it into the living room. She couldn't help but notice how low those pants sat, the curve of his hips showing from the top.

"What do ya wanna watch?" she asked, still staring at him, adjusting her glasses.

"Actually..." He grabbed a deck of cards from the dining room drawer and sat on the living room floor. The popcorn bowl was set in the center of the coffee table.

"What we playin'?" she asked.

"What you wanna play?"

She sat across from him on the floor, between the coffee table and the couch.

"You choose." She watched him shuffle the cards.

"Well, first, I haven't said hello to the little one." He crawled around to her and lifted her nightshirt. His gentle touch felt comforting as he laid a hand on her stomach. He scooched closer to kiss her on her soft lips and remove her glasses before returning to his side of the coffee table, shuffling the deck of cards. He caught her staring at him with a smile. He smiled back and asked, "What?"

"I just love you. So much."

"I love you too, darlin'."

He dealt the cards as he shoved a handful of popcorn in his mouth and they decided on which game they were playing. Partway through the game she was looking to draw an ace of diamonds. He was smirking so she asked with a mouthful, "You have it, don't you?"

He shrugged.

"Sawyer, are you hiding the card I need?"

He didn't answer, his smartass grin only widening while he looked at her with his chin tucked.

"Sawyer, give me the diamond. Please." Her head tilted to the side.

He dropped the card down the front of his pants and said, "Whoops. Your ace is in the hole. Now it's a diamond in the rough."

"Oh my God, Sawyer!" She giggled, making him laugh.

"If you want it, come get it." He bit his lower lip.

Oh, that sexy bass tone he lowered his voice to...it had her willing to do anything. She crawled over to him, yanking at his pants. He playfully fought her off at first, almost carefully wrestling her, but she wasn't giving up. She pulled the drawstring on the front of his pants and reached down them, feeling for the card.

"I found what I was looking for."

"Um, that's not the card, baby."

She kissed him, both of them laughing, and he tipped her over onto the area rug then leaned over her, propped up on his elbow. Her nightshirt rose to her panty line and his hand slid up her outer thigh. She pulled him down for a long kiss while reaching down his pants. Pulling away, she teasingly whispered, "I got my diamond," and showed him the card. He laughed and stood, reaching for her hand. Upon pulling her to her feet, he asked, "Wanna cuddle in bed? I'm sure it'll lead to more diamond mining."

"Sawyer, you never have to ask that. The answer will always be yes." She giggled.

"I wasn't too rough with ya, was I?" he asked sweetly, pulling her to him.

"Never. You played your cards just right."

CHAPTER 31
Repeat That, Please!

"Why is it always so cold in doctor's offices?" Marina tucked the white sheet under her hips as she laid back on the table.

"I don't know, to keep the germs to a minimum probably. It's not right to make a pregnant woman shiver though." Sawyer looked through cabinets looking for another sheet or blanket. He found a sheet and left it folded in half, laying it over her legs.

"Thanks, babe."

He smiled at her, sitting in the corner chair just as the doctor came into the room.

"How's everyone doing?" Dr. Chen asked as she washed her hands.

"Doing well, thanks. You?"

"Yeah, doing well. Sorry that we couldn't get you scheduled right away. Any morning sickness?"

Sawyer was nodding his head yes.

"A little but it's nothing I can't handle. It's slacking off now." Marina answered, snickering at Sawyer.

"Make sure you take your prenatal at night before bed. That should help. Especially with the ones I'm prescribing you today. It'll help you sleep better at night too and not be so drowsy during the day." Dr. Chen sat on the stool and pulled the ultrasound machine closer. "This will feel cold," she warned as she squirted gel on Marina's bare belly. Sawyer walked around to Marina's other side and held her hand, excited.

"Okay, now let's see this little one." Dr. Chen rolled the transducer around until a small, noticeable formation showed on the screen.

"There it is. Your sweet bundle of joy." She pointed to the monitor screen.

Sawyer couldn't even speak. He was choked up and just squeezed Marina's hand, smiling at her, then looked back at the monitor.

"That's what we've worked so hard for, babe." Marina was so excited that she could barely contain herself.

"Actually..." Dr. Chen squinted and moved the device around, pressing Marina's stomach in different directions.

"Is something wrong?" Sawyer asked, concerned.

"Well, I wouldn't consider it a negative thing but...I think you're about to be even more excited, actually."

"Why?" Marina sat up on her elbows.

"I'm seeing double," Dr. Chen said, then turned and smiled.

"Wait...so...are you saying...?" Marina asked, then paused, looking at the screen.

"Twins," Dr. Chen said, nodding.

"Say what? Repeat that, please," Marina requested as Dr. Chen kept nodding yes.

"I'm sorry, did you just say twins?" Sawyer was shocked.

Marina's eyes were huge. "I was thinking we'd only have two kids altogether so..." Marina was in shock as well.

"You only have to go through this once!" Sawyer was stoked.

Marina laughed and said, "Perfect!"

"Darlin', this is great. I'm so excited." He kissed her forehead, then her cheek, then her lips. She loved that he was so happy.

"I'm going to get huge, aren't I?" Marina's excitement quickly turned to worry.

The doctor nodded and said, "Probably."

Sawyer said, "Oh, baby, it doesn't matter as long as you stay healthy and they stay healthy too."

"It matters to me. I'll need to keep exercising and watch how much I eat."

Sawyer sighed and shook his head but wore a smile.

"Well, for blood sugar reasons, yes to an extent, but we'll keep an eye on your health the whole nine months. You'll be okay," Dr. Chen assured.

"You okay, darlin'? What are ya thinkin'?"

"I'm just thinking of how much work it'll be having two babies at the same time and we're going to need double of almost everything on our baby shower list, but I am so excited. We've been double blessed." She squeezed his hand, which prompted him to hug her tightly. A happy tear ran down her cheek.

"We've got this." His forehead rested against hers as he held her face in his hands.

She nodded, squeezing his arms.

"Looks like y'all have two names to choose now," Dr. Chen said as she handed them a printout of the sonogram photo.

"Two more stars to name in the sky," he said, looking at Marina with a twinkle in his eyes.

CHAPTER 32
Splattering Love

"Whatcha doin'?" Marina asked, stepping out onto the porch.

"Trimmin' this tree. This limb keeps tryin' to snag my hat right off my damn head." He was barefoot and wearing black pocketed joggers with the pant legs hiked up to his calves. The sun shone down upon his tan skin as she stood leaning against the porch beam watching him.

"Those overalls look adorable on you." He cut the branch while staring at her instead of paying attention to where he was cutting.

"Aww, thanks. Actually, I was thinking just now about how hot you look in those pants."

"Oh yeah?"

"Definitely, yes." She wore a handkerchief rag pulling her hair back from her face that matched her t-shirt under those overall shorts.

"What are you doin', darlin'? You should be relaxin'."

"I'm about to paint the nursery."

"You supposed to be sniffin' in those fumes? I doubt it's good for ya. Give me just a minute and I'll come do it."

"I've opened the windows and I won't be in there for long

periods of time. I'll put a fan in the window too. It's nice outside today so fresh air flowing through the house would be nice. It would be nice to paint together."

"Yeah, you got it, baby." He dragged the big branch to the edge of the field and plunked it down. "Hey, my dad texted a while ago saying they had something important to ask us, so don't let me forget to call him later," Sawyer mentioned, walking up to the porch and brushing his hands together.

"Maybe we can video call them after we paint so we can show them the nursery."

"Sounds good." He gave her a smooch before they headed in to paint.

"Well, look at you. Plastic is down, paint and rollers are ready to roll, we just need the ceiling taped off yet. Thank you for not using a ladder, darlin'. I'll do that real quick." She watched him tape the ceiling off; him reaching up, those shoulders and back muscles being put to use. He climbed down after sealing off the last corner.

"I might be a little excited." She wrapped her arms around him from behind as paint dripped from the roller he picked up.

"This is pretty damn exciting, isn't it?"

"Mmhmm." She swiped paint from the roller with her index finger and smeared it across his bare chest. He chuckled and wiped some on her face as he turned to her.

"We gonna get messy?" he asked in a low rumble.

"We always do when you talk to me like that."

"That's true."

"I don't wanna get these hot joggers all paint-splattered though."

"Well, there are two solutions: either I take 'em off and paint in my underwear, or they just get painted because I do have another pair just like 'em."

"If you paint in your underwear, we won't be getting any painting done. It's difficult enough with you in these joggers."

"Can you get these cute overalls all paint-splattered?"

"They're old so I don't care." She shrugged a shoulder.

"I was hopin' you'd say no so you'd have to paint in *your* underwear." He flung paint all over her.

She gasped as it splattered across her chest and in her hair then said, "Oh, it's game on, cowboy." She picked up the other roller and dipped it into the paint. He was ready to fling back and did just that as soon as she splattered him. He jumped back, trying to dodge it but paint splattered across his black pants.

"Truce?" she asked, batting her eyes as she looked up at him.

"For real or are you psyching me out?" He chuckled, his stance defensive.

"For real. At least for now till we get the room painted."

He gave her an unsure look, one brow lowered, and made her laugh.

Together, they rolled an entire wall, having chosen a pale yellow since they didn't know the sex of the babies yet, but Marina decided she wanted the opposite wall painted a seafoam-aqua-green color. The accent walls brightened the room, leaving the other two walls gray.

"You wanna find out the sex when it's time to be able to?" he asked, setting the roller down in the tray.

"I don't know. I kinda like the idea of a surprise."

"We'd have to pick more name options then." He wiped his yellow-speckled hands on his pants.

"Yeah, I'm okay with that."

"Our moms will wanna know. You know that, right?"

"Yeah, I know. I'll do whatever you wanna do, babe."

"It's up to you, love."

"Then I wanna wait for a while at least. It'll be hard to buy things we need like clothes if we don't find out, so maybe I'll decide to find out later." She shrugged.

"Deal. I think the walls look great." He settled on her compromise.

"Me too. Let's call your parents."

When their faces appeared on the screen, they greeted Tom and Caroline from the freshly painted nursery.

"Oh, my goodness! That's lovely! I'm guessing you two haven't decided on finding out the sex?"

"Nah, we're gonna wait for as long as we can stand to." Sawyer held out the phone so his parents could see both him and Marina.

"Surprises can be a wonderful thing." Caroline was excited. It was all becoming a reality.

"I agree, Mom. We have a few weeks before we can find out anyway."

"We're just thankful to be pregnant. Hopefully, these babies stay healthy. That's all that matters," Marina said.

"Absolutely," Tom agreed.

"So did you two pick a theme or y'all just sticking to a color?"

"I'm thinking horses." Marina looked at Sawyer.

"I like it." He nodded. "So, what's the news you two wanted to share?"

"Well, it's more of a question and offer," Tom drawled, obviously hesitant and measuring Sawyer's reaction.

"Okay..." Sawyer was almost reluctant to hear it.

"We were thinking you two might need help once the babies arrive. We wanted to ask what your thoughts would be on us buying a small place down there to stay at for a couple of weeks at a time to help out. Raising babies is a lot of work," Tom said.

Caroline chimed in as Sawyer and Marina looked at each other, pondering the idea. "We don't want to overstep or be in the way but we'd like to be able to help and spend time with our grandbabies. We completely understand though if it seems smothering. We thought, since we're retired, we should offer."

"No, I like the idea." Marina smiled at Sawyer, who raised his brows.

"Just think it over and discuss it. Let us know whatever y'all decide. No hard feelings, we just would love to take some pressure off the two of you," Tom said.

"You'd really buy another house here just to help out?" Marina asked, surprised at their grand generosity.

"Of course. We love it here in Tennessee too much to leave it completely, and there's the whole smothering thing too, but we'd love to be closer more often," Caroline said.

Marina looked at Sawyer, smiled, and nodded discreetly. He smiled at her then told his folks, "That's quite the gesture. You guys sure you're up for the challenge?"

"Absolutely!" They both hollered.

"If it's okay with Sawyer, I'd love that." Marina gladly accepted their kind offer.

"Jeez, no pressure." Sawyer laughed then said, "Of course. We appreciate it."

"It's settled then. We'll look for a little place nearby soon." Tom was obviously thrilled at the prospect of being closer to his growing family.

"Oh, Tom, I've been looking for a week. I think I've already found the perfect one," Caroline said.

"Of course, you have, dear." Tom chuckled, shaking his head.

"Thank you both." Caroline was thankful for their acceptance of the idea and practically squealed with joy.

"We'd love to have y'all close more often. It'll be good for everyone," Sawyer agreed, "We can still have date nights and maybe a nap." Marina could *almost* see the daydream bubbles above his head and laughed.

"If your children are to act anything like you, Sawyer, you'll need all the help you can get," Caroline said.

"Uh oh!" Marina laughed but Sawyer wasn't amused.

"That's what grandparents are for." Sawyer's wiseass grin spread wide.

CHAPTER 33
All Is Fair

"You've got this!" is what the barn note read as Sawyer got ready to help Marina with chores. She knew she was to stick to stuffing hay in bags and putting the hose in troughs; just the easy stuff that didn't require her to go into pastures with the horses. He would've preferred for her to just take it easy but she was too stubborn not to help him at all now that she was feeling better in the mornings.

"Thanks for the note, darlin'." He kissed her on the cheek as she poured him a cup of coffee and handed it to him.

"You're welcome. Are you excited?"

"Yeah. It'll be fun."

"You guys are going to be the talk of the town after this fair."

"Think we'll rock it out?"

"I know y'all will."

"Thank you for your support." He sipped his hot coffee.

"You'll always have my support, Sawyer. I really do believe in you guys though."

"I appreciate you." He kissed her forehead and pulled her in for a hug. "Thanks for the coffee...and the note."

"You're welcome."

Later that afternoon, the crowd was growing considerably and quickly at the fair. The aroma of funnel cakes and popcorn filled the air and Sawyer let out a huff of breath as he stretched his arms and cracked his neck with a loud pop.

"Are you nervous?" Marina asked, straightening the collar on his fitted black, three-quarter-sleeve button-up shirt. It had teal on the inside, which showed since his sleeves were cuffed and the shirt wasn't fully buttoned up.

"You look so sexy in this outfit. Those ripped-up jeans are gonna be a hit."

"Yeah?" He smirked. "I wore them just for you."

"Aww, just when I thought you couldn't get any sexier, you pulled out all the stops today, cowboy." She handed his black hat to him.

"Thank you, baby. You look mighty fine yourself." He slapped her rear with his hat before placing it upon his head, biting his bottom lip. She batted her eyes and smiled. "You gonna get chilly in this dress tonight?"

"Nah. Watchin' you up there on that stage is all the fuel I need to stay warm. It's long to cover my legs and I brought a sweater just in case."

"You sure you don't wanna sing with us? It's only fair that you get to experience this too."

"Oh, I'm sure. There are way too many people out there." She giggled.

"It's packed, huh?" He looked nervous, biting the inside of his cheek.

"Pretty much. But that's a good thing. Sawyer, I love sharing the stage with you, but this is your spotlight. It's your time to shine, so get out there and be the star you were born to be. I'll be right there, front row, cheering you on."

"That stage looks huge." He looked around Marina to the side of the stage where he was about to enter.

"Deep breaths, babe. It's just more space to move around on, which is a good thing too. No falling off like you could've on the tailgate."

"True. Okay. I can do this. Your support means the world to me." He put his earpiece in and said, "I hope I remember how to use this damn thing."

"No overthinking, Sawyer. Pretend it's just a busy night at the bar. You ready?" Anna walked up and patted Sawyer on the arm.

"I guess so." He nodded and grabbed his guitar. The other guys joined Sawyer at the open curtain at the bottom of the steps.

"Where's your guitar?" Sawyer asked Jake, who was chugging water.

"Already on the stage."

"Oh, I guess I should've done that."

Todd took Sawyer's guitar, walked it up, and set it on the stand on the stage then joined everyone in the back for a pep talk. Anna said a few words of encouragement then Marina kissed Sawyer, wishing him the best of luck. She went out to join the crowd, in the front row with Becka, Raquel, Olivia, Stacy, Trina, Justin, Bob, and Gladys. Everyone was excited, about to burst with anticipation.

Todd stepped out onto the stage to announce the band's entrance.

"I present to you, as their first public performance outside of a local bar...are y'all ready? Here's Backroad to Backcountry!" Todd left the stage and the band ran up the stairs and out to their instruments. Sawyer took the microphone from its stand at center stage as Jake flipped the switch on his amp.

"How we doin' tonight?" he shouted. The crowd cheered, the distinct peal of female excitement clearly outweighing that of the masculine half of the crowd.

"We're gonna start with a few cover songs and then throw in a few originals that we wrote. Is that okay with everybody?" He threw his hands up into the air and the crowd cheered. He put his head and arm through his guitar strap, eager to get started, and the band put those instruments to use. They started with *What My World Spins Around* by Jordan Davis. They were naturals in the big spotlight. If they were nervous, it didn't show at all; the adrenaline rush had kicked in and Sawyer was completely in his element. Jake joined him up front at the second microphone as they jumped right into *Freedom Was A Highway* by Jimmie Allen and Brad Paisley. Both guys were on their A-game, making it obvious they were having a blast. Then Sawyer decided to slow it down a bit but keep the ladies' attention with *Mind On You* by George Birge. *Love Drunk* was a hit and the band had fun with that one. Jake joined Sawyer in singing *Red* by HARDY and Morgan Wallen. There's no way Sawyer was about to be on a big stage without singing a Wallen song. Another band original made its debut next, an upbeat song with the electric guitar carrying some heavy weight, that they called *Intoxicating*.

"Intoxicating"
(Verse)
Your scent fills the air
It stops me in my tracks
Come here, let me take you in
Now there's no goin' back

(Verse)
My fingers through your hair
Getting lost in your eyes
I'll pull you in close
Dancin' with you, time flies

(Chorus)
You're intoxicating
You get my pulse racing
I can't get enough
I'm addicted to you
Obsessed with all that you do
I'm so in love

(Verse)

Don't want you going anywhere
Stay in my arms all night
I'm still lovin' on you
Twisted in these sheets so tight

(Verse)
Oh, your eyes (intoxicating)
And your smile (intoxicating)
Everything about you
Is driving me wild

(Chorus Repeat)
You're intoxicating
You get my pulse racing
I can't get enough
I'm addicted to you
Obsessed with all that you do
I'm so in love

Justin told the girls he'd see them in a bit and squeezed his way out of the crowd at the edge of the stage as Sawyer put his guitar on the standing rack and thanked the crowd, thankfulness as a visible emotion. Screams echoed for an encore, which the band had pre-planned anyway. He threw his fist in the air and hollered "We got you!" Trev revved up that keyboard and the crowd knew the song from the first few notes and shouted in excitement, the volume reaching deafening levels. Marina loved *Waiting For You* by Russell Dickerson but knew there would be a key instrument missing so was curious to hear how that was going to work. When that part neared, Justin surprised the girls, joining Sawyer on stage with his saxophone. The girls went wild in the front row. They had no idea he played and were most definitely pleasantly surprised. He killed it! Sawyer took his mic off the stand and jammed, guitarless, next to Justin. Their whole performance that evening was incredible. They had an energy that was even more intense than when they played at the bar. Their naturally smooth charisma spread contagious smiles.

"Thank you all! You've been an amazing crowd!" Sawyer wrapped up the evening by throwing out guitar picks with Jake and Chris tossed his drumsticks out into the crowd before they left the stage still pumped up. Marina and the gang rushed backstage to congratulate the guys on a job well done. Todd made his rounds, shaking the guys' hands, and told them, "You guys are going places."

"Thanks, Todd. We appreciate that. This was a blast and I can't wait to do it again." Sawyer shook his hand, then Anna's.

The guys agreed.

"Justin! What the hell? You play the sax?" Marina was still shocked.

"Yep, sure do. This was fun."

"I'm so glad you were up there rockin' with us." Sawyer patted Justin's back and squeezed in a side hug.

"Me too, I'm glad you invited me."

"We'll have to write a sax part into one of the songs we write so you can get more stage time. It's only fair. I'm excited all of us can do this together."

"So, I take it you want on the schedule for the next fair come summer?" Anna asked, cheekily.

"Hell yeah!" all the guys shouted.

"Now, how about a funnel cake?" Sawyer shouted, nodding at Marina and rushing toward the scent of deep-fried goodness.

"You've earned it, cowboy." She laughed, taking his arm and matching his quick stride.

CHAPTER 34

All Hands-on Deck

Marina started the coffee pot in the barn and let it play the Morgan Wallen playlist as she filled feed bags. She couldn't sleep all night so she thought she'd be helpful in the barn. She found a barn note that read "All hands on deck." She pondered what it meant as she stuffed the stiff hay into the mesh. Sawyer came into the barn a few minutes later, adjusting his hat on his head, and poured a cup of coffee.

"What are you doin', darlin'?"

"Chores. Well...trying to help."

"You don't need to. I keep tellin' ya I'll do it."

"I want to. Hey, I have an idea. I saw on social media where a ranch stapled the thick mesh across a corner in the fencing to stuff the hay in."

"Instead of bags, huh?"

"Yep."

"Sounds easier for us and the horses. Good idea. I can get the mesh today when I go to the hardware store or we can just use burlap."

"What's the note about?"

"Well, now that Dad closed on the house, they need help moving all their stuff in."

"Are the guys able to help?"

"Yes, ma'am. I don't want you lifting a thing. But if you wanna help Mom with small stuff and getting lunch for everyone, unpacking the light-weight stuff, that would be great."

"You know I'd be happy to help."

"Thank you, I appreciate it."

"You don't have to thank me." She tipped his hat back.

"Sure, I do." He kissed her as she lifted to her toes. "Pretty soon that belly will be getting in the way of us kissin' this close," he teased with a grin.

"Oh, stop." She rubbed her belly and handed him the feed bag.

"Good morning, little ones." He bent down and rubbed her stomach then readjusted his hat and opened stall doors, grabbing his coffee and taking a sip as he walked horses out. Legend detoured, turning to greet Marina. He slowly lowered his head and nuzzled her belly with his muzzle, lips twitching against her shirt.

"Aww, I miss you too, buddy." She rubbed the side of his neck. Sawyer was at the barn door when he said, "What the hell? I lost one," and turned to click at Legend. "Legend. Come on, let's go."

"He wanted to say hi to the little ones."

"I'm sure he did." He grinned.

Legend turned around, careful not to bump Marina, and clopped his hooves toward Sawyer, his head still low. Sawyer patted down his side as he reached him at the barn doors.

"I know, she misses you too. Sorry, buddy."

Marina let out a sigh and pouted her bottom lip out. She sure did miss riding that horse and thought it was sweet how animals could sense her pregnancy. Even Whiskey hadn't been as hyper. That could've been due to Sawyer having him neutered recently too, though. Whiskey was getting big and would be an adult before the babies were born. Hopefully, he'd be calm around the babies too. Speaking of the little devil, he chose that moment to come spinning his wheels into the barn, his tongue hanging out, panting. She bent over to pet his fluffy head and asked, "Where have you been, you little troublemaker?"

Sawyer hollered in a gruff tone, "Whiskey! Where'd you run off to, you little shit?" Whiskey's ears perked and the side of his upper lip tucked under, innocently showing his teeth.

Marina snickered and whispered, "Uh oh. What'd you do?"

Sawyer came marching into the barn wearing a scowl, took his hat off, and waved it at the dog.

"Damn you."

Whiskey tucked his nub tail and hauled ass past Sawyer and out of the barn. Sawyer shook his head, his flared nostrils, tight jaw, and pursed lips giving away how pissed he was.

"Should I even ask?" Marina shut the feed room door.

"I was working on a project in the garage and he chewed the shit out of it. I have to start all over. Goddamn it!"

"A project, huh?"

"Yes, ma'am."

"What project?" She didn't recall seeing one in the garage with his woodworking clutter. She wrapped her arms around him and he instantly seemed calmer.

"It's supposed to be a surprise for you."

"Oh? Well, don't spoil it then."

He smirked and gave her a kiss before his phone rang in his back pocket. He grabbed it and, pointing a finger at Marina, said, "No treats for that dog today," as he stepped away.

"Yes, sir." She nodded, trying not to crack a smile.

"Hey, Dad. Okay, I'll give the guys a holler." He ended the call just that quickly and called Chris as he walked out of the barn.

The small enclosed trailer was attached to Chris's truck.

"This is all they're moving in?" Marina asked as Chris opened the big door.

"Nah, this is what they bought online. Furniture to furnish the place. There isn't much they're bringing down with them though, is there?" he asked Sawyer.

"Nah. Dad said he loaded the back of the truck, he's not even hauling a trailer."

"Must be nice to have a house here and one in Tennessee." Chris chuckled.

"It's sweet they're doing this." Marina looked over to her right from the driveway at the cute house his parents had bought. It was located only a few convenient miles away from their own home.

"Yeah, we'll need all the help we can get with the twins."

"We'll help whenever y'all need us to," Chris volunteered.

"Thanks, man." Sawyer patted Chris's back then they counted to three before lifting the new couch.

Jake pulled in and, upon exiting his truck, hollered, "I told you guys to wait before lifting the heavy shit and I'd help. Y'all don't listen worth shit."

"We got this." Sawyer shrugged. Marina ran to the house to open the door for them as Jake hoisted the small dining room table over his head and carried it in behind them.

"When are your parents gonna be here?" Jake asked, taking his time through the doorway, careful not to scratch up paint.

"Anytime."

"I thought you said they weren't planning to bring a trailer?" Marina asked, still holding the door open after Jake went through.

"They aren't." Sawyer came back out the door as Chris helped Jake set the table down in the dining room.

"Oh, shit." He stopped.

Tom and Caroline pulled in with both vehicles and a trailer attached the same size as the one the guys were currently unloading...and a horse trailer.

"Hope you boys don't have plans today," Sawyer hollered to them. They joined him on the porch and both said, "Oh shit."

CHAPTER 35

Oakley

"I thought y'all were packin' light." Sawyer hugged his parents as Marina excitedly came out to the driveway to greet them.

"Well, we kinda did. The trailer isn't full," Tom said, shaking Jake's hand.

"We need to holler at the other guys?" Jake asked.

"Nah, you three guys can handle it." Caroline gave Jake a big hug.

"Glad y'all made it safely." Marina tried peering through the horse trailer window but whatever was in there was being shy. "Whatcha got in there?" she asked.

"Well, it's your Christmas present. Yours and Sawyer's both," Tom said, walking to the back of the trailer.

"Huh?" Sawyer raised a curious brow.

"Yep. Slightly early, I know, and another mouth to feed. Returning the favor. Saw this beauty at a stud farm I went to in Kentucky. Couldn't pass him up." Tom opened the back door and set the ramp down. It clunked to the dirt. Tom clicked and a bay roan stepped down the ramp.

"Wow, he's beautiful!" Marina was excited.

"Yeah, he is. Jeez, Dad, he had to have set you back a bit. Y'all didn't need to do this."

"Sure we did. And he didn't set us back as much as you might think. Turns out I did vet work for the owner years ago at a small ranch and Dave has bought a few from him before. He gave me a hell of a deal."

"Wow. Thank you, Dad."

"You betcha, son."

Sawyer joined Marina in petting the roan.

"He's pretty beefy. Nice and thick." Sawyer patted the horse's side, its coat thick with winter fluff.

"They called him Oakley. He's only three but very well behaved. He's a big baby," Caroline said.

"I like that name." Marina scratched under his chin.

"He stayin' here or at the stables?" Jake asked, looking the horse over.

"I don't know yet. Probably our place for now," Sawyer pondered aloud, watching Oakley loving Marina's attention.

It was a long afternoon, moving Sawyer's parents into their second home. Oakley was hitched out at the trailer, grazing in the grassy yard as furniture was rearranged inside the house. Tom and Caroline insisted on unloading the few boxes they brought themselves as Sawyer was anxious to be getting the new stud horse home. They loaded the horse just in time for the rain to come.

Oakley made himself at home in the barn for the night and was rearing to be let out to pasture the next morning.

"He sure does have a pretty coat, doesn't he?" Sawyer leaned his arms up against the fence next to Marina, watching Oakley.

"He sure does. He seems to be interacting well with the others."

"So far so good."

"We got so much rain last night." Marina noticed huge mud puddles throughout the pastures. Oakley noticed them too and trotted over to one. His head lowered and knees folded as Sawyer shouted, "Don't do it!" but down Oakley went. Sawyer jumped the fence and hollered to get the horse moving but Oakley ran from Sawyer and laid in another puddle. Rolling in the mud, that bay roan coat was now orange-red clay.

"Aww, shit." Sawyer hung his head as Marina snickered.

"I had a feeling that was gonna happen as soon as he trotted over there." She laughed.

"Wow, he's a totally different color now. Look at him! He's got mud dripping from his nostrils even. What a mess!"

"He's gonna need a good hosin' down. Glad it wasn't Dixie," she said as Sawyer climbed out of the pasture. He stopped midway and pointed. Marina turned around to see Dixie upside down with fluffy hooves flailing and kicking in the air, her white fluff tainted orange and mud flying everywhere.

"Aww, shit." Marina pouted playfully, stomping a foot and making Sawyer laugh.

"We've got ourselves *two* characters now," he said, putting a hand on the small of her back and adjusting his black hat, giving in to defeat.

CHAPTER 36
Showering Love

White and blue twinkle lights lit up the interior and exterior of Backcountry. Real pine trees had been hauled in and an artificial snow-making machine sprinkled white wonder upon the trees. Aqua glittery snowflakes hung from the ceiling, completing the winter wonderland look. It was simple yet elegantly extravagant for a December baby shower. The group of friends were happy to throw together a party for the expecting couple. Sawyer was told the party started a half hour after everyone else was to get there so the food and décor were set and ready before they arrived. Sawyer had stored a surprise for Marina in the back storage room the day before when he and the guys hauled in the trees. Marina had been throwing ideas around for a shower and was planning on the winter wonderland theme but hadn't set a date yet. Gladys and Bob arranged for the bar to be reserved just for the shower, which Sawyer suggested for a Friday night so Marina wouldn't be suspicious. Becka and Raquel had it easy with planning since they had been discussing with Marina and knew what she wanted. The rest of the band was all set up on the stage, Gladys had pizzas in the brick oven, and Lana was ready with Bob behind the bar.

Sawyer and Marina came in, arm in arm. She was glowing; her

small baby bump showing in her white off-the-shoulder sweater. Her tall heeled black boots paired adorably with her snowflake-printed leggings. She complimented Sawyer's aqua long-sleeved tee. He even wore his white hat to match her sweater.

She gasped, looking up at the snow falling upon them. He set his guitar case down and took her hand as she wore the biggest smile on her face. Flakes decorated her hair and she brushed them off her face as she gave Sawyer a sweet kiss.

"Oh, my goodness!" She looked around the bar, the trees, the lights, the baby gifts wrapped and placed under the trees amongst the piles of snow.

"This is amazing! I can't believe you guys did this!" She was tearing up with joy. She grabbed Sawyer's scruffy face gently and said, "You're absolutely amazing. I love you."

"I love you too, so much."

"Aww, thank you, everyone. Y'all are a blessing. We really lucked out on friends and family, Sawyer."

He chuckled. "We sure did, darlin'."

"Here I thought it was going to be a typical Friday night. I love it when you surprise me." She rested her hands upon his chest, looking up at him.

"Good because I love surprising you. We're still playing tonight too."

"Yay!" She excitedly clapped her hands.

"There's another surprise later," he said with a gentle kiss on her forehead and squeezed his arms around her tightly.

"Another?"

"Yep. What do ya say we get this party started?"

"Let's do it!"

"We playin' first?" he hollered to the crowd of friends. All of them cheered, but when the pizza came out just then, Marina tugged at Sawyer's shirt, making the choice obvious.

"Pizza first," he announced with a laugh.

After pizza, he grabbed his guitar case and ran to the stage, meeting the band up there. Marina made rounds, chatting with everyone while Sawyer got prepared. Andrea told Marina as they walked past the stage, "I'm so glad you're over morning sickness. I'm sure that was miserable."

"Thanks. Yeah, it was tough."

"I ate a lot of pizza and cereal." Sawyer chuckled and nudged Gladys with his elbow when she delivered his beer to the stage.

Marina poured herself hot cocoa from the cocoa fountain... yes, a cocoa fountain that looked like a horse ice sculpture. Sawyer and the girls pulled out all the stops. She sprinkled a handful of mini marshmallows on top, complete with a candy cane stir stick, and took a seat at a stage-front table with Becka, Raquel, and Andrea. Savannah and Aliza sat at the next table with Tom and Caroline. Lana decided to take her apron off since everyone was helping themselves with drinks and sat up at the bar with Sabrina. They seemed to be getting along well. Stacy and Trina joined Gladys and Bob at the center table after indulging in the hot cocoa.

Sawyer took the mic and adjusted his white Stetson, guitar strapped on the front of him and his right arm resting on top of it.

"We can't tell y'all how much it means to Marina and me that y'all are here tonight, sharing this special celebration with us. We want to thank you all for your love and support. This has been a journey for sure and we're happy to be able to share it with y'all who mean so much to us. I appreciate the help with getting the bar ready for tonight too and for everyone keeping this event a secret. We've been blessed and we couldn't be more excited." Everyone cheered and clapped. "You know y'all will get another speech at the end of the night. Hope y'all don't mind babysittin'," he said with a chuckle before strumming his guitar and allowing himself a full laugh.

Love You Like I Used To by Russell Dickerson is how they started the evening; a sweet reminder that he loves her more each day. *Best Shot* by Jimmie Allen let Marina know it would be a night of lovey songs sang just for her. She was the reason for so many good things in his life so he had to show her through song with *She's Why* by Russell Dickerson. He and Jake sat on stools while singing *Mean To Me* by Brett Eldredge and *Home Sweet* by Russell Dickerson. They ended the performance with *Look Like A Love Song* by Russell Dickerson since Justin brought his sax. Trev worked his magic on the keyboard like a DJ mixing up sounds and even broke out the tambourine. Every song they played was a perfect fit for the event.

"Marina, darlin', are you ready to open some gifts?"

"I am!" she shouted. He set his guitar down and jumped off the stage to her.

"You two sit, we'll bring them to you." Raquel and Becka made their way to the pile of gifts and brought them over to the table as Jake carried over the larger boxes.

"I think that's everything," Jake said as he took a seat at a table with the other guys.

"Well, besides what's in the back," Sawyer reminded.

"We'll get those after y'all open these."

There were cute little outfits, cozy blankets, all the major necessities too. Sawyer and Marina had already added cribs, a dresser, and a rocking chair to the nursery but hadn't bought much of anything else because their friends instructed them not to. Now they knew why. What possible surprise could Sawyer have in store for her? It seemed they had everything now. Sawyer nodded at Jake to help in the back room and Chris and Trev jumped up to help. Pairing up, they carried out two wooden cradles that matched their home décor; the modern farmhouse look.

Marina's jaw dropped. "Oh, Sawyer! They're beautiful! Where did you find these?" She stood to look them over.

"I made them."

"That's the project you were working on? Oh, my goodness, these mean so much! You having made them makes them so much more special. Thank you."

"Of course, darlin'. I'll make them rocking horses for their first birthdays."

"Good because our moms worked together to make the horse and star mobiles for above their cribs and matching quilts with the colors that we painted the nursery. Rocking horses would be a perfect fit."

Their sweet embrace had the room feeling the love. Raquel gifted the sequel novel she wrote for them along with the baby gift she had brought. So many special gifts were opened for the two new additions. They were going to be spoiled rotten by so many people. Sawyer took Marina by the hand and they stood on the stage in front of everyone.

"We know this time of year is busy for everyone with Christmas comin' in hot tomorrow, so for all of you to take time to celebrate with us…it means the world; we just want you all to know that. We might as well count this as our group Christmas celebration too." Everyone cheered.

"It's beautiful in here tonight and these babies are already spoiled by so many wonderful people. I can't thank you all enough." She sniffled with a smile that could light up a room; a hand on her baby bump.

"I've come to realize our biggest celebrations have been with y'all and most of them here in this bar. I hold this place dear to my heart as well as all of you. Guys, how about we jam out a few Christmas songs before we call it a night?" The guys stood and headed for the stage.

"Sawyer, I have a surprise for you too," Marina said quietly as she took his arm.

"Oh?"

"Just have a seat next to me on a stool up here." She nodded toward the stools behind them and his grin spread wide.

Jake set an extra stool by the two that were already on the stage then sat on one with Sawyer's acoustic ready on his lap. Sawyer and Marina each took the other stools after she took the mic off its stand.

"I wrote a song for you, Sawyer. I'm no songwriter so I hope you enjoy the attempt. Jake was kind enough to put a melody to it so I can't chicken out now."

"Yep, it's too late now so just breathe." Sawyer's pearly whites shone under those sparkling lights.

She snickered before nodding to Jake who began strumming a beautiful acoustic melody. Sawyer took her hand as she sang to him, their eyes connected.

"His Notes"

(Verse 1)
The notes he writes
Brighten up my day
It's something I look forward to
Reading sweet words I know he'll say

(Chorus)
His heart is always in the right place
There's passion written on his face
We fell in love in record time
He's smoother than fine wine
In my mind, he's penning quotes
I'll forever cherish his notes

(Verse 2)
The notes he strums
Heal my broken soul
The words he sings
Makes me wanna lose control

(Chorus)
His heart is always in the right place
There's passion written on his face
We fell in love in record time

He's smoother than fine wine
To my heart, he's singing quotes
I'll forever dance to his notes

(Bridge)
Feel my heartbeat?
I feel a rhythm of emotions flow
This heart is beating for him
Yeah, this heart is beating for him because

(Chorus)
His heart is always in the right place
There's passion written on his face
We fell in love in record time
Oh, he's smoother than fine wine
The sound of our love floats
He saved me with his notes

With Jake's last strum, the crowd stood clapping and Sawyer's hand clung to his chest. He was so incredibly touched by her gesture.

"Baby, that was beautiful. Thank you so much." He stood and pulled her to him for a passionate kiss, making the crowd and the rest of the band clap and whistle even louder. They both thanked Jake before Marina joined the crowd and Jake handed Sawyer's guitar back to him.

"Y'all are stayin' to help me clean up the joint though, right?" Sawyer covered the mic but hollered back to the guys on purpose, making everyone laugh.

"We'll clean it up Sunday with your help, cowboy." Gladys hollered back.

He tipped his hat and chuckled. "Yes, ma'am."

The guys had the room rockin' with *Rockin' Around The Christmas Tree* then *Jingle Bell Rock* before Justin joined them on stage with his sax to end the night with a couple of slower paced

Christmas songs; just the sax and Sawyer on acoustic. They sounded great together and the crowd sang along to the music like carolers. The atmosphere sure felt like Christmas, with magic and love in the air—snowflakes too.

"It's been wonderful staying with you guys," Aliza told Caroline. Savannah and Aliza had stayed with Tom and Caroline the week of the baby shower since Christmas was the day after.

"It's been wonderful having you two."

"It's nice you two live so close to Sawyer and Marina part-time, especially with the babies coming," Savannah said, sipping on hot cocoa.

"I think it all happened with perfect timing," Tom agreed.

"It's less stressful on Marina to not have extra people in their home for as long so thank you for opening your home to us," Aliza said.

"Oh, of course. I'm sure they enjoyed y'all staying the few days you have."

"Thanks. We did have a good time. She's getting tired out pretty easily but she looks wonderful," Aliza said.

"I can imagine. She was a trooper through the rough few weeks at the beginning from what Sawyer said." Caroline stirred her hot cocoa with a candy cane.

"I'm glad that didn't last long for her."

"Oh, I know, poor thing."

"Marina said your son has been absolutely wonderful. She sure praises him," Savannah said, eating a secret recipe cookie.

"I'm so glad. Not that I would've expected less, but he's very protective and nurturing." Caroline smiled.

"He gets that from his mom." Tom laughed.

Marina came up to the table and said, "Now I know why we all made so many extra secret recipe cookies."

Caroline laughed as Sawyer joined them at the table, a mouthful of cookie and another in his hand.

"Sawyer and Jake Christmas shopped together," Caroline mentioned.

"I bet *that* was comical. They both hate shopping. What could y'all have been shopping for?" Marina asked Sawyer.

"Our ladies," he answered with a closed-mouth smile, cheek still full.

"I received the gift I was wishing for though." Marina kissed his cheek.

"All you have to do is wrap yourself...better yet, just sit under the tree wearin' nothin' but a bow. That's gift enough for me." He chuckled when she playfully elbowed his arm.

"So, you must have gotten knocked up on that romantic trip to Bali," Savannah said with a shimmy.

"He said he was going to plant the magic seed that first night we were there. It had to have been one of the four days." Marina laughed.

"The abstinence thing did the trick. Who knew?" Sawyer said with a shrug, brushing cookie crumbs off his shirt.

"And we are beyond thankful." Marina nodded.

"I'm thankful y'all decided to do the baby shower on Christmas Eve. Just one trip for us and all the friends could all celebrate both occasions at once. Great idea," Savannah said, pointing out crumbs on Sawyer's shirt that fell from his beard after he brushed them off. Marina brushed them off his shirt and said, "I agree. Everything turned out perfectly. So, all of you are coming over tomorrow morning then?"

They all nodded.

"What time?" Aliza asked.

"We're always up early, so whenever," Sawyer answered.

"We'll come over around ten or so, that way y'all can have your own little Christmas morning together," Caroline said, folding her hands under her chin with her elbows on the table.

"Sounds good, Mom, thanks." Sawyer kissed her on the top of her head. "Next year the twins can sit in a little red wagon and we'll hook the pony up to it for photos. It'll be epic."

"That will be adorable." Marina squeezed his arm.

"Hey, Marina, darlin', I need you over here for a minute." He scooped her by the small of her back and they walked over to the doorway of the liquor storage room. He stopped in the doorway and pulled her to him, sporting a smirk, then pointed above their heads at the mistletoe.

"Did you hang that there?" she asked with a smile, arms wrapped around his back.

"I sure did." Everyone whistled and clapped when the couple shared a sweet kiss.

CHAPTER 37

Was That A Fumble?

"I got your wings, darlin'." Sawyer kicked shut the door when he entered with his arms full of grocery bags. Marina came out of the kitchen in a Miami football jersey and black leggings. It made him smile that her jersey fit snugly across her baby bump.

"Thanks! I can't believe you left the house in that Tennessee jersey," she bantered.

"Hey, now. Don't make me eat all those wings without sharin'?"

"You wouldn't dare." She glared playfully.

"You're right. I wouldn't dream of getting between a pregnant woman and food she was cravin'."

"I knew you were a smart man." She winked and he chuckled. Grocery bags were plunked on the countertop before he wrapped his arms around her for a quick, intimate kissing session before building an all-out taco bar.

Becka and Raquel rang the doorbell.

"Y'all don't have to knock, just come on in," Sawyer greeted them as he flung open the door.

"Wasn't sure if you were dressed," Becka said, entering the living room.

"Either of you, for that matter. Y'all are animals." Raquel giggled.

"I guess I can't argue with that." He took the dessert tray from Raquel as Marina came around the corner and greeted her friends with a hug. Trev, Trina and Jake came through the door a few moments later, Jake saying, "Knock, knock" as they walked through.

"*They* don't care if we're naked," Sawyer teased.

"Chris and Stacy were—" Trev's explanation was cut short by Chris hollering, "Yo!"

"—right behind us," Trev finished.

"We have to wait on Justin to eat?" Jake snatched a tortilla chip as Marina was pouring them into a large bowl.

"Nah. Kickoff is in like, twenty minutes." Sawyer turned on the big TV.

"Aww, you've added friend photos to your mantel!" Stacy stood looking at wooden frames.

"Of course. They look good up there, I think." Marina set a pile of napkins on the coffee table.

"They do. I love all of these. Nice touch."

"Thanks. Y'all are all so important to us."

"Well, it shows with these. You've included everybody. They look great." Trina agreed.

"Don't look at the photos hanging in our bedroom," Sawyer said with a smirk as he winked at Marina.

"Now I do wanna go look," Chris teased, making Sawyer chuckle and Marina shake her head.

"Need any help?" Becka asked Marina from the kitchen.

"We just have to put that crock pot over here on this island counter with the tacos, if you wouldn't mind."

"Gotcha. What's in it?"

"Queso dip."

"Oh, hell yeah!" Jake was excited and tried dipping a chip in it as Becka was moving it.

"Food looks good." Chris hovered over the taco bar.

"Go on ahead, I know you guys can't wait." Marina gave a surrendering wave.

"Drinks are stocked in the fridge." Sawyer doused a wing in buffalo sauce just as Justin let himself in and nodded hello to the girls in the living room who didn't feel like squeezing their way between the guys and food. Sawyer handed Marina a plate and backed up, letting her in at the counter.

"Now, see! Sawyer's a gentleman," Trina teased as Trev headed to the kitchen. He stopped with a raised brow and said, "Well come on then, I ain't waitin' long."

She jumped up and ran to the kitchen.

"Y'all better hurry up, six minutes till kickoff!" Justin hollered. "Hey, by the way, I kind of invited my crush. Hope that's ok." Justin gave Sawyer a back pat.

"Sure." Sawyer chuckled.

The doorbell rang so Justin ran to answer it, Whiskey on his heels.

"Did he say crush?" Chris inquired, peeking around the doorway with Jake.

"Who the hell would it be?" Trev peeked around with them. Justin invited her in and the group was surprised to see it was Lana, happily waving her in as Justin took her coat.

"Nice to see ya, Lana. Hope you're hungry." Sawyer got a beer out of the fridge, balancing a full plate in the other hand.

"Likewise. I'm starving. Your home is lovely."

"Thanks."

"Thanks for letting me hang out tonight for the Super Bowl. It's pretty cool I get to hang out with the popular band around these parts. Y'all have been the talk of the town...and the bar."

"Is that so?" Jake asked, not convinced.

"Absolutely. The bar has been packed almost every night since I started working there. Customers are requesting you guys play more than just one night a week."

Justin handed her a plate and she dug right in.

"We're all so busy and tired after a long workday, I don't think we could squeeze another night in," Chris said, balancing his plate as he dumped hot sauce all over his mountain of tacos.

"Maybe we'll have to do special occasions or something more often." Sawyer headed out of the kitchen while Trev grabbed the dining room chairs and added seating to the living room, everyone heading in to take a seat.

"We could do a monthly fundraiser night for your nonprofit," Jake suggested.

"Not a bad idea!" Marina was on board.

"We could do that," Sawyer agreed as he turned the TV volume up just in time for the kickoff.

"Tennessee is gonna whoop some ass!" Jake shouted.

"Excuse me?" Marina raised her brows, her mouth full of tacos as she sat on the couch next to Sawyer.

"It's adorable y'all are rooting for opposite teams." Trev snickered.

"That jersey looks damn good on him though. He's lucky." Marina gave Sawyer a pretend cold shoulder.

"And you're lucky you look cute in yours." He winked and she couldn't help but laugh.

"Damn! That was a good run!" Jake was getting all excited already.

First quarter: check! Second quarter: "What the hell was that?" Jake stood up, getting pissed.

"That was a bullshit call," Sawyer added, thumping his beer onto the coffee table.

"His foot was totally out of bounds, dudes," Chris sat back all chill.

"Nah, I don't think so." Sawyer was anticipating a play review, elbows on his knees.

"I agree with Chris," Marina said, sipping water.

Sawyer wrinkled a brow. The review called it out and the Tennessee rooters of the group were yelling at the TV.

"That was such a close call it was hard to tell." Trina got up for a beer.

"That could make or break the game though!" Trev hollered from the living room. "It doesn't matter to me who wins, I just like to get her goin'," he whispered to those present and chuckled.

"It's all in fun anyway. Of course, I'd rather my team win though." Sawyer laughed.

"Oh, Shit! Run!" Jake just about spilled his beer as he jumped up to yell at the TV.

"He fumbled! Get it! Somebody get the damn ball!" Raquel shouted, rooting for Miami.

Justin asked Lana if she wanted a drink and nodded for her to join him in the kitchen. Sawyer peered over with a smirk.

"Recovery!" Marina jumped to her feet all excited.

"Son of a bitch," Sawyer mumbled, slapping his hand on the arm of the couch.

Lana followed Justin into the kitchen to grab a drink as she was unsure of what she wanted. He got closer, flirting and about to make a move, maybe a kiss, when Chris came around the corner but quickly turned around, aware of what he was walking in on. Lana turned her attention to the doorway as Chris's man-bun flashed by and Justin let out a sigh. He had worked up the courage finally then lost the chance when he lost her attention. Chris tried to stop Stacy from going to the kitchen for a nacho refill but she was oblivious to the hint thrown. Jake was distracted by Chris's attempt to intercept and wore a puzzled look on his face.

"Should we take bets? Was that a fumble?" Jake asked, sitting back down on the couch.

"He won't do it," Sawyer said, eyes still on the TV.

Chris just nodded with a defeated frown. Stacy hustled once she realized that Justin was trying to have a moment alone with Lana. Maybe it was his irritated scowl that made it obvious.

"Half-time show will suck." Raquel blurted as the clock neared the end of the second quarter.

"It's always somebody shitty. It's either nobody worth listening to or somebody skanky. Nobody wants to see that shit.

Maybe if they kept it country, they'd have more viewers and not waste their money," Sawyer said, waiting for Justin to come back in the room so he knew it was clear to go grab another beer.

"Kids can't even watch it these days," Marina agreed.

"Maybe someday we'll get to perform for it." Jake shrugged and Trev laughed.

"Hey, ya never know. Y'all are good enough so if you wanted to run with it ya could." Trina swatted Trev's arm.

"I love how you two piss with each other." Chris chuckled.

"It's all in fun. There's nobody I'd rather do life with." Trev side-hugged Trina as she looked over at Marina, who flashed an assuring smile.

Justin and Lana entered the living room and Justin hollered, "Score!"

Lana laughed and everyone cheered.

"Y'all a couple now?" Chris asked, as if impatient.

Justin proudly put his arm around Lana and said, "Yep. Finally got me a girlfriend." The ladies clapped and Trev said, "Could've had one a long time ago if you weren't so damn picky."

"This is true," Justin agreed. "But I have a feeling this one is worth the wait."

"Aww." Marina gushed with joy for them.

"The good ones are." Sawyer patted Marina's knee with a big smile.

"I agree." Jake took Becka's hand.

"Well, we takin' bets for the win since none of us give a shit about this halftime show?" Chris dug his wallet out of his back pocket.

"Sure!" Sawyer pulled his out, as did the other guys. The girls busted out the dessert tray and let the guys have the fun of gambling. Marina showed off their latest sonogram in which they decided to find out the sex of the babies after all.

"So one twin wouldn't cooperate but we know for sure one is a girl."

"Ahhh! That's so exciting!" Stacy shouted, Becka clapping.

"You didn't want us to throw you a gender reveal party?" Trina asked, disappointed.

"I feel like after that beautiful baby shower it would've been asking too much." Marina shoved a cookie in her mouth.

"What? Nah, we would've loved to throw y'all one," Raquel said as she traded Becka a cookie for a different kind.

"We know and we appreciate the offer. We didn't really want to find out the sex until we got to that appointment that day. Now we just have to be prepared for the second to be either."

"White onesies it is!" Stacy held her beer up, signaling for a cheer.

The third quarter was boring so the guys did more eating than cheering but the last quarter was intense.

"Tackle his ass! Jesus!" Jake was on his feet again.

"He's gone! Go, go, go!" Raquel was rooting for Miami along with Marina and Becka. The guys stood shouting and punching the air with their fists as the girls snickered at how devoted the guys were to their team.

The house rang loud with yelling and laughter and much shouting at the TV; Marina, Becka, and Raquel were the only examples of sobriety that evening.

"Looks like we're the designated drivers tonight," Raquel told Becka.

"Mmhmm, for sure."

Sawyer and Jake were in a man-giggling fit over their team winning and the hard time they were giving the girls.

"Alright, cowboy, scoop up your winnings and help me clean up the kitchen." Marina kneaded Sawyer's shoulders from behind him. He couldn't sit still, he was laughing so hard, leaning into Jake as Jake also laughed so hard that his laugh fell silent as he bent over at the end of the couch.

Trina rolled her eyes and flipped her braids from her face. "Trev, let's go get your losin', drunk ass in bed."

"Y'all need a ride home?" Raquel offered.

"Nah, thanks though. I only had one so I'm good." Trina assured as she tossed Trev's jacket at him.

"You need help in the kitchen, Marina?" Stacy stood and pulled Chris up by the arm.

"I'll help her. We got this," Becka volunteered as she headed to the kitchen with Marina.

"I think I had a few." Chris was slowly counting on his fingers and had four up already when Raquel said, "I'll drive y'all home."

"Oh, good, because I had as many as he did." Stacy almost lost her balance trying to put her shoes on. "You need help in there first?" she hollered.

"Nah, we're good. Y'all get on home safely. Thanks for coming over." Marina popped around the corner and waved. Justin gave Lana her coat and they said goodbye on their way out. Sawyer and Jake were starting to simmer down; their cheeks hurting from laughing so hard. Numbers were down to the four of them, all of which helped clean up before Jake took Becka home...and stayed with her. Sawyer shut off the TV and the living room light.

"Gosh, darlin', I'm pretty sure you could take advantage of me tonight." He swaggered over to her in the bedroom doorway, a sexy grin on his rugged face.

"Well, I planned to anyway."

"Really?" He pulled her to him by her hips.

"Absolutely. Not with you wearing this jersey though."

He looked down into her eyes, a smoldering look about him, those bright blues less sharp and drowsier than usual. He pressed his pelvis against her, pinning her in the doorway, careful not to press on her baby bump.

"I see they're already trying to cramp our style." He smirked and she said with a giggle, "Sawyer! You're horrible!" His head tipped back with a laugh and she fisted the front of his jersey before shoving him into the bedroom. He let himself fall backward onto the end of the bed then rolled onto his elbows as he crawled up farther.

"You're drunk." She cat-walked to him.

"I'm feeling déjà vu right now."

"Except the first time we were already naked before we got this far." She stripped her clothes off and crawled to him as he sat back against the headboard. He unbuttoned his jeans but could barely do that. He chuckled at his fumbling fingers.

"Looks like you'll be doin' most of the work tonight, darlin'." He could barely keep his eyes open and his speech was getting slower.

"I can do that."

"Can't promise I won't fall asleep. So sorry if I do."

"I'm going to have my way with you whether you're awake or asleep." She pulled his jeans down just past his butt as he lifted a bit for her.

"Oh, dear God. Please do."

"I don't recall asking for your permission." She upturned her nose with a sultry pout as she crawled on top of him.

"Oh, damn! I am so turned on right now."

"Yeah, you are." She pulled him from his briefs and said, "You bet against my team tonight, sir. You're going to be punished. And I told you to take that jersey off."

"Is that so?" He grinned, slowly stripping the jersey off.

"You wanna know what I'm going to do to you?"

"Nope. I wanna be surprised." His heavy eyes closed, then opened a crack, then closed. His chest fell more relaxed. Did he seriously just fall asleep? She covered her mouth laughing for a moment before stroking the side of his bearded face. What a gorgeous man he was; absolutely breathtaking even when passed out drunk. He woke back up moments later as she was moaning, finishing on top of him. She felt him stiffen even harder with rousing surprise.

"Mmm, I love you, woman. So glad you weren't kidding. It's my turn." He flipped her onto her back.

"Don't be fallin' asleep again, you'll crush me."

"I won't be fumblin'. I got my second wind so I'm good for

about five minutes." He nipped at her lips, making her giggle as he positioned himself between her legs. "I'm about to score a touchdown. Think I'll earn the extra point?"

"I already won." She laughed as his brash grin fumbled from his face.

CHAPTER 38
Horsin' Around

Sawyer had just gotten to the feed store when Marina called.

"Miss me already, darlin'?" he asked in a low tone as he and Justin walked an aisle.

"Of course, but I'm calling because Gin is in distress. I think she might be in labor."

"Oh! Ok thanks, I'll be right there." He hung up, shoved his phone into his back pocket, and told Justin to come along as he dashed for the door. They jumped into Sawyer's truck and sped all the way home, dirt kicking up behind the tires.

"Doc. I have a mare in possible labor so if you could be on standby…Great. Thanks."

He flopped his phone over into the console. "Doc isn't busy so he's headed over, just in case. Already putting his boots on."

Sawyer wasn't horsin' around behind that wheel and Justin had a hold of the "oh shit" handle every sharp turn they took. Clouds of dust rolled as Sawyer hit the brakes next to the stables. He barely had the truck in park and shut off before hopping out and tossing his hat inside onto the seat. They ran into the barn and to Gin's stall. The door was open, Willow's nose curiously huffing breaths around the next stall corner. Marina was sitting in the straw petting the uncomfortable mare.

Gin's eyes were big, her neck stretched out, and her breathing labored. She'd let out a whinny here and there that sounded like a cry for help.

"How long?" He hiked the thighs of his jeans to squat down to lift Gin's tail.

"I found her this way seconds before I called you. I wasn't sure what's normal for a mare in labor but she's definitely in a lot of pain."

"I imagine it isn't cozy." He ducked down lower, peering under the tail.

"Having hooves punching out of your hoo-ha...yeah." Justin snickered.

"Got a muzzle. I can't feel hooves though.

"Uh oh." Justin crouched down to take a look as Sawyer was diving in up to his forearm, then further to his elbow.

"Shit. I think a leg might be folded."

"Oh no!" Marina felt pity for the mare and little one.

"Shit. I have one." Out popped one little hoof next to the muzzle.

"Justin, run and grab my phone from the truck and holler at Doc for me."

"You got it." Justin took off running out of the barn.

"Whiskey at the house, darlin'?"

"I put him in the office right after I called you. I didn't want him getting in the way."

"Good thinkin'. I hope Doc hurries, it's been a while since I assisted Dad in a birth."

"Aww, you've got this, babe. You won't have to work so hard when we have ours." She giggled.

"True." He wiped his forehead with his clean arm then continued feeling around for the other hoof.

Justin returned to the barn and announced, "Doc's ten minutes out. Maybe less. He got caught up on his way out."

"Thanks."

Gin whinnied a loud one so Sawyer pulled his arm out.

"Aww, poor girl." Marina tried to calm her, slowly running her hand up and down Gin's neck.

"Sorry." Sawyer patted her croup. "Marina, you be careful around her."

"I will."

"I think we might need her to get up. Did Doc say what to do?"

"Nah, he just said he would be here in about ten minutes."

"Okay. Let's get her up. Maybe I can feel the hoof and get it pulled forward." He swatted her rear and hollered, "Up!"

She struggled, but with some coaxing, she rose to her feet, straw falling from her coat.

"Good girl. Sorry about this." His hand entered again and poor Gin let out a big huff, her ears pinned back.

"I found it! I can't tell which direction it's oriented in though. Ugh! She's pushing but I need her to stop."

"Not sure she can control that, babe."

"Well..." He was stretched into a sideways position attempting to straighten the hoof out.

"Ok, so...it's bent under, which is good. It's probably not broken or anything weird." Sawyer grunted, trying to twist and pull. Gin kicked at Sawyer, connecting the edge of her hoof with his shin.

"Son of a bitch! Okay, okay, I know, I'm so sorry but we've almost got it. So close." Sawyer was determined. Justin reached to pull Sawyer's t-shirt sleeve up before it could get messy.

"Thanks. Not sure this blood would come out of a white shirt."

"I'd just soak it in an ice bath. It would have a chance." Marina shrugged.

"See? No biggie." Justin chuckled.

"Justin, keep her tail up for me. Man, it sucks not being able to see what I'm doing. I don't wanna hurt either one of 'em."

"She'll be okay, Sawyer. She's tough. Do whatcha gotta do."

Marina nodded and he tugged. The second hoof was in his hand now along with the first.

"Here we go." Sawyer pulled, the muzzle coming out with the hooves, slowly inching closer. Ears were out, then the whole head. "That's it, push. Push!" Sawyer tapped her rear and she let out a huff and a whinny as Sawyer pulled. When Gin would break, Sawyer would stop pulling until she started pushing again. Doc came hustling into the barn and reached the stall just as the colt was eased to the ground by Sawyer and Justin. Sawyer stuck two fingers in its nostrils and shook but it didn't move. Doc grabbed a bucket and told Marina to go fill it with water, so she took it and ran for the faucet. Gin turned and was sniffing at and licking the colt. Marina came in with the bucket as Doc finished clearing mucus from the colt's mouth. He then took the bucket and splashed it on the colt. That did the trick.

"Thought I was gonna have to hang it upside down for a sec there." Doc chuckled and everyone was relieved. "Good job, cowboy." He patted Sawyer on the back. Sawyer laughed and shook his head then gave Doc a hug with his cleaner arm. "You didn't even need me. I'll take a look at him after mama checks him out, though."

"It was a team effort. Thanks, everyone." Sawyer fist bumped Justin, both having bloody hands. He side-hugged Marina with his cleaner side and she grabbed his chin and kissed him.

"Good job, babe. I'm proud of you."

"Thanks, darlin'."

"He had a leg folded but Sawyer got it straightened out," Justin told Doc.

"Well, that will cause distress alright. It's a good thing you got started without me then; that colt might not have survived much longer." Doc crouched down to examine the colt, which was lying down but had its head up and bobbing around. Gin was licking him, ignoring the steaming afterbirth hanging from her back-end. "I'll examine mama here too but we'll give them a few minutes." Doc waved for everyone to step out of the stall.

"I'm glad she wasn't out to pasture. We may not have noticed in time." Marina leaned against the doorway, watching mother and colt.

"Yeah, that's true. The ranch hands couldn't make it in today and neither could Sabrina, so it's a good thing you came over, darlin'."

"Y'all did good. Your Dad would be proud of you, cowboy."

"I think so. Nerve racking, ya know, to have other lives in your hands. Not sure how you do it every day, Doc. It's amazing but it would be so sad when it doesn't turn out with a positive outcome."

"Yep. You can take a breath now, though. Looks like all is well. He's a pretty color. Any idea what the sire looked like?"

"Nah, we picked her up at that ranch up north, remember? But the sire wasn't there."

"Well, ya got a little gray appaloosa from a brown one. Many possibilities."

"That's true, Doc. Thanks for rushing out here."

"No problem. Glad I was able to swing by."

"I can't say I've ever witnessed anything like that!" Justin rubbed his hands together, a surge of excitement rushing through him.

"Me neither. It was intense, miraculous too. I'm so glad we were able to watch," Marina said, still leaning against the stall.

"I think I'm just ditchin' this shirt," Sawyer said, looking down at the discolored mess smeared across the front of him. Doc chuckled and Justin nodded and said, "Yep. I don't blame ya."

"She seems relieved of pain now," Marina observed.

"Oh, I'm sure. Now that her concentration is on that little one, she won't think much of it. The pain has subsided now for the most part." Gin had him pretty well cleaned off when Doc stepped inside the stall to examine them both. He was stepping back out when the colt attempted to stand. Marina got it on video with her phone and they all quietly cheered the colt on, but his knobby knees folded and he plunked to the ground.

"Aww, almost. Come on, little guy," Marina quietly encouraged. He planted those tiny hooves and used every ounce of strength he had when Gin nudged him to stand.

"Easy, little fella." Sawyer watched, smiling.

"I love how they stumble around trying to catch their balance like a drunk." Justin laughed.

"Tonic," Marina said.

"Huh?" Doc was confused.

"Get it? Gin and Tonic."

The guys chuckled at the colt's newly assigned name; fit for wobbly legs. He was nursing and kicking in no time, head bunting up underneath Gin. He was already feisty and would no doubt be one for horsin' around.

CHAPTER 39
The Cure to Her Worries

Marina let out a frustrated sigh as she stood at the bathroom sink, having trouble reaching close to the mirror to apply her makeup. She stood sideways, allowing her belly more room as she leaned over the sink. Suddenly, Sawyer was behind her in the doorway. She looked up at him in the mirror as she applied her mascara.

"Aww, darlin'. You're so cute."

She laughed and replied, "This is getting more difficult."

"I see that. I'm sorry." He came up behind her, wrapping his arms around her to place his hands upon her belly, his chin resting on her shoulder.

"Nothing to be sorry about, babe. This is a blessing. I still can't believe I've wrangled you and you're all mine and I'm carrying a piece of you inside me. How did I get so lucky?"

"I'm the lucky one. I have the best woman in the world, the most beautiful woman by my side and we get to experience this life together. We get to create a family and share so much love. I thank my lucky stars for you every single day."

"Aww, me too."

He tipped her chin to him for a kiss and said, "You're glowing, you know that?"

"I am?"

"Oh, yeah. You know, to be honest, I'm jealous of you."

"Really? Why's that?" She turned to face him.

"Because you get to experience all of it."

"You want morning sickness and to have to pee every five minutes?" She giggled.

"Actually, I could do without that part but if I could've taken that in your place I would've."

"You're so sweet."

"I envy you for being able to do this. For both of us. I'm thankful mostly. I know how much you're risking and sacrificing for us to have a family. I'm proud of how well you've handled everything and how well you've taken care of yourself and our little ones. You cut off having coffee the day you found out so I know that was hard for you."

"Oh, Sawyer. That's so sweet of you. I wish I could share all of the good parts with you, like feeling them kick and move around. It's the craziest yet most amazing feeling in the world."

"Well, I'm certainly glad you get to experience it. You deserve the good parts, especially since you have to experience the not-so-good. Not much longer to go, darlin'." He rubbed her belly. "I just wanted to peek in and marvel at how beautiful you are and tell you how much I appreciate you."

"You're amazing. That means so much to me, I hope you know that. I appreciate you, too. You're so attentive and caring." She wrapped her arms around him, rubbing his back. " My feet are swollen just from standing long enough to put my face on, but quitting coffee has been the hardest part of this pregnancy." She looked down at her feet.

He chuckled then puckered out his bottom lip in pity. "How about you rest on the couch while I rub your feet?"

"Yeah? You'd do that?"

"Of course, I'd do anything for you. Rubbin' your pretty little feet is no big deal." He took her hand, leading her out to the couch.

"It's chilly in here, it must be cold outside."

"The temp is dropping fast. It's overcast too. This last cold front of the season has the horses all worked up. I left them in the stables where it's warm. This is why I always wait to start planting the garden." He went in for her cozy blanket and spread it out across her lap, then sat next to her and put her feet up across his legs. She stared at him, smiling while he gently rubbed her feet, her pink-painted toes loving the attention as much as her sore heels.

"Looks like it's time for a new paint job." He wiggled her big toe and made her laugh.

"I can't reach them very well anymore. It took a lot of yoga moves just to trim them."

"I'll repaint them after your foot massage."

"You're really going to paint my toes?"

"Yep. Think I'll look sexy doin' it?" He grinned then laughed when she said, "Of course."

She smiled adoringly at him, watching him rub her feet. He looked over at her and smiled. She felt like the luckiest woman alive to have a man so perfect. He was her twin flame and she felt privileged to even be in his presence, let alone anything more. Somehow, she had found the one that she couldn't live without. They were comfortable just being in each other's presence, not even having to talk much. She adored every single thing about him; the sound of his laugh, the way the sunbeams dancing across his face would wake him early every morning, the way he moves with the music, how smart, talented, and funny he is, not to mention how thoughtful and kind, the way he carries himself and treats others, all of it. He was the whole package and he belonged to her. She was lucky enough to share his bed every night and they had created new life together. She had been blessed in every way.

"Sawyer."

"Hmm?" He looked up at her, letting her know he was listening.

"The way I feel when I'm with you, whether it be just in the same room or right up against you, that peaceful floating-with-the-butterflies feeling...that's how I want to feel every single day of my life."

He smiled and took her hand then said, "I'll make sure I do everything I can to make you feel that way every single day." He lifted her legs and scooched closer to her. She laid her head over onto his shoulder, arm twisted with his.

"It's gonna be a clingy cuddly day today. Hope that's okay," she said.

"Absolutely." He chuckled, putting his arm around her. "I'm always in the mood to cuddle with you, you know that. I'll even cook for you today too."

"You don't have to do that."

"Well, I'm able to so you'll stay your pretty pink swollen toes right here today. I don't want you worrying about a thing."

"You're the cure to all of my worries, Sawyer."

He kissed the top of her head and snuggled close to her under the blanket. The fireplace lit up the dim room, orange flickers entertaining them while high winds howled outside.

CHAPTER 40
Snoozin' and Kickin'

The barn note on Marina's office desk read "Trail training today. Should be back before lunch", but when lunchtime rolled around, Sawyer still wasn't back.

"You try calling him?" Justin asked.

"Not yet. Maybe I should though." She looked at her phone but there were no missed calls or texts. "Which horse did he take out?"

"Oakley and I think he's leaving him over here as of today. War was too busy licking the ferrier's neck."

"Hmmm. I think I will call. I'm getting worried."

"I'm getting hungry. Thought he was getting us lunch today."

"Yeah." She leaned back in her chair, hand on her growing belly, and called Sawyer, but he didn't answer. She stepped outside and still couldn't see him so she asked Justin, "You wanna go lookin' for him or you want me to?"

"You aren't supposed to be on horseback so I'll just take a four-wheeler down in a minute." His phone was ringing.

"Is that him?" she asked.

Justin shook his head no and said, "Oh, it's that stud farm Sawyer needs to talk to. Let me take this first."

Her phone began to ring but stopped. She rushed over to it

and it was Sawyer so she tried to call back but no answer.

"Ok, I'm worried now. I'm going out to the trail." She slid her phone into her back pocket and he nodded. She tried to start the four-wheeler but it wouldn't start so she got the gas can to put gas in it but the can was empty.

"Those little shits," she mumbled, referring to the ranch hands. She looked out at the field, debating on walking the distance, but it was too far, out then back; just the thought of it exhausted her. She entered the stables, watching for Justin because she knew he would try to stop her. It sounded as though he were still on the phone anyway. She tossed a blanket up onto Bourbon's back, then a saddle. Bourbon stood still as she fastened the bridle. Her belly was getting too big to comfortably hop on like normal so she pulled a step stool over to give her a boost. She got comfortable in the saddle before Bourbon clopped down the stable hall and out the door. Marina took it easy, nice and slow, appreciating how nice it felt to be back in a saddle after months of not being allowed to ride. She knew Sawyer would be pissed but she had to make sure he was okay. She was cutting across the field to the trail when she spotted his hat, sticking up higher than the rustling knee-high grass. Bourbon came to a soft halt when she reached Sawyer. He put his index finger to his lips, telling her to stay quiet. Oakley was comfortable, lying next to Sawyer with his head across Sawyer's lap, eyes closed and lips loose and floppy. Oh, my goodness, how adorable it was. She took her phone from her pocket and snapped a photo.

"Why didn't you answer?" she whispered.

"My phone is on my leg under his head," he whispered back.

"The fresh spring air knocked him out after all that training, huh?" She giggled.

"I reckon so. Or he got lazy and didn't wanna train anymore. Training horses is like tuning an instrument in a way. The trainer needs not to be tone-deaf. He said he was tired and needed a break, so that's what we did. Why are you on a horse, ma'am?"

"I was worried about you." She just knew he was going to say something about the matter.

"Four-wheeler, darlin'."

"Well, I tried but those ranch hands didn't fill the gas container or the four-wheeler."

"Dumbasses. I'm sorry, darlin'."

"I'm not complainin'. I'm in a saddle." She grinned excitedly.

"You're in trouble for it too."

"Is that right?" She adjusted her black cowgirl hat.

"Yes, ma'am."

"I don't believe you're in a position to do anything about it right now, sir."

"You're right about that because I can't feel my legs, but as soon as we're both home tonight—"

"What? You gonna give me a spankin'?"

"You know me so well." He grinned, making her laugh. "You're lucky I can't get up right now."

"You'd give me that spankin' right here in the field?"

"Damn right. Don't make me take this belt off, Marina." He looked at her with smoldering eyes.

"Oh, Sawyer." She giggled and spun Bourbon around. "Get that horse up and let's eat lunch."

"He's so peaceful though."

"He's starting to snore." She clicked and Bourbon began walking toward the stables. Sawyer tipped his head back laughing. He scratched and petted Oakley's face for a few minutes, tracing the swirl of shedding fur on Oakley's forehead with his finger before the horse woke up.

"Have a good nap, big guy?" he asked as Oakley sat up and straightened a folded knee, dazed and confused.

"Take your time gettin' up. I'll need a minute to gain feeling back in my legs."

Justin had given in and gone to get lunch for the three of them after texting Marina to check on her. As they were eating lunch at their desks, they heard little whinnies and chatters.

"Is that the colt?" Sawyer asked.

"It sure is." Marina smiled, setting down her salad fork as the colt snuck into the office next to Justin's desk. He turned to find the colt's muzzle just about touching his nose. He slid back his chair in surprise. Tonic walked his spindly legs over to Sawyer's guitar that was propped up near his desk and lipped the strings then jerked back his head when the sound startled him. That spiky short gray mane bounced back and forth as his neck stretched out and his lip wiggled at the strings again. His fluffy short tail rose almost like a deer.

"That's adorable." Marina's nose wrinkled as she watched with a smile until a loud whinny came from outside.

"Mama's callin' ya back, little dude." Sawyer got up from his chair and clicked his tongue, getting Tonic's attention. The colt trotted alongside Sawyer out of the office and into the pasture, that little tail still held up.

"He must have gotten out through the fence." Justin shrugged.

"We're gonna have to keep a closer eye on that one." Marina stabbed her salad with her fork.

Sawyer came back in, the colt right behind him.

"Shoulda named this one Trouble. He showed Gin he was okay but he's a bullheaded one."

"Kinda like his owner." Justin chuckled.

"Ya can't argue with that." Marina giggled.

"Not sure why you're gigglin', Marina. I meant you."

She looked at Justin with an innocently confused look while Sawyer laughed.

Later that evening, Marina saw Sawyer standing in the backyard, hands in his pockets, staring off toward the line of crepe myrtles that separated the yard from the pastures. She slid open the patio door and asked, "Whatcha doin', babe?"

He turned and nodded for her to join him. Taking his arm in hers, she asked what they were supposed to be looking at and he pointed to the hammock.

"I don't see-oh my goodness, is that Tonic?"

"Yep. He's sleeping in the hammock with Whiskey."

"What a trip that little guy is. He's so fun. Makes me wanna go cuddle with him."

"He sure is cute. It's nice being around a colt again. It's been a while."

"Whiskey loves the horses."

"He's been running around with Tonic half the day. They tuckered themselves out. I'm just gonna leave 'em there."

"The sprinklers are gonna turn on in a few minutes," Marina reminded.

"It won't reach 'em, I don't think." He and Marina sat at the patio table, watching and waiting. The sprinklers came on a moment later and the sound woke up the snoozers. Whiskey leaped off the hammock and ran through the spraying water. It took a minute for Tonic to crawl his spindly legs out of the unstable swinging hammock but as soon as all four hooves were on the grass, he ran through the sprinklers with Whiskey, who was barking and biting at the water as he ran. A little back-kick and a jump from Tonic made Sawyer and Marina laugh.

"We should buy a giant ball for the horses to kick around. Even the animals have fun around here." She squeezed Sawyer's arm.

"It'll be even more fun soon." He rubbed her belly, her hand over the top of his, and together they felt a big kick. His eyes widened and she was just as excited.

"I love it when they do that." Marina glowed with pride for her little ones.

"Does it hurt?"

"Sometimes. Not right now though."

He kept his hand on her belly, enjoying the moment. "I've felt and seen them moving before but not like this."

"They're getting bigger in there so the kicks are stronger. Not much longer and we'll be holding those kicking little feet in our hands." She rubbed his shoulder.

"I can't wait."

CHAPTER 41
Fresh for the Pickin'

"Thank goodness it's getting warmer." Marina met Sawyer out at the barn, taking in the smell of fresh-cut grass. She wore leggings and a t-shirt and flipped her sunglasses up onto her head as she entered the shade near the barn door.

"It'll stay warm now, too. Leggings today, huh? You look cozy." Sawyer approached her for a morning hug and kiss and greeted her growing belly.

"Can't fit into much of anything else anymore. Almost overnight I got even bigger. These leggings have to stay ridin' under my belly. Soon my t-shirts won't come down low enough, but at least my flip-flops still fit." She tugged on the bottom of her shirt and shrugged. "This sleeping propped-up crap is for the birds. Can't wait till I can't lie down flat again. I'm loving all the foot massages though."

"You're adorable." He pulled his work gloves off, gave her a smooch, and said, "You can wear my shirts."

Jake and Becka pulled into the drive on a motorcycle a moment later and Sawyer slapped the gloves in his palm with a smile and said, "Well look at that."

The loud roar of the bike motor fell silent as Sawyer and Marina approached them.

"What's this?" Marina asked, hands on her belly.

"My new motorcycle."

"I see that, but I meant the two of you together." Marina smiled big as Becka got off the bike and greeted Marina with a hug.

"Nice ride!" Sawyer walked around it, checking it out.

"You talkin' about me or the bike?" Jake bantered as he cleaned his sunglass lenses with his t-shirt, making Sawyer laugh.

"So, you two are getting pretty serious then?" Marina thought she was speaking low-key but Sawyer overheard.

"Yep." Becka nodded.

"Good. This just got a whole lot easier then," Sawyer started, confusing Jake. "Not to take the attention off your sweet bike, but I'm too excited to wait."

"Okay, spill it," Becka said.

"Marina and I wanna ask you both to be our babies' Godparents."

Becka and Jake's eyes instantly grew huge.

"Seriously?" Jake clapped and shouted. Becka's jaw dropped before she cried out, "Aww, of course! Thanks for asking. Wow, I feel so special." She looked as though she could cry and gave Marina the biggest hug.

"Wow, man, what an honor. Hell yeah!"

"Yeah?" Sawyer raised a brow.

"Absolutely." He bear-hugged Sawyer, almost knocking him off balance.

"Thanks, Jake."

"No, thank you. Shit, I appreciate you trusting me that much. That's a huge deal. I'll treat them as my own, you know that."

Sawyer nodded. "You were the first to come to mind."

Jake placed his hand on his chest. "I appreciate it, bro."

Sawyer patted Jake's back.

"So, if y'all could stay together, it would be so much easier," Marina joked, making them laugh.

"Not that we feel we'd ever need y'all to take over with

parenting but we feel better knowing our kids will be taken care of if anything were to happen to us." Sawyer sounded relieved with assurance.

"Of course they would. Y'all never need to worry about that." Jake returned the pat.

"Okay, back to this bike..." Sawyer sat on it, checking it out. Jake offered for them to take it for a spin but they politely declined for the babies' safety. Marina tried talking Sawyer into taking it by himself but he said he'd rather wait until she could ride it with him.

"You look sexy on that thing," Marina said before biting her lip.

"Do I?" He chuckled. "I think I'll stick to horses though. Maybe we can borrow it for a date night sometime."

"Absolutely," Jake said. "Chris and Stacy opened up their farmer's market this morning. We're headed over there."

"Oh, that's today? I forgot. Pregnancy brain is a real thing."

"It sure is." Sawyer laughed. "We can go too if you want, baby." Sawyer got off the bike, letting Jake back on.

"Sweet! I want some peaches."

"I need apples for the horses."

"Cool. So, we'll see ya over there," Becka said as she hopped onto the bike after Jake and put her arms around him.

"Sure thing. Enjoy the fresh spring air." Marina waved as Jakes's foot drug the ground while he spun the bike around, flinging dirt behind them before hitting the road.

"Load up in the Jeep, Peaches."

CHAPTER 42

That's What I Get

It was a hot, muggy morning and Marina was straightening up the house before her cousin arrived. Paisley was passing through on her way from South Florida to Alabama and asked to stop for a few hours to visit while taking a break from driving. It had been several years since Marina last saw her so she was anxious for Paisley's arrival. They kept tabs on each other's lives through social media but Paisley had a different way about her; a troubled past that had forced space between them. Marina distanced herself from trouble and drama while Paisley always seemed to find it when not creating it herself.

Sawyer had left to get his hair trimmed at the local barbershop after walking Luke through the chores that needed doing at home and at the stables. The ranch hands were going to help Luke out.

Sawyer returned to the stables then took Luke home and made a few stops after being stuck in a traffic jam in the center of town for nearly thirty minutes. He continued on to pick up Marina's prenatal script from the pharmacy along with the dark chocolate she was craving, grab eggs from Stacy at the farmer's market, and stop at the coffee shop for a fancy coffee. He tried to finish it before getting home so he wasn't drinking it in front of Marina but receiving phone call after phone call prevented him from drinking more than half of it. He pulled into the driveway at home and began exiting his truck but juggling several things in his arms wasn't as simple of a task as he planned. He put his hat on his head and held the coffee in the crook of his elbow before grabbing the three cartons of eggs stacked on top of one another, the bag of chocolates, and his keys from the console. He stepped out and shut the truck door with his knee, almost tripping over Whiskey. He started to drop the eggs and spilled his coffee trying to catch the eggs, causing the coffee cup to crush, dousing him in hot coffee so he dropped the eggs after all. Whiskey scooted out of the way just in time to not get splattered.

"Son of a bitch!" He was a hot mess. Literally. Whiskey was clearly thinking about cleaning up what he could, inching closer.

"Go on." Sawyer pointed to the house and Whiskey went on ahead as Sawyer picked up the mess and threw it in the trash can in the garage before going inside. He had paid no attention to the extra vehicle in the driveway.

Marina and Paisley were out back chatting at the patio table, which was the reason for Whiskey being outside. Marina heard Sawyer come in, cussing, so she slid open the door and went inside to greet him. Paisley stayed outside but was looking in through the open doorway.

"Hey, babe. How did-oh, my! What happened to you?"

"Well, I tried to make only one trip from the truck but Whiskey had a different trip in mind. I should've just made two trips." He was washing his hands and arms at the sink then removed his egg-and-coffee-stained shirt as he walked through to their room, a slimy yellow mess following across the wood floor.

"Fuck it, I'm just gonna shower." He picked yolk slime out of his hair with a wrinkled nose, not sure how it got up there.

He was unbuttoning his jeans as he walked toward their bathroom when Marina said, "Um, my cousin is here."

"Huh?" He unzipped, then stopped and turned around.

"She's passing through and stopped for a quick visit so you might want to undress in the bathroom."

"Oh! Ok. I'll clean that mess up when I get out. Sorry about the eggs. Your chocolate survived though." He stripped the rest of his clothes off in the bathroom.

"I see your coffee didn't," she said as she shut the bathroom door for him.

"Uh, yeah, well, that's what I get for sneaking one behind your back," he hollered.

She laughed as he turned the shower on then let Paisley know she had a mess to clean up quickly. She mopped up the scrambled mess while he was in the shower and took the mop bucket outside as Paisley came into the house. She followed the sound of the shower and kept a watchful eye for Marina as she entered the bedroom. With a quiet, slow slide of the bathroom barn-style door, steam rolled, warming her face. She watched Sawyer running his fingers through his hair, rinsing shampoo from it, and rinsing his face before shutting the water off. The glass shower door was steamed over for the most part but she saw enough of him and that tan, wet, muscular body to not want to leave the bathroom. That was her point to begin with though—corner him in a vulnerable state and make a pass at him, especially after seeing him in person when he walked through the house.

"Darlin', would you hand me my towel?" He flung water from his face with his eyes closed then opened the glass door as Paisley reached toward him with his towel, her tank top strap falling off her shoulder suggestively.

"What the hell?" He shouted as he snatched the towel and held it in front of him. She slid the door shut behind her quickly, shutting herself in the bathroom with him.

"What the hell are you doing? Get out!"

"Shhh, it's okay. Keep your voice down," she whispered.

"What?"

"Shh!" She was waving her hands at him to quiet his shouting.

"This is not okay! Get out! You make a habit of barging in on dudes in the shower?"

"No, of course not."

Sawyer's brows were still raised, his eyes wide and his heart racing with anger.

"Why are you still in here?" He wrapped the towel around himself, tucking it in the front.

"I was hoping to get you alone."

"No shit!" He was about to panic.

"You're even sexier in person, my God."

"Oh, hell no. This is not happening." He stepped toward the door, which she was still standing in front of.

"Move," he ordered in a low, serious tone.

"I don't want to. Don't you find me attractive? I mean, you must since your wife is hugely pregnant right now." She reached for his towel but he stepped back.

"Please move. I'm in no mood." His nostrils flared and he saw red.

"Now that we've officially met, I'm Paisley," she began as she started lifting her tank top.

He reached over her, opening the door with his fingertips while holding his towel, and hollered, "Marina!" He squeezed his way through the doorway, trying to avoid her touching him, but he felt her hand brush across his side.

"We don't have to tell her about this," Paisley said, following him out of the bathroom while pulling her shirt down.

"The hell I don't. Don't touch me." He marched through the house, wet footprints following him, his skin still wet from not having a chance to dry off.

"Marina!" He had reached the dining room when Paisley grabbed his arm.

"Sawyer, don't be a tattle-tail-Tina. Seriously, please don't—"

He whipped around, halting Paisley in her tracks right behind him as Marina walked in the back door. He stuck his finger in Paisley's face and growled, "You came into my house and disrespected me and my wife. She and I don't hide shit from each other. I don't suspect you grew up with the same manners as Marina was taught so let me explain how a guest is *supposed* to behave in a stranger's home."

Paisley stared at him with wide eyes as Marina stood in the doorway, surprised. Marina knew it was serious because the only female he had ever talked to that way before was Gabby.

"What the hell is going on?" Marina's eyes darted between the two of them, interrupting before Sawyer could finish scolding. Sawyer crossed his arms and looked at Paisley, expecting her to answer Marina, but she didn't. She stood, tongue in cheek and a hand on her hip, rolling her eyes like a teenager.

"Why not speak up? You were bold with audacity two minutes ago when you walked in on me in the shower. Who knows how long you were watchin'?"

"You what?" Marina asked Paisley.

"It was a mistake, I thought it was you..." She shrugged nonchalantly.

"Bullshit!" Marina interrupted. Paisley huffed as Sawyer shook his head.

"What is it with our cousins being troublemaking jackasses? I haven't seen you in years, Paisley, and I welcomed you into our home, last minute, no less, and then you hit on my husband. That's the reuniting thanks I get? You really haven't changed at all but you outdid yourself this time. You're still the little hoe that you've always been, trying to steal everyone else's men. Forget friendships or relationships. You don't give a shit as long as you think you can get a piece of hot ass, but let me inform you about somethin'..." Marina got in Paisley's face and Sawyer took a step back. "You won't *ever* have a chance with *my* man. Family or not, don't you ever set foot on this property again."

"I was just lookin' for a good time, Marina. Just once with him. Don't be so uptight." She looked at Sawyer with a flirty grin. He turned his head in disbelief.

"So that's the reason you wanted to 'reconnect' as you passed through? You just wanted an opportunity to snag my man? So did you think you'd steal him for good after this 'just once' or did you just need to add another notch on your belt?"

"A notch on my belt? Really?"

"You should have enough notches to circumnavigate the entire Earth by now." Marina glared at her and Sawyer had to turn away so he didn't laugh.

"Wow." Paisley huffed.

"This isn't how I wanted y'all to meet. I was really hoping you had changed. I gave you the benefit of the doubt but I was wrong to do so. That's what I get for giving second chances. Your mother would be so ashamed of you."

"That's low." Paisley's finger pointed back.

"You're lower!" Marina snapped back. "I want you to leave. Right now." Marina couldn't even look her in the eyes anymore and Sawyer nodded his agreement. She snatched her purse and phone from the coffee table and left out the front door.

"Well, that was a short visit. I would've walked away to get dressed but I wanted to make sure she didn't try to harm you. She seems like a nut job." He wrapped his arms around Marina.

"I'm so disappointed. Maybe she's on drugs again."

"I know you're disappointed. I'm sorry we had to meet that way."

"Me too. I knew I couldn't trust her. This is why I've never really talked about her. Dammit, she pisses me off!"

Sawyer ran his fingers through her hair and kissed her forehead.

"Always someone trying to come between us." She rested her face against his bare, damp chest.

"Nobody's comin' between us, baby. She was very persistent though, not moving away from the door until I yelled for you." He chuckled and she looked up at him, a less-than-amused look on her face. He laughed and bear-hugged her.

She cracked a half-smile and said, "That's what I get for

having a hot husband. I'm having to beat them all away with a stick."

"And you thought Drew was the trouble-making cousin. Thanks for cleaning up my mess by the way." He looked down at her but couldn't keep a straight face.

CHAPTER 43

In the Heat of a Dream

"This heat is killin' me already, Sawyer. I know I shouldn't complain but I was hopin' to not be pregnant during the heat of the summer. My internal thermostat is set to inferno." She wiped her forehead with the back of her hand as she sat under the patio umbrella.

He chuckled. "Sorry, darlin'. I'm assuming you don't wanna hang out with me by the pool then."

"Sunbathing is a no-no when prego but I might dip into the pool when you do for a minute."

"I tried layin' out yesterday on a few hay bales outside of the barn so you wouldn't be jealous but I didn't want a waist tan line from my jeans."

"I know, I was watchin' ya." She grinned, chin resting on her palm. He leaned up, pulled his shades down, and smiled at her.

"Okay, I'm ready to get in." She stood and stripped off her coverup, sporting a bikini, giving in to the temptation of a momentary cool down.

He whistled and sat up on the lounge chair.

"Want me to rub sunscreen on ya like old times?"

"I don't plan to be in the pool long enough."

"Oh? Why's that?" he asked as he stood and walked into the shallow end with her.

"As good as you look in these aqua shorts…we'll have to cool off inside."

"Mmm, I like the sound of that." He pulled her to him when their waists met the water's surface. Her large belly separated their closeness but it didn't keep their lips from connecting. He rubbed her belly and looked at her with raw, heated lust in his blue eyes.

"Look at you glow." He laid her hair back behind her shoulder and they shared a long sweet kiss. "You ready to take this to the bedroom?" he asked with a low groan in her ear.

"Yes, sir. I have a feeling it'll be a while before we cool down."

"You're right about that." He took her hand as they exited the pool and she handed him a towel from a patio chair as she dried off herself.

"I had a *really* nice dream last night," she said, looking up at him with batting lashes.

"Oh yeah? What did you dream of?" His smirk grew as she elaborated.

"I dreamed that I was walking through the field and here you came, riding Tango bareback, completely nude."

"Really? That's hot!" His smirk turned into a sexy sideways grin.

"Yep. You looked magnificent, like a God up on that horse."

"Maybe one of these days I'll surprise you and make your dream a reality."

"Yeah?" Her brows raised with excitement.

"Yeah, under one condition though."

"What's that?"

"You ride nude with me."

"I could do that."

"Make sure your cousin isn't here first." He tossed his head back laughing but she just looked at him, tongue in cheek.

He slid open the patio door and allowed her to enter first.

"For now, how about you ride *me* in the nude?" he asked as he slapped her rear, earning himself a yelp as they entered the house and shut the door behind them.

CHAPTER 44
It's Time!

"Want help?" Marina waddled out to the barn as Sawyer was finishing up chores.

"Good morning, darlin'. Nah, I just have to let them out to pasture. Thanks though. You're up late."

"Yeah, but I woke up well rested and found myself buzzing with a sudden surge of energy. I just went out back and watered the garden."

"Hmm, I read that's a sign labor might happen soon."

"Let's hope. I sure feel miserable, like I have a whiskey barrel strapped to the front of me. This heat doesn't help either."

He laughed, unable to do anything else to relieve her discomfort. "I can imagine. Any day now."

"They aren't due for another week. Let's hope this week flies. It sure has been a long summer." She sat on the bench just outside the barn doors, her knees apart to accommodate her huge stomach, and watched him lead the horses out. She leaned back and sighed; her burst of energy already expended just by walking out there. He strutted alongside the horses' clopping hooves, those jeans stretched tight around his thighs and his t-shirt desperately clinging to his chest and biceps.

He headed back toward the barn after leading the last two out and said as he straightened his Stetson, "Ya know...I've also read that having sex might throw ya into labor faster too."

"Oh, you read that, huh?" She smiled.

"Sure did." A quick raise of his brows as he flashed a bright smile made her laugh. He brushed his hands off onto his jeans and reached for her hand. After pulling her up from the bench, he rubbed her belly and said good morning to the twins. She loved that he did that every morning.

"I wanna watch the horses for a minute." She steered toward the fence and Whiskey ran from the barn to follow. She petted Dixie at the fence, Sawyer by her side, and pointed out dark clouds heading their way from the west. "I really miss riding."

"You'll be able to again soon."

"I can just see the horses wiggling their lips at the babies when they first meet."

"It'll be good for the twins to grow up around horses. I'm glad I did. It led to my career and led me to you too."

The breeze picked up and swept her hair across her face and he couldn't help but push it back, admiring her glowing beauty. The sun lit up her hair from the east as it rose to its mid-morning position, about to be covered by darkening clouds.

"Maybe we should put this energy to use. Might be the last time for the next six weeks." She took his hand and began walking to the house, her bare feet feeling the soft grass as they walked side by side.

"Six really *long* weeks."

She suddenly stopped walking, jerking his arm to a halt.

"You okay?" He turned and asked, but her eyes were big and her jaw dropped. "Marina?"

She looked down at the puddle she was standing in.

"Um." Her heart started racing.

"Is that...?" he asked, his eyes wider than hers.

"Uh-huh."

"Your water just broke?"

"Yep." She stood frozen, staring at him.

"Shit! Um, okay, let me...oh my God, I'm so excited! Let's get you rinsed off and into clean clothes. I'll grab the go-bag." He took her by the arm and they rushed to the house.

"You in any pain?"

"Not yet." They entered the house and, as she got undressed, he darted around the bedroom gathering stuff. "I'll be in front of you cheering you on, behind you to have your back, and beside you going through everything together the best I can." He slapped the doorway with his hand before rushing out the front door, causing her to giggle while trying to catch her nervous breath. She quickly washed herself in the shower and got dressed. He had the SUV started already, car seats in the back and the go-bag ready to roll. He helped her into the car, a towel underneath her just in case. She had never seen him move so fast. He called Bob on their way after alerting the hospital they needed to contact the doctor.

"It's time! We're on our way to the hospital. You and Gladys on Whiskey duty? Yes, sir. I left the door unlocked. Thanks. You ready to do this, darlin'?" he asked her excitedly.

"As ready as I'll ever be. I'm so excited to meet them."

"Oh, me too!" He called one mom at a time, checking on Marina and holding her hand the whole way.

"Promise me, Sawyer, if anything goes wrong, you'll choose the twins over me."

"Please don't talk like that, darlin'. I can't make a promise I know I couldn't keep."

He let the valet park the car and, with the go-bag over his shoulder and her arm in his, they hustled into the hospital. She began feeling uncomfortable pains as a nurse brought a wheelchair for her to sit in, but she could still breathe through them. Sawyer helped her ease into it before the nurse quickly wheeled her to a room. Sawyer got her checked in at the desk, fumbling pages with shaky hands, anxious to get in the room with her. Her contractions were getting closer together quickly, the pain worsening with each. He was signing papers as quickly as he could; flipping and signing, flipping and signing.

"Sawyer!" she screamed from down the hall.

"I'm comin', baby!" He practically chucked the clipboard and pen at the nurse and hollered, "Sorry!" as he took off running. He followed the sounds of her moaning loudly through a contraction and almost passed her room, his boots squeaking on the floor as he stopped quickly at her door. He rushed to her, taking her hand and sitting on the edge of the bed next to her after flopping the bag to the floor.

"I'm right here, darlin'. I'll breathe with you."

She took a deep breath in through her nose and let it out slowly through her mouth. He led her breathing rhythm, letting her squeeze his hand.

"I'm so ready for this! Are you ready?" he asked excitedly.

She shook her head no.

The anxiety churning in his gut manifested itself in a laugh. "Too late now, just keep breathin'."

A nurse came in to check her dilation and hook her up to monitors. She informed Marina that she was at about seven centimeters.

"Ten is what I need to be at though, right? Oh, God." She looked at Sawyer, a bit more relaxed between contractions but her nerves swirling clearly in her eyes.

"You got this. You're doing great." He ran a small towel under cold water from the sink, wrang it out, and laid it across her forehead.

"Have you done this before?" the nurse asked, certain that he had.

"No, ma'am. Neither has she. I've been researchin' though."

"You're a keeper." The nurse smiled and Marina grabbed his hand in preparation for another contraction.

"He sure is," she grunted out as she started the breathing exercises again. She leaned her head back, breathing along with Sawyer, but he could tell the pain was getting worse.

"You think you want an epidural? You have time," he asked.

"I'd rather not."

"It's up to you. I rather you not be in much pain."

"You'll have to decide soon," the nurse informed them, jotting something on her chart.

Marina nodded, unable to answer without interrupting her breathing. Her body would relax when the contractions let up. The time between seemed to fly too quickly.

"I know I already don't wanna go through this again," she said.

"I don't blame ya, darlin'. I'll get snipped so you don't have to worry about it."

"You'd do that?" She turned to face him, surprised at his offer.

"Absolutely. It's the least I could do."

"Are you sure?"

"It won't deflate my manhood." He grinned with confidence.

"I love you."

"I love you too, darlin'." He kissed her lips just before another wave of contractions took over. She squeezed his hand hard, breathing deeply in through her flared nostrils then out through her mouth. He comforted her and helped in any way he could but still felt helpless as he watched the spikes on the monitor to know when the next wave was coming. He tried convincing her to get an epidural but she turned it down. "You're stubborn, that's for sure. I admire you wanting the full natural experience but just know that I won't think any less of you'd if you rather take the easier road."

"I'm sure. It's risky."

He nodded. "You're a brave woman, I hope you know that."

"We're almost there. I hope anyway. I can do this. You're such a big help, Sawyer, thank you." She smiled up at him, her love for the father of her children almost overwhelming her.

"You're welcome, Peaches." He winked and smiled briefly. "It wrenches my heart though to see you in so much pain. I'm so sorry."

"It's okay, it's temporary pain so I'll be okay. Their little faces will be so worth it."

He felt tortured with anticipation, his knee bouncing rapidly, just as rapidly as his heart was racing. He deeply admired her courage.

"We chose a girl's name. We didn't settle on another. You bettin' it's a girl or boy?" He tried distracting her from the pain.

"I don't know." She didn't have time to really think on it as her thoughts were interrupted by another contraction slamming into her.

"Geez, that one came fast," he said to the nurse, who agreed and paged for Marina's OB-GYN. Dr. Chen came in quickly with another nurse who gloved her in preparation.

"I made it just in time! Let's check your dilation." When her contraction subsided, Dr. Chen announced dilation was at nine.

"Wow, almost there, baby! If it's a girl, you want somethin' unique and nature related like the other name we chose?" he asked.

"Yeah, something special to us."

"You'll have an hour or so after they're born before a name must be added to the birth certificate," the nurse said.

"Good to know, thanks. It might take us that long to decide. We've only had nine months."

"The second wouldn't cooperate in the ultrasounds?" the nurse asked.

"Nope." Marina laughed. "So probably not a boy because Daddy here isn't shy."

He laughed and the nurse blushed, probably imagining what an unshy Sawyer looked like. One last contraction, and it was a long one, before the doctor told Marina, "Okay, it should be time to push, so when you feel the urge, do it. Take a deep breath in and release it slowly over the count of ten as you push. Ready?"

Marina nodded and took that deep breath. Sawyer talked to her, cheering her on the whole time as the doctor counted. Marina had white knuckles from squeezing Sawyer's now-purple hand so tightly. The first twin was born within a few pushes; a blue-eyed little girl. A second nurse let Sawyer hold her up next to Marina. They both sniffled with happy tears and named her right away. It took several longer pushes, with Marina already being exhausted, for the second to be born, which was also a girl. Sawyer and a nurse both laid the girls upon Marina's chest, her face wet with sweat and uncontrollable happy tears.

"You did it, darlin'. I'm so damn proud of you." He held her face and kissed her salt-stained lips. "I love you," he whispered before kissing her again.

"Thank you, Sawyer. They're beautiful. I love you so much." She looked at their twin daughters with love in her eyes and added, "I love them so much too. I'm gonna need a fancy coffee after that. It's been nine months."

"Anything you want, darlin'. You definitely deserve it." He kissed her forehead, laughing.

Sawyer heard the doctor order the nurse to fetch her suture items and more towels, which the nurse did in a rush.

"We need to choose her name," Marina reminded.

"Sawyer, could you go ahead and cut the cords?" one nurse asked.

"I'd love to." He cut the cords bedside, then took the babies one by one to the weighing table. The nurse logged weight and measured length. He turned back to Marina with a name idea but the color in her face was fading. Her eyes looked exhausted and her body limp. He left the twins with both nurses when the doctor had a nurse call in another doctor, which alarmed Sawyer.

CHAPTER 45
It's Complicated

Sawyer noticed an alarming amount of blood that Dr. Chen was trying to control. Towels were stained red and were dropped to the floor. He felt a rush of panic come over him along with a bad gut feeling as everything moved in slow motion.

"Marina, are you feelin' okay?" he asked as he rushed over and took her hand.

"Not really, I'm cold." Her words were slow, strained, as if it took all of her energy to drag each one from her lips. Her eyes went glassy before closing and the heart monitor screeched a deafening alarm.

"What's happening?" Sawyer started panicking. "Marina? Marina!"

Another doctor and nurse rushed in, gloved up. Chaos suddenly flooded their joyous world and he wasn't getting answers.

"Sir, we need you to step out," one nurse said as another started chest compressions on Marina.

"No! I'm not leaving!" He stood his ground, holding onto Marina's hand.

"You have to."

"I said I'm not leaving!" He shouted as he backed up out of a nurse's way.

One nurse made a call on the room phone that hung on the wall then the overhead speaker system to the entire hospital announced "code blue." The air had been sucked out of his lungs; he couldn't breathe. He felt as though he were being suffocated. Fear rushed over him like a raging mudslide, blurring his vision and drowning him in anguish. He looked at her and his world stopped in that moment. The doctors and nurses were rushing around the room and one told him to leave or they'd call security. He still refused, frozen in place, so security was paged. Two security officers rushed past the family and Jake in the hall and into the room. The family was concerned by the flurry of activity, but it wasn't until Sawyer was pulled from the room by the arms yelling Marina's name as his feet slid across the floor that they started to panic, realizing that code blue was in regards to Marina.

"What the hell is going on?" Aliza ran up behind Sawyer as the officers escorted him down the hall and outside to the sidewalk, Caroline, Tom, and Jake following. Once out the front doors, Sawyer yanked his arms free from the officer's grip.

"She coded." His chest heaved as he glared daggers at the security guards who stood watching him from just outside the sliding doors.

"What?" Aliza's hand flew to her chest, her eyes wide with panic.

"Her color just...left her. She turned white and there was a lot of blood." He was about pulling his hair out of his head as he paced back and forth.

Aliza hugged him, crying and muttering, "No! Not my baby!"

"My daughters are in there still." Sawyer leaned his back against the wall, using adrenaline to hold himself up.

"They're both girls?" Caroline asked through her tears, a glimmer of joy coming through in her voice.

"They are. We didn't get to name the second. This should be one of the happiest moments of our lives but I'm more terrified than anything. I can't just stand out here waiting, she needs me. I need to be in there!" Sawyer headed for the door but the security guards stopped him.

"You see his size, right?" Jake asked the guards, but they just stared back, arms crossed. They too were largely built men, but only together the size of Sawyer.

Sawyer's eyes met Tom's with desperation as Tom took hold of Caroline's hand.

"You should be in there, son."

"You two aren't gonna stop him, so you might as well help him suit up." Jake pushed off the wall with his foot and joined Sawyer in front of the guards at the door before quickly pushing the automatic door open button next to the guard on the left. "Just let him in. You aren't going to keep him out. That's his wife and kids in there," Jake said and patted Sawyer on the back. Sawyer knew Jake's words were falling on deaf ears so he darted between the guards like a running back, bolting down the hallway and busting through the door to Marina's room as her back arched off the table, two paddles in Dr. Chen's hands. He ran to her and took her hand as soon as she was cleared. The staff was moved by his determination and, surprisingly, allowed him to stay by her side.

"Marina! Don't leave me!" Sawyer shouted with panicked tears streaming down his face. Fate was trying to pry the reins from his hands but he held on with the strength of a thousand cowboys. He found the courage to keep holding on to the belief she'd be okay.

"We have a pulse," her doctor called out.

He released a huge sigh of relief. "Stay with us, darlin'. What the hell happened?" he asked, turning to face Dr. Chen.

"She lost a lot of blood and needs a transfusion. It put her into cardiac arrest when her blood pressure dropped so low," she answered, checking Marina's vitals.

"A transfusion? Can a family member donate right now?"

"Are one of them a blood type match?"

"I'll go ask." He ran to the door, flinging it open with more force than necessary, and called into the hallway.

"Any of you a blood type match for Marina? She needs a transfusion."

"I am. I'm ready," Aliza answered.

"What's her blood type?" Caroline asked.

"A positive," Aliza answered.

"I'll donate too then," Jake volunteered. Sawyer thanked them and went back in with Marina while a nurse came out to lead Aliza and Jake down the hall to give blood. Tom and Caroline stayed in the hall in case Sawyer needed them. The twins were wrapped up and handed over to Sawyer while the doctors tended to Marina. They lit up his eyes, even as saddened as they had become. He found himself smiling and was now concentrating on their little faces momentarily; those tiny noses and precious pink lips gave him a sense of calm in the chaos. The muddy, raging waters were flowing less aggressively now as he tried to remain calm for the twins so that the panic he was feeling didn't agitate them.

"Is she stable?" he asked Dr. Chen.

"She is. We'll take her to the recovery room after a while."

"Shouldn't she be waking up?"

The doctor didn't want to panic him. "It may take a little while. Her system was in shock," she answered calmly. "We need to monitor her closely right now."

He nodded. "Thanks, for everything."

"Of course."

He sat with Marina for half an hour, terrified she'd code again.

"Can I call family in to meet the twins?" he asked from his position bedside, holding both babies.

"Marina probably shouldn't have visitors quite yet but if you'd like to take them out into the hall, that would be okay. We do need to get them cleaned up soon though."

The doors opened and all of the parents were there in the hall. Jake was still giving blood, but Sawyer updated them on Marina's condition and they all slumped in relief. Tom let the ladies hold the twins first. He gave Sawyer a big hug, congratulating him as the moms gushed over the girls, which brought a big smile to Sawyer's face.

"Oh, sweetie, they're absolutely precious!" Caroline handed a twin over to Tom and gave Sawyer a big hug, not wanting to let go of him.

"They sure are, Mom, thank you."

"You two did good. These girls are going to be so spoiled." Tom was grinning ear to ear.

"I have no doubts about that." Sawyer chuckled.

"How's Marina then? She looking any better?" Aliza asked, swaying slowly with the baby in her arms.

"She's breathing okay and stable. Her color is still pretty pale so she needs that blood. I think they'll do that in here before moving her. I wanted y'all to meet the girls before they get taken to the nursery to get cleaned up."

"Thank you for that," Aliza said, handing over the baby to Caroline. "I got back here just in time but poor Jake is missing out."

"I appreciate you guys giving blood. I'd rather she have your blood than that of a stranger. I know it's pretty safe these days, but still. Hopefully, they can get it to her quickly. I've never seen her look so weak and sickly."

"That must have been so scary," Caroline said. "I'm so sorry you had to see her like that."

"Terrifying. I'm just glad I was with her. Not sure it mattered to her, but I'd rather her not have to go through that alone."

"I'm sure it meant the world to her, son," Tom assured.

"I was the last thing she saw before she went unconscious."

"Then she was aware you were there with her," Aliza said.

"She felt the presence of all of you, you and the girls," Caroline added.

Sawyer just nodded then took the girls back to love on them a moment before handing them back in to the nurses. He told the parents he'd see them in a bit then excused himself to go back in with Marina. The family waited in the waiting room, along with Jake, for a while. Sawyer joined them as Chris, Trev, Justin, Becka, and Raquel arrived. That lobby was full of cheerleaders for Team Marina along with balloons, flowers, and gift bags. Sawyer plunked down in a chair across from Jake, starting at the floor.

"You okay, Sawyer?" Chris asked with his elbows on his knees next to Jake.

Sawyer shook his head no.

"Something else happen?" Aliza asked, concerned.

"They're starting the transfusion and kicked me out. She's still not awake, which really worries me. The doctor said they're going to run tests but I can tell she's trying not to freak me out. It just does all the more though."

"Any more heart issues?" Aliza was still just as worried as Sawyer.

"No, thank God, but her blood pressure issue is dangerous. It was fine going into labor. I don't get it. She's healthy and took great care of herself."

"She did and you catered to her, you treated her with care and respect, you spoiled her and cooked healthy meals, and you know damn well she appreciated all of that. You kept her stress level down. It's weird that this happened," Raquel praised, trying to lift his spirit.

"I feel so helpless."

"I know. It's understandable you feel that way but you've helped as much as you can," Becka said.

"You just worry about taking care of those babies and yourself. That's what she'd want," Trev said as he sat next to Sawyer.

"She didn't take her engagement ring off during that time that y'all were apart. She didn't give up on you. She won't give up now either because you're not giving up on her," Becka said, encouraging Sawyer to stay positive. He didn't say a word; he couldn't because what she said choked him up, so he pulled her in for a bear-hug as she was about to walk by him, about smothering her with his biceps. He let her go, blinking the dampness from his eyes.

"I can't wait for you guys to meet the girls," he said.

"Oh, we're super excited," Jake said enthusiastically.

Sawyer smiled and the room fell into a comfortable hush for a while, the ladies talking quietly amongst themselves.

"Sawyer, can we get you anything?" Aliza asked.

"I don't think so, but thank you."

"Coffee run?" Raquel asked.

"Actually—."

"On it." She patted his shoulder on her way out, as did Becka as she followed suit.

"Thank you!" he hollered.

He sat slouched in the chair, leaning to one side, his head against his hand and his boot heel clunking at a nervous pace.

A nurse came into the lobby and asked for Sawyer. He whipped his head around and jumped to his feet. Aliza was on the edge of her seat, hands wringing in her lap as she waited for any news.

"The transfusion is almost finished but Marina still hasn't regained consciousness. When we're finished, we'll move her to recovery. By that time the twins will be ready to join you both in the room."

"Okay, thank you." He was still noticeably upset as the nurse smiled with a nod and walked out. He turned back toward everyone.

"Why hasn't she woken up yet?" His chest rose and sank quickly, repeatedly, as if he was about to have a panic attack.

"She will, son." Tom was trying to be comforting.

"Oh, sweetie." Caroline stood and hugged Sawyer.

"I'm so scared, Mom." He hugged her tight.

"I know, I know. Oh, honey, I'm so sorry. She just needs some time to regain her strength. She'll need it for those babies. Her body just went through so much."

"I hope that's all it is. I need her to come back to me." He clung to Caroline for strength.

"She will, sweetie. You just have to stay strong. Be strong for her," she encouraged quietly.

He nodded and sniffled then patted her on the back, clearing his throat.

"No matter what, we're here for you. We'll be close by whenever you need us to be," she said.

"Thanks, Mom."

"Of course."

"Sawyer, you know you can call whenever and I can fly here," Aliza added.

"I appreciate it."

"Aliza, you're always welcome to stay at our place, whenever," Caroline said.

"Thank you. I'll take you up on that. I appreciate the hospitality this last couple of days. I'm glad I was able to drive up when I did. She'll be okay, everything will be ok. No new bad news so we just have to stay positive."

"I wanna be. I'm so worried about her though. The worst-case scenario keeps taking over in my mind. I told her she needed to switch doctors, I really wish she would've." Sawyer blinked repeatedly, looking up at the ceiling.

"We'll never know if that would've made a difference, Sawyer. Try to think about those precious new faces right now. That's what I'm trying to do. I need to go pick Savannah up from the airport. I'll be back right after. Keep me updated if anything changes, please."

"Yeah, of course." He gave Aliza a hug and she wiped a tear off his cheek before leaving.

"We should go with her, Tom. She shouldn't be driving while her daughter is in this condition," Caroline told Tom as she stood and straightened the bottom of her blouse. He nodded and joined Caroline near the door as she hollered for Aliza to wait a second. Sawyer told them thanks for going with Aliza on their way out and sat back down in the chair. Only the guys remained there in the lobby with him. The silence was deafening for several minutes before Sawyer spoke.

"What if I have to raise these babies by myself?"

"We'd be here for ya, man. Anything you need, anytime." Trev patted and rubbed Sawyer's back in comfort.

"I wouldn't expect y'all to be helping out with three a.m. feedings."

"We would though," Chris said.

"Yeah, absolutely. Even *when* she recovers, if you two need a break, anytime, day or night, you just call." Jake sat across from Sawyer, trying to make eye contact but Sawyer was staring at the floor.

"Please tell me this is all a nightmare and that I'll wake up and she'll be lying next to me in our bed."

"I wish I could, man." Jake was getting misty-eyed watching Sawyer's heart break.

"But she'll be okay. She's gonna pull through. She's strong and she has these babies to come back to...and you. You're her love story. It doesn't end this way for you two love birds," Justin assured.

"I appreciate you guys. I really do. More than you'll ever know. I'm sure y'all have work and other shit to do but you're here supporting me and it means the world." He scooched his chair inward and the guys followed suit. They football-huddled, their heads down, tears falling from Sawyer's blue eyes. "I've been needy this year, haven't I?" He wiped his sniffling nose with the back of his hand.

"Nah, you just have a big heart that keeps taking a beating, and that big heart belongs to that woman. That's pretty damn special. Not everyone is lucky enough to experience a love like you two have," Chris said.

Sawyer smiled, "Yeah. I am lucky to know that feeling. I feel like our life together has just begun. We haven't had much time together and the time we've had has flown by. I can't go the rest of my life without her. This is my fault. I brought up having kids and she wanted nothing more than to give me that. Now she could miss out on life and seeing her daughters grow up. How am I supposed to carry on if the worst happens? How can I live knowing I did this to her and our girls?" Sawyer was starting to panic again, breaking down, rubbing the back of his neck.

Jake put a hand on Sawyer's knee and said, "Sawyer, you can't be thinkin' that way. Those little girls need you. They'll get you through."

"So will we," Justin added.

"That's right. Now breathe with me, big guy." Jake inhaled through his nose deeply, then out his mouth, Sawyer following along, his nostrils flared as if it helped him hold it together. "I'm surprised you aren't throwing things or punching holes in the wall," Jake joked.

"I've noticed there's nothing except chairs in here to throw," Sawyer said.

A nurse stepped into the lobby, arms around a clipboard.

"Sir, we're moving your wife now but visitors will have to leave for the evening."

"Okay, thanks."

"The twins will be on their way in a few minutes."

Sawyer nodded then texted the others, letting them know not to come back that evening. The guys stood, each taking their turn for a hug.

"Call us if you need anything, even just to vent." Jake had a hand on Sawyer's back as they headed for the hall.

"Anytime too. Update us on any changes in her condition," Chris added.

"Thanks, guys."

"Get some sleep, you're looking like Hell," Trev said over his shoulder as he walked down the hall.

Sawyer laughed and flipped him off, making Chris laugh.

The last to leave, Justin wrinkled his nose and said, "You don't look that bad."

Sawyer chuckled, shaking his head, "Thanks for the laugh, Trev!"

"Anytime, bro," Trev hollered, passing the giftshop on his way around the corner as he put his ball cap on backward. It gave Sawyer an idea. He entered Marina's recovery room with a floral arrangement and placed it on the end table next to Marina. He wrote her a sweet note on the floral card that read "Music has a beat, same as our hearts. We shall always keep dancing through life together. My heart beats for you so I'm wishing on our lucky stars for you to come back to me." The twins entered right after he tucked the card back into the bouquet.

"Here are your girls. Can I get you anything, Sawyer?" The nurse was one he hadn't seen before; must be it was shift-change time.

"I'm good, thank you. Oh, um...so feeding them...?"

"Do you know if she planned to breastfeed?"

"I don't think so. Let's bottle-feed for now. When she wakes up, I'll ask her what she prefers."

"Okay. They're definitely hungry."

The nurse seemed reluctant to answer at first. Was it because he said *when* she wakes up?

"I'll get the formula and be right back to help."

"Perfect, thanks." He scooped them both up, one on each arm, talking to them and smiling. Their little mouths were like baby birds, instinctually turning toward his chest. "Sorry, girls, I have nothing to offer y'all till these bottles come."

The nurse came back in with a care bag, diapers and wipes, formula, and burping cloths, too. He opened the go-bag they had brought and took out the white onesies with little yellow stars on them that they had brought for the babies. He had their diapers changed and onesies on by the time the nurse had set everything up in the room.

"I'm impressed," she said. "We have to show and instruct most first-time dads how to do all of that."

"Did I do okay?"

"You did a perfect job." She showed him how to swaddle them as they began to grow fussy and he and the nurse each fed a twin. He followed her lead. Marina's doctor came in and asked for names to put on the birth certificates. He looked over at Marina and huffed a long breath before answering.

"Those are beautiful names," Dr. Chen said, smiling as she wrote them down. "I'll let you know the results of Marina's tests as soon as I get them."

"I appreciate it."

The hospital photographer took newborn photos and the doctor came in later with footprint postcards and informed Sawyer that test results looked good. Sawyer refused to eat the entire evening. He watched football and rodeo channels as he cared for the twins. It was nearly midnight before he just grew too tired to do it anymore safely. The nurse offered to take them to the nursery for a couple of hours so he could sleep, which he gladly accepted. After the nurses kicked him out for a few minutes to tend to Marina, they left him a pillow and blanket in the pullout chair. He slid Marina over to one side of the bed and put the pillow next to hers, crawled up next to her, and snuggled to her.

"I'm gonna drift into your dreams with you as our hearts beat in rhythm tonight. I love you." He kissed her cheek before falling asleep with his hand upon her chest to feel her heart beating. There was no song more familiar to him than her heartbeat.

CHAPTER 46

Hopeful

"Good morning, son." Tom quietly entered the room, Caroline just behind him.

"How did last night go?" she asked.

"Good morning. No change for Marina. The twins stayed in the nursery for a couple of hours at a time during the night and I was up with them in between." He was sitting on the edge of the bed next to her, wearing the same clothes from the day before.

"You look tired. I wish you would've let me stay to help." Caroline set her purse and a bouquet on the window sill.

"They wouldn't let anyone else stay last night but someone might have to tonight. I'm whooped."

"Babies are hard work, especially newborns. You've got two plus the added stress with Marina." Tom gave Sawyer a pat on the shoulder.

"We brought you coffee but maybe you should have some rest first."

"I'm okay, Mom, thanks. I'll take that coffee though. This shit is horrible." Sawyer tossed the hospital coffee in the trash.

"The first night as a parent is the hardest. You'll get the hang of it quickly. Where are my grandbabies anyway?" She hugged Sawyer then sat in the chair over in the corner.

"In the nursery. They should be coming back in soon."

"Savannah's flight was delayed again but Aliza helped with chores and wanted to make another stop after the flower shop so she should be here soon."

"Okay. Everything go okay with chores? I haven't checked in over at the stables."

"I did. All is good. Chores over there were done already. Good ranch hands you have over there," Tom said.

"Yeah." Sawyer chuckled. "Justin and the guys have been blowing up my phone. I need to holler back at them real quick."

"Go ahead, we'll stay right here."

Sawyer stepped out and called Justin to make sure all was okay and update him, letting him know they could have more visitors the following day in the room. A nurse brought the twins in while Sawyer was on the phone and the grandparents gladly intercepted, getting their lovins in before Sawyer came back into the room. He couldn't help but smile at them every time he'd greet his little blessings.

He said, "I feel like this is all my fault."

"What are you talking about?" Tom asked.

"I pushed for having kids, and this soon into our marriage. I feel like I did this to her."

"Oh, Sawyer, no. This wasn't anyone's fault."

"This was out of everyone's control. If you two would've waited a few years, this still could've happened." Caroline tried to comfort him.

"We would've had more time together though. I hate that there's nothing I can do for her."

"You are though, son. You're taking care of your little ones when she can't. You're here with her, at her side, you have been this whole time."

"Thanks, Dad. You too, Mom. I still feel horrible for her. She's missed out on a whole day of her kids' lives. That's just not right. How much more will she miss out on?"

"Sweetie, she'll wake up. I know we aren't usually the type but maybe we should say a prayer if you haven't already."

"I have in my head a million times. Hasn't helped yet."

"Well, she's still with us so let's say one aloud." Caroline took Sawyer's hand and Tom's, and Sawyer took Marina's. They bowed their heads and Sawyer exhaled deeply before leading a prayer.

"Marina is a wonderful woman who deserves to be with her babies right now. I need my wife and our daughters need their mother. I can't do this without her and I don't want to. She can't miss out on their lives and I can't be the father I need to be without her. It's just not fair. Please, I'm begging you. Bring her back to us. If there is a higher power up there, I need you to hear me out. I'll do anything. I'm begging you. Let Marina wake up, please." He started breaking down again.

Caroline took him into her arms as her heart broke for her son and said, "Amen.".

Aliza showed up a few hours later, bringing everyone lunch. They all helped Sawyer out with the twins and he was able to get a short nap in, snuggled up to Marina. Aliza asked Caroline if she minded if she stayed that night to help out. She was extremely concerned about Marina and wanted to stay close. She slept in the pull-out chair and got up to help with the twins each time they'd wake. Whenever one woke, the other would wake. Aliza was impressed with how Sawyer was so attentive to them.

"You're a natural, Sawyer."

"Think so?"

"Absolutely."

"I'm nervous I won't do something right or accidentally hurt them."

"You're already doing everything perfectly."

"They're so dependent. These tiny lives...I'm responsible for them."

"You're doing great. Don't worry so much and just enjoy them. It's obvious they're comfortable with you." She cradled one in her arms as he held the other against his chest.

"Think they'll take to Marina as well? I'd hate for them to not feel as comfortable with her because she can't hold them right away."

"She's their mom. They'll sense that."

"I hope so."

"I'm proud of you, Sawyer."

"For what? I've been a wreck." He sounded disappointed in himself.

"For everything; everything you're doing for your babies, for Marina, the person that you are, and how you make her so happy. I couldn't ask for a better son-in-law. When she told me she had found the one, I couldn't have imagined one as good as you."

He stepped over to her and gave her a big hug with his free arm then kissed her forehead.

"You have no idea how much I appreciate that, Aliza. I'm thankful for you too. Thanks for staying tonight."

"Thanks for letting me."

"Oh, I would've begged you or Mom to, I'm too damn tired to do this alone. I thought I could handle it by myself."

"You never have to do it by yourself. You never have to beg either. She and I were both anxious to stay."

"I appreciate both of you. I'm a lucky guy to have so many special ladies in my life."

"You're sweet. Just so you know, you can call us with any questions or for advice anytime. We've been through this rodeo before."

"Oh, you should probably already count on that happening. I have no shame in asking."

"Good. I think they're good and sleeping. How about we lay them down and try to get some rest?"

"Sounds great," he said as they both laid the twins down before getting horizontal themselves.

CHAPTER 47
Can't Lose Her

The next morning, Caroline showed up at the hospital early, leaving Tom behind, still sleeping. She made herself comfortable in the chair in the corner of Marina's room just as a nurse came into the room with paperwork in her hand.

Caroline whispered, "Sawyer. Sawyer, sweetie. Wake up."

He lifted his head from his arm, which was serving as a pillow, and his other arm bumped the side rail to Marina's bed that he'd put up so he didn't fall off.

"Hmm?"

"I just wanted to let you know that your daughters have been cleared to go home. I have their discharge papers." The nurse handed the papers to Sawyer but he didn't take them.

"Already?"

"Oh, that's wonderful!" Caroline was quietly excited.

"Yeah, that's great. Um...I can't go home without her though." He looked at Marina and touched the side of her face.

"Do you want me to take them home?" Caroline offered.

Sawyer took a moment to think before answering, "I'd rather we stay together."

"Who knows how long that will be, dear?" Caroline felt his pain. She could tell this was a difficult choice for him to make.

"Please? At least for today, can they stay here in the room with us?" he asked with desperation in his eyes.

"Of course. Since they've been discharged the nursery won't accept them back though," the nurse regrettably informed.

"That's okay, I understand. I'll take care of them." It was obvious he was exhausted; dark circles were progressing under his bloodshot eyes.

"Sawyer, you need to be able to get rest though too." Caroline was concerned.

"I'll have Justin bring a cot in."

"Sawyer, I really think it would be best if—"

"I'm not leaving her, Mom," he interrupted with a snap.

"Okay, okay. Would you like for me to stay and help you? This is going to be a lot of work and you're already exhausted."

He huffed a ragged sigh, raking his fingers through his hair.

"That's up to you."

She nodded at the nurse who then set the papers on the end table and exited the room.

"Aliza should be back here with coffee soon."

He looked at the loudly ticking clock on the wall.

"Her and I will help you with the girls. You don't need to worry about a thing," Caroline said.

"I appreciate it. I'm sorry I got snappy."

"Sweetie, there's no need to apologize. My heart is aching for you. I can't imagine how you must be feeling. Just know I'm here for you, whatever you need. All of us are. You have wonderful friends too."

"Thanks, Mom."

Caroline walked over and wrapped her arms around her son, who gladly accepted her embrace.

"Knock, knock," Tom whispered as he and Aliza walked in. "I ran into this lady in the hall."

Aliza hurried to Sawyer for a big hug.

"Still no change?" she asked, taking Marina's limp hand.

"No, ma'am. Not yet."

"How are you holding up? You getting any sleep?" Tom asked.

"No, sir. I'm not worried about me though. I'm just worried about her. Y'all have been helpful though."

"I know you're tired. I can't tell you enough how much it means that you haven't left Marina's side. If you'd like to go home and get some rest though, we can call you if there's any change," Aliza offered.

"Mom offered as well and I thank you both, but I'm not leaving her. I want to be here when she wakes up."

Aliza nodded, knowing he would say exactly that. The nurse brought the twins in and Sawyer's face spread an instant smile. They were snuggled and sleeping soundly, tucked in cozy receiving blankets. He rushed to them and leaned over the bassinets, admiring their sweet, precious faces.

"I can't wait to hold them again. I almost wanna wake—"

"No!" all three parents whispered.

"Oh, sweetie, you never wake a sleeping baby. You learn to sleep whenever they do," Caroline advised.

"Not unless you absolutely have to wake them," Aliza agreed.

"Just don't," Tom added.

"Noted. I wish she'd wake up so she could hold them." He looked back at Marina over his shoulder. His eyes were even more tired and red than they had been moments before, it seemed.

"I know, son. She will." Tom laid a hand on Sawyer's shoulder.

"She has to." Sawyer looked up at him, his red eyes getting damp again. He was having a hard time keeping it together.

"Savannah will be up here any minute. She insisted on getting a car at the airport," Aliza said just before Savannah quietly peeked in. Tom waved her into the room and she hugged Sawyer before setting another bouquet on the stand, then said, "No offense, dude, but you look like you could sleep for a week."

He chuckled, offering her a weak smile. "I feel like I could. I missed you too."

"You doing okay?" She set her purse on the window sill.

He tossed a shrugged shoulder.

Savannah scooched past Sawyer at the foot of the bed to squeeze Marina's hand.

"She always was stubborn, ya know."

"She sure is. That's how I know she'll come back to me. To all of us. She's a survivor."

Savannah patted his solid back then went around to the bassinets to see her nieces.

"Oh, my goodness! They're adorable!" she whispered loudly.

"Thank you." Sawyer nodded proudly.

"How does it feel to be a dad?"

"It feels great. A big change for sure, but in a good way."

"Are you hungry? Can I get you anything? Have you eaten at all?"

"Um, I'm not very hungry. Thanks though."

"Sure. He hasn't eaten, has he?" Savannah turned to Tom and Caroline who occupied the chairs in the corner near the window. They shook their heads no and Caroline held up two fingers and mouthed "two days".

Savannah's eyes widened.

"I think I'll go get all of us something from the sandwich shop across the street. Is that okay with everyone?"

"That would be wonderful, Savannah, thank you," Tom said as he pulled his card from his wallet, but Savannah politely refused to take it.

"I'll go with you since the girls are asleep." Aliza picked up her purse and headed for the door, following Savannah.

"Will you text me what he might eat from there?" Aliza whispered to Caroline, referring to Sawyer. Caroline nodded, picking up her phone.

Sawyer was quiet for a few minutes, sitting next to Marina.

"I'm gonna step out and call Justin real quick." He stood and took his phone from his back pocket on his way out. He leaned his back against the wall just outside of the room with barely enough energy to stand.

"Any change?" Justin asked as soon as he answered the call.

"No, unfortunately. Will you do me a favor though?"

"Absolutely. Anything."

"Will you bring a cot and my guitar?" He rubbed his closed eyes.

"Sure thing. Anything else?"

"Maybe another change of clothes. Joggers and flip-flops. Somethin' comfortable."

"You got it."

"I appreciate it."

"No problem. I'll be there as soon as I can."

As Sawyer entered back into the room, both babies were waking. He rushed to them, greeting them with a wide smile.

"Well, hello, my precious girls." He quickly picked one up and Caroline picked up the other. He tucked the blanket lower under the little one's chin, cradling her along his forearm.

"Take this one too, Sawyer, and I'll get a picture." Caroline carefully handed over the other bundle of joy and Sawyer smiled for a picture before taking them over to Marina.

"Mom, would you help me?"

She rushed to his side as Sawyer laid the twins on Marina's chest one-by-one with Caroline's help.

"I wonder if she feels this. Think she hears us at all?"

"I don't know, sweetie, I hope so."

"Actually, this one needs changed." He carefully laid the baby down near Marina's covered feet, held a hand on her tiny body, and reached for a diaper on the stand.

"You need help?" Tom asked as Sawyer laid the wipes next to her.

"I got it, Dad. Thanks."

"This one needs changed too. That's probably what woke them. It's nice they aren't fussy though. Hopefully they'll be easy for you."

"I hope so, but I can handle it even if they're a little rambunctious like their momma." He changed the diaper quickly and traded babies with Caroline, who put the other on Marina's chest. He changed the second then held her against Marina. The twins snuggled to her.

"You'd think having them against her would wake her up." The disappointment in his voice was thick.

"Never know, I'm sure it helps. It's good for the twins too, to have skin-to-skin contact with their mom," Tom said.

Aliza and Savannah came in with food shortly after and were excited to see the twins awake.

"Can we hold them?" Aliza set food on the stand along the wall.

"Of course." Sawyer handed one to her carefully, supporting the tiny head, while Caroline handed the other to Savannah.

"Oh, my goodness. They're so tiny." Savannah held her close and admired her sweet face. "Look at these bright blue eyes. She has your beautiful eyes, Sawyer."

"She does, thank you."

"This one has Marina's eyes," Aliza observed.

"She does. That's how I tell them apart."

"You gonna tell us their names?" she asked.

"Nope. I think Marina should hear them first." He smiled.

"Fair enough. Y'all didn't know the sex of the second one going into delivery though, right?"

"No, we didn't. I chose the name after she was delivered. I was asking Marina her opinion when she crashed. I didn't even get to run it by her. The doctor needed a name for the birth certificate so I chose one. I hope she'll be okay with it."

"I'm sure she will since you chose it," Aliza comforted. He smiled and nodded, appreciating the support.

"Thank you both for getting food." Tom dug through the bag, taking sandwiches out and passing them around.

"Absolutely. Sawyer, go eat," Savannah instructed. He hesitated.

"Sweetie, please come eat," Caroline told him.

"Why don't you ladies eat first and I'll take the girls?"

"No, sir. We know you; you won't end up eating. Go on ahead." Aliza could be stubborn too.

"Yes, ma'am." He took a sandwich from Tom and ate it quickly. He was hungrier than he thought and thanked the ladies for the food, greeting Justin as he came in with a bag and handed it to Sawyer.

"Hey, everyone." Justin waved around the room in greeting.

"Thanks, man." Sawyer took the canvas bag of clothes from him and set it on the floor in the corner out of the way and set the bouquet Justin brought on the stand.

"Aww, look at them. Can I hold one?" Justin asked excitedly.

"Absolutely," Aliza said, handing a little one over to him.

"Wow, they're so small. Those tiny little fingers...the office is about to get a whole lot noisier."

Sawyer laughed. "Yeah. Bring your earplugs."

"Those sliding doors might help too," Justin joked. Sawyer laughed his first real laugh in days. Justin stepped over to look at the other twin.

"They look the same except for their eye color."

"They sure do. I don't know if that changes later on or not but for now, it's how I tell them apart."

"Names?" he asked, trading babies.

"He won't tell anybody," Tom blurted.

"Why not?"

"He wants to tell Marina first."

"Ah, gotcha. Well, they're adorable."

"Thank you." Sawyer looked so proud every time.

"I think the guys and Becka wanna come up here soon, so give Jake a holler and he'll call the rest. He's chomping at the bit to meet these two."

"Okay, I'll text him right now."

"Who did that?" Aliza asked, pointing to three long-stem red roses in a vase in the window sill.

"I did. One for each one of my girls on the twins' birthday. Luckily, they had some in the gift shop downstairs," Sawyer said.

"That's a sweet gesture."

"That's the furthest he's been this whole time," Caroline stated.

"Dad would've loved that," Savannah said.

Sawyer nodded. "I wish I could've met him."

"He would've loved you," Savannah said sincerely, Aliza nodding in agreement.

"I appreciate that." Sawyer looked a little choked up.

"I'm guessing you bought the biggest bouquet the gift shop had?" Savannah said, nodding at the huge bouquet on Marina's end table.

"I did. I hope the flowers don't die before she gets to see them."

Two nurses walked in and one said, "I'm sorry to have to do this but we need everyone to leave the room for a few minutes so we can tend to Marina." Everyone left the room, taking the twins with them, and waited in the hall. Sawyer the last one out. He couldn't leave without giving his wife a gentle kiss on the forehead.

"You've been so strong, Sawyer." Caroline rubbed his shoulder.

"I feel a wreck, Mom."

She looked at Tom, heartbroken.

As the nurses opened the door a few minutes later, Jake, Chris, Trev, and Becka walked out of the elevator and rushed to see the twins. Upon everyone entering the room, Becka handed Sawyer a potted plant then took one of the twins into her arms. Jake quickly snatched the other after giving Sawyer a hug.

"Congrats! This is amazing. I'm so excited for you, bro."

"Thank you."

"There's nothing on Earth cuter right now than these two little faces. I love them already." Becka was gushing over them.

"Any change for Marina?" Chris asked as he hugged Sawyer then took the twin from Jake.

"No." Sawyer hung his head.

"I'm so sorry."

"Thanks, me too."

"Doctors have any new news or know why she hasn't woken yet?" Trev gave the hand-shake-turned-hug then took the twin from Becka. Sawyer just shook his head, his hands in his pockets. Trev stood next to Chris and they held the babies out on their arms next to each other.

"Wow, they sure do look the same but aren't quite identical, huh?" Chris observed.

"Their eyes are different," Aliza said.

"Yeah, that's cool. You can tell them apart," Trev said.

"Little Miss Teal Eyes has a freckle in the middle of her back like her mama," Sawyer said.

"Aww." Becka was still gushing, holding little fingers.

"I'm glad y'all came. I appreciate the support."

"Oh, Sawyer, you don't need to thank us," Becka said. "Shoot, we were all excited to come."

"Yeah, seriously. There's nowhere we'd rather be." Jake patted Sawyer on the back with a bright, excited smile.

"This has been really tough; I don't know what I'd do without y'all."

"We're glad we can be here. You would've survived without us though. You're tougher than you think," Chris said, handing a baby back to Becka, who was begging to have her back.

"Our weekend getaway proved otherwise," Sawyer said.

"You would've gotten through that without us too, just would've taken longer." Jake laughed then hugged Sawyer again and Sawyer held on to him longer this time, trying to keep from getting emotional.

A nurse came into the room and said, "We're going to move y'all to the big recovery suite. It's bigger so you can set up a cot if you wish. She's all taken care of so you're welcome to go back in and gather your things. We'll be right back for her."

"Great. Thank you." Sawyer nodded.

"I brought the cot. Your guitar too. I left them in the truck for now because I figured there wasn't much room in here, plus it's been raining."

"Thanks, Justin."

"The suite has a shower in it so that'll be easier for you," Caroline added.

"Yeah, I probably should take one."

"Everything you need is in that bag," Justin said.

"I appreciate it."

"They expect her to be here a while then if they're moving her?" Caroline asked Aliza, concerned.

"I hope not. My baby girl needs to be with her babies at home. I hate seeing her like this and your poor son is a mess."

"That's the truth." Caroline looked over at Sawyer.

Everyone helped gather the bouquets and the twins' stuff before the nurses came in and rolled Marina down the hall and around the corner to a bigger room. The whole gang followed; a parade of supporters crowding the width of the hall. Aliza and Caroline helped Sawyer set up the room while everyone else waited in the hall to keep out of the way.

"I'm going to go get the cot and your guitar real quick now that there's more room," Justin peeked in and said.

"Thanks. You want help?"

"I'll help him," Chris volunteered and headed for the elevator with Justin.

"She should be set for a couple of hours. We'll be back later," one nurse said to Sawyer in the doorway on the way out. He noticed the room number was 230.

"Thank you both."

"It's nice they come in to take care of her like that. The aftermath of birthing isn't for the faint of heart," Caroline said.

"No, it isn't. I could've helped her but it's hard when she isn't able to get up," Aliza said.

"I wouldn't mind helping either, or just doing it myself, but I'd have no clue what to do," Sawyer said, sitting in a chair next to Marina's bed and taking her hand.

"The nurses help and they'd explain what to do but with her in this condition it's difficult."

"I feel so helpless." Sawyer was sinking into a sad funk again. It came in waves but stayed longer than it was gone.

"Sawyer, why don't you go ahead and shower? You'll feel better. The twins have a ton of help and love right now. Take a few minutes for yourself. I'll get you coffee, or if you want to just rest that's okay too." Caroline rubbed his shoulders, standing behind him.

"I could use a coffee, Mom. Thanks."

"You could use a nap though too," Aliza said.

"I'm afraid I won't be awake when she wakes up."

"Sawyer." Aliza was almost scolding him with her eyes.

"What?" He rubbed his chin scruff.

"She or we would wake you. You really do need rest, especially if you want the twins staying here with you tonight."

"I can't. Everyone is here visiting. That would be rude."

"I'm glad your mother taught you manners, but don't be ridiculous. Everyone knows you need rest. That's the best way to help. Take care of yourself." Aliza had a hand on her hip.

"She's right," Tom spoke up.

Sawyer looked at the two moms then caved. "Fine. Since the nurses won't be back for a while and y'all are here with the twins, I'll try to take a nap. Coffee can wait."

"Thatta boy." Caroline tousled his messy hair and winked at Aliza. "We'll let everyone know you need some rest," Caroline said as they left the room.

The guys poked their heads in to tell him they'd be in the lobby for a bit and be back later as Justin and Chris brought in the items they fetched from the truck. Sawyer thanked them and Becka snuck in quickly to hug Marina, almost making Sawyer cry. She gave him a big hug on her way out. The family took the twins with them to the lobby, staying close by, and Sawyer took a long shower, bracing himself on the wall while letting out exhausted tears. The water rained down upon him, rinsing heartbreak down with it. He shaved, perfecting his short beard line at the sink even though he wasn't in the mood to primp. He didn't want to look his worst for Marina when she woke. He threw on his favorite gray sweat joggers that Justin had packed for him as well as a clean t-shirt and set the cot up. The nurses had left a pillow and two blankets for him, one of which he laid on and the other he covered up with. He was out as soon as his head hit the pillow. The nurses were aware he was resting so they waited as long as possible before going back in. He didn't hear them enter the room when they finally did. They left Sawyer to sleep undisturbed and let the family know he was sleeping soundly. The twins were napping as well, snuggled in the arms of Tom and Savannah as everyone visited quietly amongst themselves in the lobby. Chris and Trev made a food run for everyone and returned with better coffee than the hospital offered.

"Sawyer's gonna appreciate that coffee," Jake said.

"Probably the food too. Hospital food sucks." Trev laughed.

"The coffee is even worse." Tom nodded.

"That man is so exhausted he probably doesn't even notice," Caroline said.

"I can't imagine he'd care anyway, as long as it's caffeine," Aliza chimed in, helping pass out food.

"Is someone staying here tonight with him?" Savannah asked.

"I can. He'll need help with the girls, I'm sure. Unless you would rather, Aliza."

"It doesn't matter to me. Go ahead. Please let me know if there's any change with Marina."

"Oh, absolutely. I definitely will. You all coming back in the morning if her condition is still the same?" Caroline asked the group. They all looked around at each other, nodding yes.

"It's been almost three hours. Should we take Sawyer's food to him before it gets cold?" Caroline asked.

"Probably should," Justin agreed, packing up.

Everyone went back up to the room. Caroline peeked in first and Sawyer was just sitting up on the cot.

"Hey, sweetie. You have a good nap?"

"I did, thanks." He yawned and stretched his arms out forward.

"You must have been sleeping hard because the nurses came in a little bit ago."

"I didn't hear a thing. How are the girls?"

"They're just fine. They slept almost that whole time too but they could use some mom and dad time and we brought you food and real coffee."

Sawyer chuckled. "I'm ready for it."

"You got a shower and shaved too, I see."

"Yeah, I feel better."

"You look it, too." She smiled then waved out the door for the crew to join.

After eating, Aliza and Savannah held the twins to Marina for a bit until they got hungry. Sawyer sat feeding one in the chair while Aliza fed the other. Friends left for the night and a nurse came in to announce that visiting hours were about over. Tom, Aliza, and Savannah said their evening goodbyes and headed out after handing the baby over to Caroline.

"Text me when y'all are awake in the morning and we'll come back," Aliza said on their way out.

"Will do. Thanks." Sawyer was appreciative of all of them.

CHAPTER 48

Flyin' Through the Storm

It was a long night of feedings and changings, constant interruptions from nurses, too, which made it impossible to sleep. Caroline took the cot as Sawyer scooched in bed next to Marina. It was a tight fit but he slept on his side and snuggled up to her. Feeling her heart beating was comforting enough to allow him to sleep between little hunger cries and diaper changes. Caroline got up with him each time, taking on one twin while he took on the other. They'd walk the room, bouncing and burping, soothing and humming the little ones back to sleep. They discovered that the twins slept more soundly snuggled up next to each other in one bassinet. They should've attempted this strategy earlier; they would've gotten more rest. Sawyer was desperate at this point. It felt as though they were finally getting sleep just as the sun poked through the blinds, right across Sawyer's face. An eye opened slowly and along with it came an unhappy groan. He stretched his arm up into the air. It had been wrapped around Marina since he laid down. The other arm was completely numb, having it up under his head. His face rested against her shoulder. He looked up at her, lifting his heavy head to see she was still not awake. Caressing her face, he gently kissed her cheek and sat up to see his mom waking. He smiled at her.

"Morning, Mom," he whispered.

"Morning. You look like you got a little sleep."

"Seems like just now though. Damn sun."

"I figured that's what woke you. I'm so glad you don't snore."

He chuckled. "Think Dad will bring decent coffee again today?"

"Absolutely, I'll text him. Oh, looks like Aliza already texted this morning. They're all up and around, waiting on us to let them know we're awake. She said they're bringing coffee and donuts. Anything in particular?"

"Nope, I'll take anything."

"Okay."

The nurse came in to take Marina's vitals and tend to her so Caroline slipped her shoes on and told him she'd wait downstairs for the family to help them carry stuff up. Justin texted saying all the guys and Becka would be up there soon. Sawyer asked the nurse to show him what to do to help Marina so he could help her once she woke up. The nurse didn't mind showing him but warned him of the mess he'd be dealing with. He sure had a better appreciation for what her body went through after that. Not that he didn't before, but he realized what the nurses dealt with daily too. The nurse did mention *if* Marina wakes up this would all need to be done in the shower. He politely corrected her with *when* she woke. She replied with, "Yes, sir, forgive me. Miracles happen every day." He thanked her for her help as she left the room then stood with his arms crossed at the window, wondering why it seemed as though the staff was giving up on her. Her vitals were good and test results came back ideal. It made him instantly nervous and he started brainstorming on ways to wake her. In a way, he felt determined, and in another way, he felt worried and helpless. He stared out the window at the trees beyond his reflection, heavy rainfall danced on the window and thunder rolled overhead. Lightning flashed bright as the sky grew darker by the minute.

"Nothing can grow or bloom without rain. Nature needs to

let it all out sometimes too. Then the sunshine dries everything up, shining a new light on life. We just have to wait it out." A starling landed on the window sill outside and ruffled its metallic feathers. The tiny bird remained perched as he stared at it. It wasn't afraid, it didn't flinch or fly away when he moved. The rain didn't bother it or intimidate it, didn't chase it into hiding. Nothing was weighing it down.

"You know, Marina, darlin'...starlings build nests together, unlike other bird species. They do it all together," he said as he watched another starling land. The birds groomed each other, most likely mates. He turned to her and walked over to her bedside, took her dainty hand, and placed it upon his chest right over his compass tattoo so she could feel his heart beating.

"Wake up, my love, so we can do this together. Wherever you are right now, find your way back to me. Let our love guide you home." He raised the head of her bed a little more before grabbing his guitar and sitting in the chair next to her bed. He took a drink of water and set the glass back down on the end table, then cleared his throat and propped his guitar on his leg. He began strumming, the sound of the music drawing the family back into the room. They all stayed back in the entrance behind the wall, Aliza and Caroline each holding a bundle of joy. He sang a heartfelt acoustic version of *Losing You* by Kane Brown. He played that guitar as though her life depended on it and the pain and worry in his voice had the whole family wiping away tears. Nurses heard the somber sound and gathered in the hall to listen. The guys and Becka snuck in behind the family and Justin recorded Sawyer singing to her. The starlings flew off together, weightlessly, and a single tear rolled down Marina's cheek as Sawyer neared the end of the song. Aliza gasped and Sawyer startled, not having realized they were all behind him the whole time. He looked at Aliza and then back at Marina while still strumming. Marina's damp pretty eyes opened and looked at him. He struck a wrong note as he set the guitar down in a hurry and grabbed her hand. His heart was racing.

"Sawyer," she whispered.

"Marina, baby." Sawyer started sobbing, his head down, pouring tears upon the white sheet. He held her hand in both of his. The guys had held back emotion until Sawyer cut loose. Everyone was crying with joy and relief.

"You came back to me." He sniffled.

"Of course. I didn't go anywhere."

He stood and embraced her as she wrapped her arms around him, tears falling from her eyes at his amplified reaction. He held the side of her face, looking into her eyes, not wanting to ever let her go. His lips kissed her hand, then her forehead.

"I knew the notes would work." Everyone was hovering in the entryway, letting the couple have a moment. He stroked her hair and asked, "Was it really the music that woke you?"

She nodded yes and said, "That and I had a dream that we were flying through the air together during a storm and the music was playing while we were flying. It was strange but peaceful."

He lost it. Completely lost it; bursting into tears with his head down. He cried harder than he ever had before and he didn't care that it was in front of everyone. She laid a hand upon his face after a moment then tipped his chin up.

"How are our baby girls?"

"They're perfect. Just like their mama. They need you. I need you too. I'm so glad you're okay."

Aliza couldn't wait any longer, she rushed in to hug Marina.

"Oh, honey, I love you so much."

"I love you too, Mom. Why is everyone hovering in the doorway and crying?"

"Sweetie, you've been unconscious since the girls were born. It's been three days."

"What?"

Sawyer nodded while wiping his face.

"I have? Really?" She looked upset and confused.

"Yeah, darlin'." He squeezed her hand.

"Why? What happened?"

"You fainted after our second was born. We were about to name her when you crashed and then coded."

"My heart stopped?" She was clearly unaware of anything that had happened; no recollection of the events whatsoever.

"It did. After reviving you, you wouldn't wake up. You've had us so worried about you, Marina."

"I'm so sorry to have put y'all through that."

"Oh, baby, don't apologize. It's not your fault."

"So, you saved me once again with your notes. I told you I'd always find my way back to you, Sawyer."

He leaned his forehead against hers, his nostrils flared and jaw tight, trying not to lose it again. Her fingertips felt his scruff.

"No, you saved me by coming back to us." He looked up at her.

"Can I see the girls?" she asked with a smile.

"Absolutely, I'm so sorry, I'm being selfish." Sawyer sniffled and waved everyone in.

"You're never selfish." Her sweet smile caused him to crack one. Her face lit up seeing everyone there. She wore the biggest smile and blinked her blurry wet eyes. Caroline and Savannah brought the girls to her and she sat up, adjusting herself slowly with Sawyer's help.

"Are you in pain, love?" Sawyer asked, eager to soothe any aches.

"I guess a little but I'm okay."

He hit the nurse call button as the girls were handed over to her. She cradled one in each arm, tearing up looking at them both.

"Hi, girls. You're both so beautiful and perfect. I'm sorry I missed your first few days. I hope you were both good for Daddy."

"They were perfect. Not very fussy or anything. They just didn't sleep for long periods at a time."

"Thank you for taking care of our princesses. I'm sorry I wasn't able to help."

"Darlin', you came back to us. That's all I could ever ask for."

She looked around the room at everyone and at the beautiful floral arrangements that lined the window sill and all of the end tables in the room. She noticed the roses and smiled at him.

"You and that damn guitar, always creating magic," Justin said. "Welcome back, Marina."

Everyone cheered and clapped. Sawyer looked so happy; his smile couldn't have been wider. He kissed her again, this time a good one as she held onto their daughters.

"Thank you all." She admired the precious little faces of the miracles she and Sawyer created. "They have different colored eyes."

"They do. Little Miss Blue Eyes was born first. They were twenty-three minutes apart. They've been discharged already so I had to choose a name for Little Miss Teal Eyes without you."

"We're dying to know their names already," Aliza spoke for everyone.

"The suspense is killing us," Tom agreed.

He laughed, smiling down at Marina and their babies before explaining, "I made everyone wait because their mama should be the first to know."

"What did you name our little stars?" Marina smiled with anticipation.

"Little Miss Blue Eyes here is Stormy Skye like we had agreed on, and Little Miss Teal Eyes is Summer Starr. I hope that's ok. You're the one that's good at naming things, I know you enjoy being creative so..."

There were *aww*s echoing throughout the room.

"I love it, Sawyer."

"I'm glad you do. I would've felt bad if you didn't." He chuckled, a relieved grin crinkling the corners of his eyes.

"You did great." She reached for a kiss.

"So, explain the creative names," Justin ordered.

"Good things come to us with stormy skies and we love looking at the stars together. We met in early summer and these two were born in the summer."

"It's perfect. Now we have two more stars to name in the sky."

"I already did. I got bored waitin' on you to wake up. They're part of the Pegasus constellation as twin stars."

"The winged horse. Perfect. They were twenty-three minutes apart, huh?" Marina asked, smiling.

"Yes, ma'am, your favorite number, and now that you're awake and we know you're okay, everything is perfect. All signs point to how life should be."

"So, the girls have the same initials," Savannah pointed out.

"Oh, crap." Sawyer's brows turned in, making Marina laugh.

"It's okay, babe. I like it. I love their names and I love you." She stretched up and kissed his cheek then said, looking down at the twins, "I love them too. We did good."

"We sure did. And you...I am so extremely proud of you. The hell you went through creating, growing, and bringing these two into this world...I can never express how thankful I truly am." He looked at her with such admiration in his eyes that she thought she might burst with his love for her.

"He never left your side. Not even stepping outside for fresh air," Aliza said. "He did beat the shit out of a vending machine in the hall though."

Everyone laughed while Sawyer hung his head in shame.

"Thank you for being by my side through it all."

"I wouldn't be anywhere else."

She was trying to hold back from getting emotional at the sincerity of his words.

"Has everyone else got to hold them?" she asked.

Everyone replied at the same time that they had.

"Not trying to make you feel bad, Marina, but you really know how to get this man down. He was a mess once again," Trev spoke up.

"Oh, shut it, Trev." Sawyer chuckled, playfully shouldering his friend.

"And once again, we're all so glad you're back," Chris added. Everyone made light, making Sawyer and Marina both laugh.

"We're not going through this again," Sawyer told her.

"Who's getting' snip-snipped now?" Chris joked.

"Yes, sir." Sawyer nodded.

The nurse came in to give Marina pain meds, which Sawyer helped her with since she wouldn't let go of the girls. Stormy started getting fussy so Sawyer grabbed a diaper and the wipes and took her from Marina.

"Luckily it's not a stinky one so y'all are safe," he joked as he changed her. Those tiny feet looked even tinier in his big strong hands. Marina watched him, his touch gentle and protective, and couldn't help but be amazed at how fast he had become a pro at the whole dad thing. She adored him taking on fatherhood like a champ right out of the gate. He wrapped Stormy back up, just like the nurse had taught him, and put her back into Marina's arms.

"Thank you." She looked at him, her eyes asking for a kiss from him, which he clearly caught onto.

"Marina, if you'd like to rest, or just want time with Sawyer and the girls, we can all scoot," Tom said.

She nodded. "You're all amazing. Thank you all for being here helping Sawyer, for supporting us, praying for me, for everything. The flowers too, they're beautiful."

"You're welcome. We're so glad you're back with us." Caroline kissed the top of Marina's head, adjusting the purse strap on her shoulder.

"You sure had us all scared." Aliza got a hug in too, holding a little longer than the rest. Everyone said their goodbyes then Sawyer walked them to the door to thank them again. Aliza told him to let her know when Marina was getting discharged or if he wanted her to come back to stay the night with them.

Marina hollered, "I've had enough rest, Mom. I'll be able to manage, but thank you so much."

The doctor came in after everyone left and checked Marina's vitals. She didn't realize she was hooked up to a heart monitor until the doctor talked to her about it. She was monitored throughout the day and it was nice to just have the room to themselves, just them together as a new little family. When the twins got fussy, Sawyer and Marina fed them, burped them, and changed them, then he taught her how to wrap them up all snug and tight before he laid them down next to each other in the bassinet. He tip-toed back over to the bed and asked if she needed to get up and offered to help her.

"Maybe I should have a nurse come in."

"A nurse taught me how to help you. We got this. Just take it easy." He grabbed their go-bag with clean clothes in it. She looked at him, horrified and nervous, as her legs dangled off the bed.

"Baby, it's okay. I got you."

She swallowed hard and hesitated before taking his arm and standing to her feet.

"I don't want you seeing me like that."

"I already had to so the nurses could show me how to help you if you need help at home, or in case it was a while before you woke up."

"Oh, God." She shuffled, embarrassed.

"I know I have an even stronger appreciation for you after all of that. I told you nothing can scare me away." He flashed a smile then a nose wrinkle as he chuckled.

She laughed. "Oh, Sawyer, I'm so sorry."

"Don't be. You're the one going through physical Hell. I can't imagine how much pain you went through but I would've taken on all of this for you if I could've and I won't ever ask you to do it again."

"You're so sweet. I know you would've but I'm glad you couldn't. I wouldn't wish it on you. Those perfect precious faces are already so worth it though."

"They're beautiful, aren't they?"

"They are."

"You probably want a shower. I'm sure it would be fine if you took one."

"Yeah, it would make me feel better."

He called the nurse's station to let them know he was unhooking her monitors and locked the door to the room.

"I'll leave the bathroom door open so we can hear the girls but I'll step in and help you."

"I guess I am a little weak and sore still. My muscles feel like I've been hit by a truck."

"You used every muscle in your body birthing those girls of ours. A nice hot shower and a massage is what you need."

"Sounds nice." She stripped her gown off and was appalled at the ugly padded underwear she was wearing. She looked up at him with big eyes and a wrinkled nose as he stripped his clothes off. He laughed, offering her a shrug, and said, "Not your sexiest pair."

She laughed but was nervous to strip them off. She turned away because of how her stomach looked.

"I understand now why women say they've lost their dignity with childbirth."

"You'll be back to normal in no time, darlin'. You're stocked up right here with everything you need." He pointed at the little shelf above the toilet.

"You sure you want to get in with me? This is gonna be gross."

He smiled and held her face.

"For sickness and in health, for the gruesome and the scary..."

She laughed.

"Seriously though, it's okay. I've been by your side this whole time; I'm not quittin' on ya now."

"You're a brave man." She smirked.

Still smiling, he said, "This will be only the third time we've showered together without havin' sex."

She laughed. "True. I'm sure these underwear would've turned you off anyway."

"Nah, but we're gonna have a long six weeks ahead of us, I can tell ya that. I now understand why doctors say six weeks by the way."

"I'll just keep wearing underwear like these so it's easier. But seriously, it'll give me time to get back into shape though." She covered her stomach with her hands as he took his socks off.

"You'll have restrictions on working out though, darlin'."

"Oh, I guess I would, huh? My stomach...it looks so weird and deflated."

"Baby, you just dropped a sudden twenty pounds or more. You don't have those two youngins in there takin' up space."

"Yeah, it feels a lot different. Empty. I miss feeling them kick already."

"I'm still jealous about that."

"Aww, I wish you could've felt it." She turned the faucet on as he stripped his briefs off.

"What do I do about these?" She tried to pull off her monitor pads from her chest.

"They can stay on. I unhooked them so we'll just ask the nurse to put new ones on when you're done in the shower. They'll be easier to get off when they're wet. You want me to get in and pull the curtain so you can take the underwear off?"

"Yes, please," she answered quickly.

"Okay." He chuckled and got into the shower, pulling the curtain closed. "You know, it's nothing to be grossed out over or embarrassed about. Your body performed a miracle, that's something to be proud of."

"I appreciate you saying that, I really do. I can't help but feel self-conscious though. Especially around you."

"Why around me?"

"Look at you, Sawyer, you're perfect. I don't look the same as I used to."

"I'm not though. But that's okay, you feel however you need to feel. Just know that I think you're a badass. You're still beautiful and sexy and you're still amazing in every way. I appreciate and respect you even more now, which I didn't think was possible." He praised her, washing while waiting for her.

"Oh, Sawyer. You're an amazing man."

"Nah, it's just the truth, darlin'. Hop in before the girls wake up." He looked into her eyes as she got in and stood in front of him under the raining water. With her back into the water, he put shampoo in his hands and gently massaged it into her hair. She closed her eyes and held onto him, tipping her head back to rinse her hair as his fingers ran through it. He helped her wash her body with such care, the places she was having trouble reaching, then took her by the hand to ensure a safe exit from the shower. They got dressed and she climbed back up into the bed as he closed the window curtains, separating them from the orange sunset that looked like fire in the sky. She slid over so he could join her, but he sat on the edge first, massaging her sore muscles. Then he lay next to her, spooned closely, cuddling. He had just started dozing off when a nurse came in to hook Marina's monitor back up and woke up the twins.

"I'll get them, Sawyer. Why don't you take a nap?" Marina sat up.

"No, it's ok, darlin', I'll help you. Thanks though. You probably want some real food." He yawned. "No offense." He looked at the nurse as he stood off the bed.

"None taken," the nurse said as she stuck new square pads onto Marina's chest under the edge of her shirt. "How are you feeling?" the nurse asked Marina.

"Actually, pretty good."

"Glad to see you awake and color back to normal after that blood transfusion. This guy has been by your side throwing up wishes the whole few days."

It was one of the nurses that had been in the delivery room with them.

Marina looked at her, brows turned in with confusion. "Thanks," she said before looking at Sawyer, expecting an explanation.

The nurse left the room and Sawyer said, "Don't freak out but you had lost a lot of blood and it threw your body into shock. Your blood pressure dropped and your heart—"

"Stopped."

He nodded.

"So, I had a transfusion?"

"Yeah, your mom and Jake donated."

"Doesn't that take a while though?"

"It didn't take too long. The doctor had to get the hemorrhaging under control first anyway but they ran the blood from the donors directly into a cleansing machine to speed up the process. I rather you have blood from someone we know if possible. Then I was afraid that by waiting on the blood donation, we had waited too long. I thought maybe that's why you wouldn't wake up, because I made the wrong choice." He gave Marina a bottle and a twin.

"But I did wake up. Not that I wouldn't be grateful for any blood but I think it's great of Mom and Jake to have donated theirs to me."

"I think so too." He sat in a chair with the other twin to feed her.

"I'm so grateful you didn't give up on me."

"Darlin', I could never."

"I trust your decision making, Sawyer. I know every decision you make is with the best intentions."

"I'm glad I didn't do you wrong." He looked up at her and her eyes connected with his. She smiled and nodded.

The twins were chugging and needed to be burped frequently.

"I think I'm actually pretty hungry." Marina softly patted Summer's little back repeatedly, those tiny legs tucked up against her chest.

"That's great. What are you in the mood for? I'll just have it delivered and I'll run down to get it."

"Anything. Surprise me."

"I'm thinking I want a big cheeseburger." He had his appetite back.

"That sounds good. Cajun fries too."

"Anything you want, darlin'. You deserve it." He was thankful to be having even the simplest conversation with his wife.

"I can't wait to go home. All four of us together."

The nurse came in with Marina's discharge papers after they had eaten. The weather had cleared and the sun was peeking through clouds. Sawyer quickly packed up the room.

"I can't wait to sleep in my own damn bed," he said, shoving diapers into the bag. Marina couldn't stop the laugh that bubbled out of her.

"Me too, snuggled up to you with more room than this bed. I still can't believe you squeezed in here with me."

"I can't sleep well without you touching me. Good thing you're petite so I could squeeze in there."

"Well, I'm not going anywhere so you'll have many nights of me cuddled up in your arms."

"I'm extremely thankful for that. Now, let's get the hell outta here."

CHAPTER 49

Nothin' Like Comin' Home

Sawyer carried both car seats up the porch steps and Marina followed with go-bags and an iced latte. She opened the door and let him in first so he could set the girls down.

"Aww, did you do that?" she asked, setting the bags down near the couch. There was a big banner hanging straight ahead that read "Welcome Home!"

"Nah, our friends or family must have. That was sweet of them."

"Yeah, it was."

"That would've been hard to come home to though if I would've had to come home without you." He wrapped his arms around her and she held him tight.

"I'm so glad you didn't have to."

"So am I, darlin'." He looked down at those pretty eyes looking up at him and held the nape of her neck as he kissed her sweetly. He was lost in the moment of having his wife home and healthy until the girls started cooing. Sawyer and Marina smiled at each other a moment before unbuckling the girls from the car seats.

"Well, hi, girls. Welcome home." Marina held Stormy and Sawyer held Summer.

"These girls are a blessing. All of this, the whole process, has been a bit of a struggle, but it was great too. Absolutely worth it. My heart couldn't be fuller. I'm so thankful...for everything." He let a tiny hand wrap around his finger as he admired their little faces.

"I agree. We're a complete family now."

Whiskey came out of the bedroom to greet them, one back leg stretched back, then the other, then the downward dog stretch with his nose in the air. Who were these new miniature people? Sawyer and Marina both sat on the couch and let Whiskey meet the twins. A close sniff, then another. His nub tail wagged excitedly, adding a whine and panting for effect.

"They can't play quite yet, buddy. Y'all will have fun when they can though." Sawyer patted Whiskey's head.

"He's gonna be a protective big brother," Marina gave Whiskey a pat and a scratch behind the ear.

"Well, he better enjoy these two because there won't be anymore." Sawyer wrapped the loosening blanket tighter around Summer.

"No? You're still sure about that?" she asked, not that surprised.

"These two are it. I almost lost you too many times, Marina. I'm not chancing it again. I can't do that to you, make you go through all of that all over again. No, absolutely not. We may not be so lucky next time. I gotta say, I was so worried for a while that we might lose you and there would never be a goodbye more painful."

"Oh, Sawyer." She took him by the chin and kissed his lips. "You're so thoughtful. To be honest, I don't really care to go through any of it again either but I'm glad I was able to this time. Pregnancy was a wonderful experience but birthing I could do without. Seeing them for the first time was the most special thing in the world though."

He chuckled and said, "I'm getting' snipped next week."

She laughed until she realized he was serious.

"What?"

"Yep. I'm calling tomorrow to make an appointment. We can be healin' at the same time."

"Are you sure?"

"Yep."

"Wow, okay. I want you to be absolutely certain though."

"I am. I have to. I don't plan on being careful with you from here on out and the abstinence thing sure as hell is never gonna happen again after your six weeks are up."

She laughed at the seriousness on his face.

"Seriously though, I could never expect you to do that again, the birthin' and all. It's different than seeing a horse go through it."

"True. Are you disappointed at all that we didn't have a boy? You don't wanna try for one?" Marina asked.

"Are you kidding? First off...what if we had another set of twin girls? Nah. Second of all...I'm not disappointed at all because I can't wait for tea parties and tutu skirt dance recitals, prom dress shopping, and walking them down the aisle on their wedding day. Driver's training is still gonna be fun."

"It'll be great. Cowgirls can do everything a cowboy can do. Watching our little rising stars growing up loving horses, music, and boots just like their parents...it's going to be adorable."

"Spoiled too." He grinned.

"Absolutely."

"Hats and matching boots are first on the agenda for these two cowgirls."

"Sawyer, they're too little for boots."

"They need 'em for pictures. Surely, they make 'em small enough."

"You have picture plans already?" she asked.

"Yep. I've been coming up with ideas since they were born."

"I love that. They have the best dad already. You're patient and understanding. You'll show them how a lady is supposed to be treated. You'll always be their gallant protector too; you're intimidating enough to scare away future potential boyfriends."

He blurted, "That reminds me. I need to clean my guns."

She laughed.

"They have the best mom, too. You'll be able to heal broken hearts, give great advice, and lead by example in so many ways. You'll be the perfect role model."

"Thank you. We're going to make a great team." She kissed his cheek.

"We already do, darlin'."

CHAPTER 50

Oh, the Exhaustion

Marina had a hard time staying awake after being up with the babies for more than half the night. She tried to let Sawyer sleep because he had horses to train but she was too exhausted to get back up at four a.m. when they began crying again. She woke Sawyer but he was exhausted too and kept falling asleep before getting woken up by Whiskey barking to get their attention. When they'd cry, Whiskey made sure Sawyer and Marina were aware. Sawyer got up and staggered down the hall, sleep-drunk pretty much, bashing into walls only half awake, and rammed the front of his shoulder into the nursery doorway. He almost tripped over Whiskey, who was leading the way. Sawyer was fighting hard to stay awake on the couch, a baby in each arm, his wrists kinked holding up bottles for each. Whiskey lay at his bare feet and kept clawing at him when he'd start nodding off. After burping the babies, Sawyer carried them back to their cribs and carefully laid them down. He tossed the burp cloths to the floor and went back to bed. Only an hour later, his alarm for work went off. He shut it off quickly so it didn't wake Marina then sat on the edge of the bed, contemplating even going into work. He didn't want to wake the babies again trying to leave for work because then Marina would be on her own with them. He swung his legs back up into bed and crashed for another half hour before one twin woke. Once she started fussing and crying, the other woke. Marina was normally a light sleeper but she was sleeping heavily so he got back up with them. Joggers would do. He slipped his phone into his pocket and crept across rays of sun that lit up stripes on the hardwood floor. They had just eaten and didn't need changed again so he stood with them, one snuggled to each side of his chest, as he swayed around, almost dancing. It soothed them but Marina had heard him talking quietly to them on the monitor when he first went in there. She heard him call the twins Honey Bunny and Sugar Bear, which she found adorable. She tip-toed out into the living room where he was serenading them with a soothing hum.

"Babe," Marina whispered, putting her silk robe on.

"I got 'em, sweetheart, go on back to sleep."

She adored the way he was with them. This big, beefy man was swaying and humming with tiny newborn babies. It was beyond adorable. She cherished seeing him like this. They were already Daddy's girls. She went into the nursery and grabbed a soft receiving blanket for each and put them against their backs. Their little legs and feet were tucked up under them like little frogs as they snuggled against Sawyer's bare chest.

"I love you," she whispered as she kissed him a peck.

"I love you too," he whispered back.

Oh, how she adored him so. The sun was getting brighter as he laid them both down again. He sat on the couch and took his phone out of his pocket and texted Justin, asking him to bring the laptop over on his lunch break because he was too exhausted to go into work. Less than twenty minutes later, as Sawyer was starting to fall asleep again on the couch, Justin woke him with a vibrating text reading, "Open the door." Sawyer got up and let him in.

"Thanks, man, you didn't have to bring it over right now." Sawyer took the computer bag from him.

"Yeah, I did. One of the ranch hands offered but we both

know why." He took his boots off then sat on the couch and put his feet up on the coffee table, laptop on his lap.

Sawyer looked at him, confused.

"What was it we had to work on today?" Sawyer scratched his head, so tired he couldn't even remember his work agenda.

"Go on back to bed. I've got them."

"Really? You sure? I can call my parents."

"Hell yeah. I've got this. You two get some sleep. You've got a buckin' bronco to work with this afternoon. Can't be fallin' asleep while ridin'."

"True."

"Computer shit can wait. Go on."

"Thanks, Justin. I owe ya."

"Just buy food later."

"You got it." Sawyer tip-toed back to the bedroom and joined Marina in slumber.

CHAPTER 51
A New Look

"Let me take you shopping" is what the barn note read. She reflected on the day prior; he saw her frustration with finding things to wear in her wardrobe. She wasn't sure how long he had been standing in the doorway watching her but she went through dress after dress and jeans after jeans, even t-shirts. Everything made her stomach look undesirable in her eyes. When she noticed he was there, she covered her bare stomach with the article of clothing she was holding. She adored the look in his eye when she caught him looking at her. The knees and pockets of his jeans were becoming more tattered and they looked amazing. She wanted her hands all over that man's body but the thought of his all over hers in its current condition was an instant turn off. She had become even more self-conscious of her stomach in particular as baby weight continued to drop. He smiled out one side of his mouth and walked to her. He turned her toward the mirror by her shoulders and stood behind her, his arms wrapped around her tight, his chin resting upon her shoulder.

"You see her?" he asked softly.

"You mean me?" She shied her eyes toward him instead of the mirror, holding onto his arms in front of her.

"Exactly. She is a new mom who doesn't realize her body

performed the most amazing miracle in life. She, and this body of hers, is the most beautiful thing this world has ever seen. She doesn't need to be self-conscious because this guy right here behind her will always think this way."

She closed her eyes for a brief moment, trying to keep from becoming emotional.

"Oh, Sawyer. You're amazing. You know that?" She turned around and wrapped her arms around his back. "You have to stop working out so much."

"Why?"

"Because I look like crap and you look amazing."

"I want you to know you don't ever have to worry about looking like crap. It'll never happen. I don't want you looking down upon yourself because there's no reason to."

"I just wanna look my best for you. And to fit into my clothes again."

"I can imagine your frustration, baby. Don't worry about it for my sake though. Be proud of what your body accomplished. I'm thankful you made it through everything. You look amazing, by the way." He glanced at her backside in the mirror then back at her eyes.

"You're sweet. Thank you."

"I mean it."

"I know you do and I love you for it. I am proud, I'm just...ya know. I'll feel better once I can start working out again. I know you'll love me no matter what because that's the kind of man you are, but I still want to look my best for you." She laid her head upon his chest, the softness of his t-shirt beneath her hands. He took a moment to hold her, being his usual supportive self, and she loved every minute of it.

Marina put the video monitor in her back pocket and continued with chores he hadn't finished yet. She was able to enjoy the quiet morning and completed chores before she heard the twins waking. On her way to the house, Sawyer pulled in and got out of the truck.

"Good mornin', darlin'." He tipped his hat to her.

"Good morning. What's this barn note about?" They walked to the house together.

"Well..."

Sabrina pulled in and Sawyer waved.

"What's she...?" Marina looked over her shoulder and saw Sabrina getting out of her car.

"So, I might have asked her to watch the twins so I could take you shoppin'."

"Why?"

"Because you deserve it and she's been begging to babysit."

"What about work?" she asked as he opened the front door for her.

"I got a little done. I'll finish up later."

They greeted Sabrina and showed her the ropes before heading to town.

After two stores and not purchasing anything, Marina seemed to be giving up.

"What's the matter, darlin'?" he asked as they left the second store and got into the truck.

"I'll just keep wearing baggy maternity clothes till I can start working out hard again. My leggings are comfortable anyway."

"Why do you say that?" He reached over and took her hand.

"I've shrunk enough to not wear maternity clothes but can't quite fit into my regular stuff. I'll stick with my sundresses or something for now. We can just go home, babe." She rested her head on her hand with her elbow up on the window frame. He pulled over against the curb along a storefront and put the truck in park.

"Why are we stopping here?" She looked out the window.

"Marina, look at me." He turned her chin to face him.

"I don't care if you wear a burlap feed bag. I'm gonna love you and still think you're the sexiest woman on Earth. I want you to feel comfortable with yourself though. So, we're goin' in here and finding you stuff that you feel happy in. Okay?" She let out a sigh then a smile and squeezed his hand.

"I'll try."

"Thatta girl."

"A burlap feed bag, Sawyer?" She giggled and made him laugh.

She pulled a few items off racks and Sawyer flopped them over his arm until she was ready to try them on. He hung them for her in the dressing room then stepped out and waited nearby, leaning against the wall.

"Let's see, darlin'."

"Yeah, um, not sure about these jeans."

"Open the door. Come on."

She opened the door and stepped out, head down but eyes up, looking at him. He smiled and asked, "What's wrong with 'em? They look good. Turn around."

She turned and held her hands out, waiting for a comment with raised brows.

"Baby, they look good on ya." He crossed his arms.

"They're too tight on my stomach. My kangaroo pouch is trying to overflow."

"I think you look great."

"Ugh." She turned and went back into the dressing room and closed the door. He shook his head, not understanding how she felt horrible in them.

"Maybe with a maternity t-shirt they'd look okay but they're still uncomfortable."

"Try on that dress I picked out."

"Okay." A moment passed before she said, "Oh, no. Nope. Not happening."

"I wanna see."

"No, you don't."

"Please?" He rubbed the back of his head, frustrated for her.

"Sawyer, it looks horrible. My stomach looks disgusting in this dress. I'm not coming out there in it, sorry."

He felt pity for her, but an idea dawned upon him.

"Okay, move on to the next then." He looked in the next dressing stall beside hers, which was empty, then went in and shut the door quietly.

"This outfit isn't so bad. It's more like stuff I usually wear too." She looked herself over in the dressing room mirror before stepping out.

"Sawyer? Where'd you go?"

He opened the neighboring stall door and came out wearing a dress that had been left hanging in the stall. Her hands flew to her mouth and her eyes widened.

"Does this dress make my butt look big?" He turned to see his butt in the mirror. She busted out laughing.

"Oh, my God, Sawyer! What the hell are you doing?" She looked around for spectators.

"I figured me wearing a dress, out of my element, would make you more comfortable trying clothes on."

"Wow, you've outdone yourself this time."

"Yeah? Think so? You didn't answer me about my butt though." He scratched his chin scruff then ruffled around the bottom of the dress like he was about to start doing a ho-down.

"It looks great." She couldn't contain her smirk for long.

"Yeah?" He danced around in front of the mirror in a feminine fashion. "I need one of those big floppy southern belle hats to go with it, like we're going to the Derby."

"Sure, yeah. Woo! Look at those sexy legs."

He raised his brows and started slow dancing with her, she twirled him but he had to bend and duck under her arm.

"These jeans look hot!" He grabbed her butt.

"Thanks, they're comfy too."

"And this shirt?" He felt the material of the shirt she was wearing. It was rouched down the sides to give the stomach area more room but still gave a slimming look.

"I'm going with it. Might grab another in a different color too."

"That's the spirit. What do ya think? Should I get this dress?"

He twirled around, the skirt flowing out enough to see his boxer briefs underneath as an employee came around the corner and stopped dead in her tracks. Marina busted out laughing and Sawyer asked the girl, barely keeping a straight face, "Does this make my butt look big?"

The girl was speechless.

Marina pushed Sawyer backward, making him step back into the stall as he questioned, "What? Should I buy it?"

Marina laughed and shut his door, leaning her head back against it, then apologized to the girl who then snickered because Sawyer laughed. Marina wasn't even embarrassed; she loved his sense of humor and knew he was trying to lighten her frustrated mood. Mission accomplished.

CHAPTER 52
Time's Up

Marina had managed to get some nonprofit work done on her laptop at home most of the day so she could be home with the twins. They were on their second nap, like usual come the afternoon, so Marina snuck away to the workout room for some light exercising. Sawyer came home early, about a half-hour into her workout. He and Whiskey were always quiet when entering in case the twins were sleeping. He took his boots and hat off by the front door and looked around the house, finding Marina lying on the floor of the workout room.

"Marina?" he panicked.

"Yeah? Hey, you're home early."

He let out a sigh of relief and walked over to her as she remained on the floor, her knees up and arms above her head as she lay on her back. He hiked the thighs of his jeans and laid next to her on his side, propped up on his elbow.

"You scared me."

"Why?"

"I saw you on the floor all sweaty. I thought it was your heart."

"Aww, I'm fine, babe."

"You supposed to be working out? You seem short of breath."

"That's what happens when I haven't been able to work out in six weeks. I just need a minute."

He smiled and ran a finger down her arm.

"You're filthy." She smiled wide.

"You like it, don't ya?"

"I absolutely do." She laughed and grabbed hold of his dirt-stained t-shirt to pull him down for a kiss.

"I don't want you overdoing it."

"I'm not. I'm taking it easy as instructed."

"It has been six weeks, huh? A long six weeks too."

"Yep. That's why I'm working out."

"Don't be doin' it on my account. I've already told you that."

"Sawyer, I look a mess."

"Nope. You already look almost the same as when you got pregnant. You look amazing." His fingers wandered down her side, down to her thigh as his eyes remained connected with hers.

"Sawyer, I'm all sweaty and you have that look in your eyes."

"Yeah, so? I am too. I'm dirty as hell. How about a shower?"

"Together?" she asked nervously.

"Those are the best kind. Come on." He got up off the floor and took her hand, lifting her to her bare feet. "How about we ask my parents to watch the twins tonight so I can take you out to dinner? Maybe down to that restaurant at the beach. We can dine watching the sun set then listen to the waves as it gets too dark to see them." They walked hand in hand to the bathroom.

"That does sound nice." She seemed unsure.

"I wanna spoil you and show you off, darlin'." He turned on the faucet and stripped off his shirt. She felt the heat that had dissipated in her face from working out rev up again throughout her body. She had yet to strip off her t-shirt and yoga leggings. His jeans hit the floor, making her swallow hard.

"Need help?" He grinned, pulling her shirt up over her head.

"Sawyer, I don't know if I can do this yet. I know you healed much quicker after surgery than I-"

"Darlin', I'm a patient man but...I've been chewin' a lot of gum," he said with raised brows before popping a bubble in his mouth.

She laughed.

"I can go to the other shower if you want me to," he offered.

She pondered for a moment. He took her face in his hands and kissed her, soft and sweet. She took hold of his forearms and asked, "Think we can save the lovemaking for tonight after dinner?"

He wrinkled a brow.

"So, the lights can be dim and I'm more comfortable lying down than in a shower."

He pulled her close by the small of her back and a hand on the back of her neck.

"We can do it however and whenever you want, darlin'. No pressure. When you *are* ready, I'll be gentle with you, just so ya know." He kissed her again, longer this time.

Oh, God, she felt him against her, trying to bust out of those briefs.

"I probably should buy ya dinner first, huh?" He smirked and couldn't hold back a chuckle. She smiled and nodded. "And I'll be sure to pull out just in case, like a gentleman." His expression turned serious and smoldering which caused her smile to turn into a lip bite as he backed out of the bathroom. "Get all dolled up when you're finished in the shower." He grabbed clean clothes from the bedroom.

"Where you goin'?" she asked in the doorway.

"I'm gonna have to take a separate shower." He grabbed the pack of gum on top of his dresser and ran for the other bathroom, making her laugh.

Sawyer and Marina walked up the steps to their front porch and she pulled him to her for a good kiss before they entered.

"How was dinner?" Caroline asked softly.

"It was wonderful," Marina said.

"Aww, good."

"How were they?" Sawyer asked as Tom came into the living room.

"They were great. Just got them down for the night, hopefully," Caroline said.

"They fought it hard." Tom nodded.

"Yeah, sorry, their second nap was an hour or so later than usual today," Marina apologized.

"Oh, it's okay. Ya know, your father and I were talking...why don't you two let us keep them overnight tonight?"

"That's sweet but y'all don't have to do that. They're already asleep and all their stuff is here," Marina politely reminded.

"Just go stay the night at our place and we'll stay here," Tom offered.

Sawyer looked at Marina with raised brows, considering the trade.

"We brought an overnight bag just in case." Tom winked at Sawyer.

Sawyer sprouted a sideways grin and hustled toward their bedroom and whispered, "Marina!" She took her heels off so as to not make noise to wake the twins and hustled to him.

"Throw some shit in a bag and let's roll."

She laughed, watching him grab clothes and throw them on the bed.

"Seriously."

"Okay." She got clothes out, him already having shoved his in a bag, which he left open for her. They quickly grabbed toiletries and Sawyer snatched the bag, heading out, practically in a sprint.

"That was quick." Tom chuckled.

"Thank you both so much." Sawyer gave his mom and cheek peck and fist-bumped his dad as Marina went to slip her flip-flops on.

"Nope. Heels." He pointed to the heels she had slipped off.

"Yes, sir."

"Sawyer! I didn't raise you to talk to a woman that way!" Caroline whispered harshly.

"Relax, Ma, it's a little game we play." Sawyer wore a sexy sideways grin.

"Oh, Jesus." Caroline rolled her eyes and Tom laughed. Marina giggled, putting the heels back on, and grabbing her flip-flops on her way out the door behind him. Marina stopped and turned in the doorway to whisper, "Thank you" to her in-laws. Sawyer helped her keep steady down the porch steps as he spit his gum out and hollered back to Tom, who stood in the doorway, "I'll change the sheets!"

CHAPTER 53
The Bands' Decision (Big in a Small Town)

"Does it feel chilly in here, darlin'?" Sawyer leaned against the doorframe to the kitchen with his arms crossed after having laid the twins down in the nursery.

"Maybe a little. You want me to turn the air off?"

"Nah, you've just turned the heat on."

"What?" She smiled, unsure of what he meant as he walked toward her with swagger, his thighs stretching those jeans.

"I may have noticed you aren't wearing a bra." He came up behind her and cupped her breasts in his hands, his warm breath upon the side of her neck. Her eyes closed as she loved him being that close.

"Well, um...we have a guest though." She nodded over at the doorway where Justin came into the room.

"Damn, baby, why you doin' this to me?" He looked like he was about to throw a fit, but jokingly, as he adjusted the front of his jeans.

"It's just me, dude. Not like I haven't heard or seen y'all goin' at it before." Justin laughed as he went to the fridge to pour a glass of tea.

Sawyer raised his brows at her.

"No, that would be rude," she whispered.

"Oh, go on, let him get it out of his system. He won't calm down till he does. He's like a damn raging bull with no concentration." Justin shut the fridge door and joined his laptop at the table.

"He's not wrong." Sawyer was almost grinding up on her, making her laugh, but she looked at him with hesitance because of Justin's presence.

"Just go. I'll put my earbuds in and get some work done. Set the monitor over here." He opened his laptop and dug his earbuds out of his computer bag.

"You sure?" Sawyer grinned, taking the baby monitor from the counter and setting it on the table by Justin.

"Yes, I'm sure. We don't need your zipper busting open. Make it a quickie so we can get workin'."

Sawyer took her hand and they hustled to the bedroom, shutting the door as Justin laughed and shook his head at their spontaneous escapades.

About twenty minutes later, they came out of the bedroom. Justin was at the table still. The twins woke up minutes after Sawyer set up his laptop across from Justin and they worked for a while as Marina tended to the babies.

"Darlin', I hope it's ok, the guys are coming over this evening for rehearsal and I told Luke to join since I promised him a guitar lesson. It's long overdue."

"Sure."

"I want you to stay too," Sawyer told Justin.

Justin nodded and said, "We need to go over royalty stuff anyway. We'll have Jake pick up pizza from the bar on his way over."

"Perfect. Marina, it looks like you don't need to worry about dinner plans."

"Oh, good. I hadn't given it a thought yet."

The band and Justin got comfortable in the music room; two pizza boxes flapped open on end tables.

"It's odd we're rehearsin' on a Wednesday night," Chris said.

"Yeah, we have stuff to go over, though," Justin said.

"First, I wanna have y'all listen to this song Jake and I wrote this week. Chris, you'll need to add the drum part yet." Sawyer picked up his acoustic and nodded for Jake to grab his electric. Jake took the lead.

"Wrangle You"

(Verse 1)
Up in that saddle
Oh, how you sway
I noticed those jeans
When you walked my way

(Verse 2)
Makin' my head spin 360
You're kickin' up dust
I'm takin' the reins
And ropin' your trust

(Chorus)
Like a bronco out the gate
And off into the wind
My heart's wide open
Vulnerable again
I like a wild ride
I don't wanna tame your wild
You make dirty look good
Matching my country style
I'm gonna win you over some way
Looking forward to the day
That I wrangle you

(Verse 3)
Our heads up in the clouds

I don't wanna come down yet
Free to roam this new found love
And ride off into the sunset

(Verse 4)
You're not gonna slip from my grip
I'm gonna lasso you
You have a hold of my heart
I have ahold of yours too

(Chorus)
Like a bronco out the gate
And off into the wind
My heart's wide open
Vulnerable again
I like a wild ride
I don't wanna tame your wild
You make dirty look good
Matching my country style
Let the barriers go
I'm head over heels so
I Had to wrangle you

(Outro)
What do ya say we wrangle life together,
now that I've wrangled you?

"I like it," Trev said, knocking back his beer.

"Yeah, me too. Let's add that one to our album track list," Chris agreed while chewing.

"Cool. This album list is growing pretty quickly. So, I think we need a quick meeting," Sawyer answered.

"About?" Trev asked slowly, as if he should be concerned.

"I wanna know everyone's thoughts on this band thing. I just wanna make sure we're still all on the same page," Sawyer said.

"What do ya mean?" Jake was confused since they had discussed all of this in Nashville.

"I'll go first," Chris volunteered.

Sawyer nodded with a mouthful of pizza for him to continue.

"With the market open now and thriving, farming, horses, and cattle...dude I don't think I'm gonna have much time to travel much. Sorry, guys."

"Don't be sorry, Chris. I feel the same. With the twins, I'm either busy or exhausted, not to mention both barns and the therapy program, training horses, and the usual work load."

"It's hard to stick to Friday nights at the bar even," Jake said. "Work's been slammed."

"Shit, yeah, the bar upkeep too," Sawyer was reminded. "Look, with all that happened with Marina, I want to spend as much time as I can with her and our girls right now."

"Totally understandable," Justin agreed.

"Look, man...honestly, none of us need or want to be rich or famous. I don't want people knowing my business either. Fame makes people stupid and complicated," Trev explained his view.

"So, we're still in agreeance on all we've discussed before?" Sawyer asked.

Everyone nodded.

"We just stick to small stuff here and there? At least for now?" he asked.

"Yup," Chris answered.

"I don't wanna hold anyone back." Sawyer looked around at them all.

"Dude, we're a band...a team. We're all close friends, ain't nothin' gonna change that. We're in this together. We make these decisions together. Our friendship and respect for one another comes first. Always," Trev said.

"I appreciate the support, guys, and I completely agree. Nobody's disappointed right now with anything we've discussed?" Sawyer asked for reassurance.

"We're good, cowboy," Jake said. "Oh, and by the way, our

band, and even your therapy program, got a wide spread in *Trails & Tails Magazine*."

"Seriously?" Sawyer's brows shot up, excitement burning in his gut.

"No way!" Trev clapped his hands and yelled, "Yee haw!"

"Maybe we can sorta be famous without the travelin' and paparazzi." Justin high-fived Jake.

"We have to holler at Todd and Anna then and let them know before Luke gets here. We're supposed to be planning out an album of originals soon so I'm sure they'll bring that up. They were asking about us traveling to Nashville for a music festival to fill in at the last minute but the gig is next week," Sawyer informed.

"Nah, that's too soon to leave your twins and Marina." Jake shook his head.

"Yeah, probably not a good idea," Chris agreed.

"I have shit to do next weekend," Trev said with wrinkled brows.

"I never have shit to do but I do whatever y'all do." Justin shrugged, making the guys laugh.

"I agree, I wouldn't feel comfortable leaving my family quite yet so I'm glad y'all are okay with it. Okay, I guess we're about to have our first conference call as a band over video with our producers. Sounds pretty damn cool, doesn't it?" Sawyer wore a big smile.

"It does, but yeah, let's stay big in a small town," Jake said with a nod.

CHAPTER 54
Waiting Up

Marina quietly unlocked the front door as headlights backed out of the driveway. Light shined through the closed blinds and changed direction as Becka left. Sawyer had crashed on the couch, his arm hanging off until she quietly closed the door behind her after entering. He jumped, sitting up when she locked it.

"I'm sorry, babe."

"Hey, darlin'. You have a good time?"

"Yeah, thanks. Trivia was fun. Why aren't you in bed?" She quietly set her keys on the end table as he stood, pulling his shirt down after stretching.

"I was trying to wait up for you but I guess I dozed off." He rubbed an eye.

She set her purse next to her keys and met him for a hug and kiss.

"Aww, you didn't have to wait up."

"I wanted to know you made it home safely."

She flopped her hand at him. "Oh, I'm good. Aww, you did laundry?" She noticed a load of baby clothes folded on the coffee table next to the folded load of towels and her author copy of the children's book she wrote for the twins that came in the mail.

"Yeah, no biggie. Takes the *load* off you tomorrow." He quietly chuckled at his own joke and she couldn't help but join him.

"You're so sweet. Thank you. I'm sorry I didn't do it before I left. You didn't have to do it, babe." She had to lean against the wall to keep her balance as she took her heels off.

"Darlin', I keep tellin' ya it's not just your responsibility. We're in this together, remember? That's what companionship is; it's mutual."

"Well, I appreciate it. I see the book came."

"It did. It's awesome. You did an amazing job with it and I love that you dedicated it to the twins and your husband."

She smiled and replied, "Thanks. I sure do love you." Her head tilted to one side and her eyes blinked sleepy as she kept her back leaned against the wall. She held him on the highest pedestal; he was the best husband a woman could ask for.

"How many drinks did you have, love?" He smiled, walking to her.

"Three...I think." He gently took hold of her waist and said, "You look lovely in this cocktail dress. Did I tell you that?"

"You did before I left tonight, but I don't mind hearing it again."

"I'll say it as many times as you want me to say it. I'll mean it every time, too." He tipped her chin up, her eyes met his and she said, "You put me under a spell, you know that?"

He kissed the side of her neck. "And I get high simply on the scent of you. You smell delicious." He pulled her away from the wall and she stumbled into his arms. He chuckled at her giggling about her clumsiness. It was obvious her head was feeling heavy. She laid her head upon his chest as he wrapped an arm around her, taking her hand in his other. He led in a slow dance to music only he could hear in his head, his body accentuating the rhythm.

"Raquel has enough material now to finish up our trilogy. oh, and the girls gave me an idea tonight. We should make a date night jar." She spoke slowly.

"Oh? What's that?"

"Where we write down ideas for date nights and put them in a jar, then each week, whichever idea we pull out of the jar is what we go do; like going dancing or whatever."

"Sounds fun. We can do that." Their lips molded into one for a moment before he said, "Your soul sang a song that I couldn't resist dancing to."

"You always say the most romantic things. You love tenderly *and* fiercely. I love that about you. I'll always love you back the same way."

"I know you will, darlin'."

Whiskey shook, his collar jingling, and Marina shushed him loudly, making Sawyer tip his head back, laughing. She was so tipsy and the vertigo was setting in along with her giggles as he practically had to hold her up at that point. She watched her finger trace a line down the center of his chest before looking up at him. She bit her bottom lip and whispered in his ear, "Carry me to the bedroom."

"This night is about to get even more fun." He tossed her up over his shoulder, fully prepared to worship every inch of her.

CHAPTER 55
Under the Stars

Marina pressed her index finger against her lips, holding sleeping Stormy upon her chest as Sawyer entered the house and took his boots off. He smiled and nodded as she went to the nursery and he wrote a note before jumping into the shower after a long day at work. It was already dark outside, thunder beginning to rumble in the distance, so he was quick in the bathroom so he could help if she needed him to when he got out. He threw on a pair of jeans and tip-toed down the hall to the nursery to peek in. Marina had her back to the door and was about to lay Stormy down, asleep. Summer was already snug in her crib. He reached around the corner and placed the note in front of the baby monitor on the dresser then continued to the dining room. As Marina left the nursery, she heard the front door open. With the monitor in her hand along with the note, she read it as she entered the living room. It read "Meet me on the porch." With a smile and quiet bare feet, she stepped through the open doorway to see Sawyer leaning against the porch post with two glasses in his hand. The thunder was growing louder as they stepped toward each other and he handed her a cranberry vodka as he sipped his whiskey. Taking her hand, he hit play on the Bluetooth speaker he had set on the swing before continuing down the steps. They chugged a few swigs before setting their glasses on the step and stepping out into the grass for a dance to *Good Times Go by Too Fast* by Dylan Scott. Neither of them spoke the entire song, just enjoyed the music and lyrics as he twirled her around then pulled her back to hold her close.

The roar of the sky was louder than the music at times, vibrating the ground under their bare feet. Upon the song ending, he gently brushed her hair away from her face and laid a soft, gentle kiss on her lips. The world around them didn't exist anymore; it was just the two of them floating through space where time stood still. Only for a moment though, for it never lasted long enough.

"We can see our stars in the sky tonight. The clouds haven't covered them yet." He pointed up in the direction of their named stars.

"They're bright."

"They sure are. I can see their reflection in your eyes." He stared into her eyes, completely lost in the moment.

"How many drinks have you had tonight?" She smiled, making the moment less serious.

"Two with Justin before I left work and that's my first since getting home. I really do see stars in your eyes though, I'm not drunk."

She giggled at his seriousness. "Even if you couldn't see a reflection of those stars, my star will always be burning for you." She lifted to her toes with her arms tight around his neck.

"As mine always will for you, darlin'." He wore a serious expression like he was undressing her with his eyes. He told the speaker to play *Growing Old With You* by Restless Road as the rain began falling, harder than a sprinkle but not a downpour yet. It didn't matter, they stayed in the moment.

He fought back a chuckle at how they're always getting caught in the rain together but knowing good things come from it. Together, they'd always be stronger than any storm. She kissed him, admiring how he looked at her.

"I look forward to growing old with you." She laid her head against his chest as they slowly danced, there in the grass, under the clouding stars, in the rain.

"Me too, darlin'. For now, I wish time would stand still so we can be in this moment longer."

"Sawyer, we'll have many more moments just like this. You know how to sweep a girl off her feet, every single day."

"And I look forward to each and every one. They'll always end with you wrapped up in my arms."

They did just that; danced many dances under those named stars, sometimes with drinks in their hands, sometimes in the rain, oftentimes alone with one another, and sometimes with their daughters, but they always began with a sweet, loving note.

Acknowledgments

No matter what stress and chaos gets thrown at my life, I know I have writing and reading to bring me hope and joy. Once the inspiration is sparked, the rest of the writing flows. I wish to share my way of thinking and creativity with readers so they can find hope from the fictitious reality they may become lost in. Thank you, readers!

I would like to thank my closest friends for being an inspiration for the supporting characters in this series. I'd also like to once again thank one of my closest friends and fellow author for our coffee shop writing days. I cherish them.

Here's a shout-out to the musical artists that are mentioned in this series, you're much appreciated. The song titles mentioned are personal favorites as well. The lyrics carry volume to the storyline. I encourage readers to listen to the songs mentioned within the book to gain a better feel for the need to mention them as well as to envision the characters performing them.

Thank you to photographer Andrei Vishnyakov for providing exclusive photos of Konstantin. Our chats are always fun. On that note, thank you to Russian model Konstantin Kamynin for being the perfect vision of "Sawyer". Hugs!

Much Love, Marina Skye

About the Author

Marina Skye is from the country in a small southern town. She's a beach girl at heart but loves being around horses and volunteers with a local equine rescue center. As a romantic, this is where her inspiration for the book series bloomed. When she isn't writing, she's working one of several jobs and raising her two boys. She hopes her sons will grow to be respectful gentlemen just like the character in this series.

www.ingramcontent.com/pod-product-compliance
Lightning Source LLC
Chambersburg PA
CBHW032027290426
44110CB00012B/699